WHY CHINA LEADS THE WORLD

WHY CHINA LEADS THE WORLD

Talent at the Top, Data in the Middle, Democracy at the Bottom

Godfree Roberts

WHY CHINA LEADS THE WORLD:
Talent at the Top, Data in the Middle, Democracy at the Bottom

Copies of this book may be ordered from Ingram Books USA, Australia, Canada, UK, EU, Hong Kong, India, Ireland, New Zealand, Singapore, South Africa, from Amazon and electronic outlets worldwide.

Cover Design by PixelStudio
Editor: Michelle Balfour
Copy Editor: Dianne Giambusso
Publisher: Oriel Media
ISBN: 978-1-7358213-0-6 HARDBACK
978-1-7358213-1-3 PAPERBACK
978-1-7358213-2-0 E-BOOK
Library of Congress Control Number: 2020918248

Chinese history
Chinese governance
Chinese education
Chinese democracy
Chinese environment
Chinese labor, wages, and poverty
Chinese military
Chinese diplomacy
Chinese geopolitics

First Edition
Printed in the United States of America

To

Richard Fong San Chan

Sea Gypsy, Biologist, Banker, Philanthropist, *Jūn Zǐ.*

The size of China's displacement of the world balance is such that the World must find a new balance. It is not possible to pretend that this is just another big player. This is the biggest player in the history of the World. Lee Kwan Yew, Father of Singapore.

ACKNOWLEDGMENTS

I am indebted to my brothers, Tony and Philip, for scrutinizing the claims in this book, to my Quora readers for their criticisms and suggestions, and to Ben Coles of Cascadia Press for guiding its publication. My special thanks go to Ron Unz, the Saker, Patrice Greanville, and Kit Knightly for exposing its ideas to their readers, and my fellow authors at Jeff J. Brown's China Writers' Group for their support and assistance.

CONTENTS

PREFACE: WHY I WROTE THIS BOOk

To put the World in order, we must first put the nation in order; to put the nation in order, we must first put the Family in order; to put the Family in order, we must first cultivate our personal lives by setting our hearts right. Confucius

***

How did China do it?

When I was born it was the world's poorest nation. In 2010 it rescued the global economy from the Great Financial Crisis and again in 2020, after the Coronavirus Crisis. Soon it will be the world's richest country. How did such a vast, poverty-stricken country transform itself in one human lifetime?

The short answer is 'planning': Beijing began preparing for world leadership in 1957 and for a coronavirus epidemic in 2003. The long answer is the subject of this book.

It tells how China hired Americans to democratize their government, engineers to run it, used consensus-building and goal-setting to get everyone on the same page, and based their legislation on statistics.

But be warned: describing a numbers-driven society calls for dozens of charts (six in the first chapter alone) and five hundred footnotes. Wonky, yes, but behind the statistics you'll encounter a unique civilization, built on principles utterly unlike ours, from which we have much to learn.

I have organized its story into five sections:

1. *Bad China, Good China* discusses the two Chinas: Bad China,

filled with resentful slaves exploited by bloodthirsty masters, and Good China, whose people claim to be the happiest on earth.

2. *Talent at the Top* introduces the men who invented their culture, one who reinvented it, and one who will lead it through 2022. They speak to you directly, in extended quotes that reveal their human responses to the immense challenges confronting them.
3. *Data in the Middle* explains how they use local experiments to solve national problems, like poverty, a process they call 'crossing the river by feeling the stones'.
4. *Democracy at the Bottom* explains the Carter Center's role in their democracy and how they democratize both politics and finances.
5. Finally, *China in the World* investigates our *image* of China: invisible famines, invisible massacres, invisible oppression, invisible pandemics, and invisible human rights violations. The final chapters analyze its huge military, ambitious foreign policy, and its design for international relations.

PART I

WHY DOES CHINA LEAD THE WORLD?

CHAPTER 1

Bad China, Good China

Imagine the impact upon European civilization of a series of Imperial dynasties maintaining the self-same style and significance from Caesar Augustus until the First World War. Now imagine such a civilization existing on the other side of the planet–unaware of Greek philosophy, the alphabet, Roman governance, Christianity, feudalism, the Renaissance, the Enlightenment, or democracy–but with its own unique cultural and institutional correlates that exceed all of them in intellectual subtlety and material success. Fernand Braudel[1].

***

Dusk was falling over Kunming and I sat in a downtown park watching apple-cheeked children chase each other around the bushes, oblivious to the descending gloom. I recalled my own carefree childhood, before the Age of Fear, when we played and wandered freely, night or day. "So, this is China?" I said, and made a mental note to query friends about cultural indicators they had noticed.

Back in California I asked Larry, an old China hand, who told me about returning to Shenzen after six months in California, chatting with a Chinese man on the plane, and mentioning that he had forgotten to pay his electricity bills. He dreaded returning to a cold, dark flat in midwinter, he said. His companion was puzzled. Utilities are publicly owned, he said, so why would they turn off his electricity? The electricity was on.

1 Fernand Braudel. *A History of Civilizations.* Penguin. 1995.

Frans was interpreting for a German engineer at a Bosch joint venture in Nanjing whose CEO was a German ex-pat, and whose assistant was a young Chinese woman who had studied at the University of Bamberg. At their final meeting, the CEO requested some German baking mix to be sent with the next shipment, so Frans asked his assistant if she would like something sent from Germany, too. Without hesitating, she responded, "I don't know what. There is nothing I need that I can't find in China!" For him, said Frans, her response was the essence of the Middle Kingdom and a measure of its distance from the European peninsula.

Peter Man, a Chinese Canadian, first visited his ancestral land in 1981 and recalled the night he treated the hotel staff to dinner. They ended up in a packed canteen that seated two hundred, and where the dishes were simple, tasty, and inexpensive. When he ordered rice, the waiter pointed to a gigantic steaming vat of it where diners were lined up. "An unlimited supply of free rice," he thought, "only in a communist country!" Then he noticed something odd. Standing quietly against the walls were neatly-dressed families holding bowls, and, as he finished his rice and put down the bowl, several of them approached him. The first to arrive was a family of three, whose child was seven or eight years old and whose father politely asked if they were done. "I was perplexed, and then my companions explained that the Yellow River had flooded and many peasants had lost their homes, their fields, and produce. Local authorities moved some of the refugees to Changsha, where the local government would resettle them. In the past, this would have been disastrous. Many victims of the flood would have starved to death or been sold into slavery. Instead, they survived by eating free rice and leftovers."

"I watched in wonder as the Family put some of the leftovers on their rice, thanked us, and walked away, leaving some for two young men lined up behind them. I did not see any police or government officials organizing the refugees. They seemed to be following some natural law that allowed the young, the old, and the weak to eat first. There was unlimited rice, so no one needed to go hungry. Everyone lined up at one table for the leftovers seemed to allot a share for everyone else in the queue mentally. I did not feel that these people were beggars or did anything undignified. Quite the contrary, I was impressed by the orderly way they shared the food and their dignified comportment. I did not know that I would return to bustling, modern Changsha, to build a digital television production facility for Changsha TV twenty years later. I spent two decades there, traveling and learning about China, and there is much that I have grown to love, but I cherish most of all the memory of the China I first saw in that canteen in my youth".

Their anecdotes recall *Good China,* where poor people own their homes, everyone trusts the government, media are truthful, people are happy with their country's direction, everybody doubles their wages every ten years and, collectively, they own everything worth owning. Imagine how we'd feel if that was our reality.

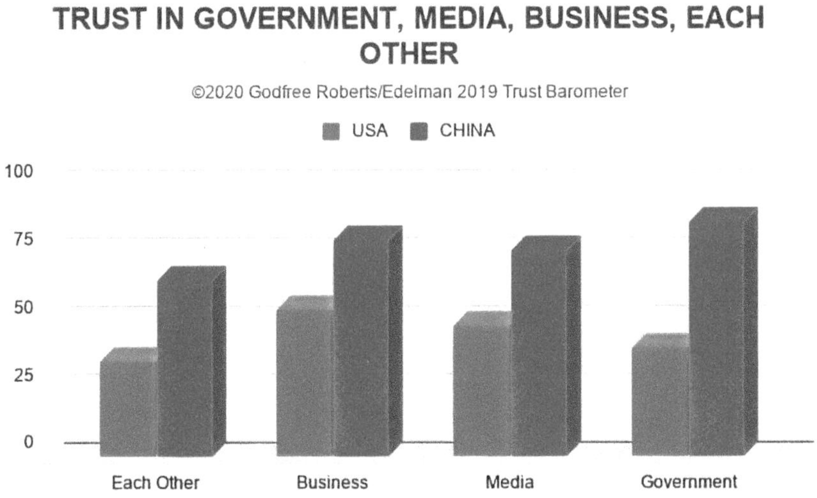

How would we feel if we could trust our government?

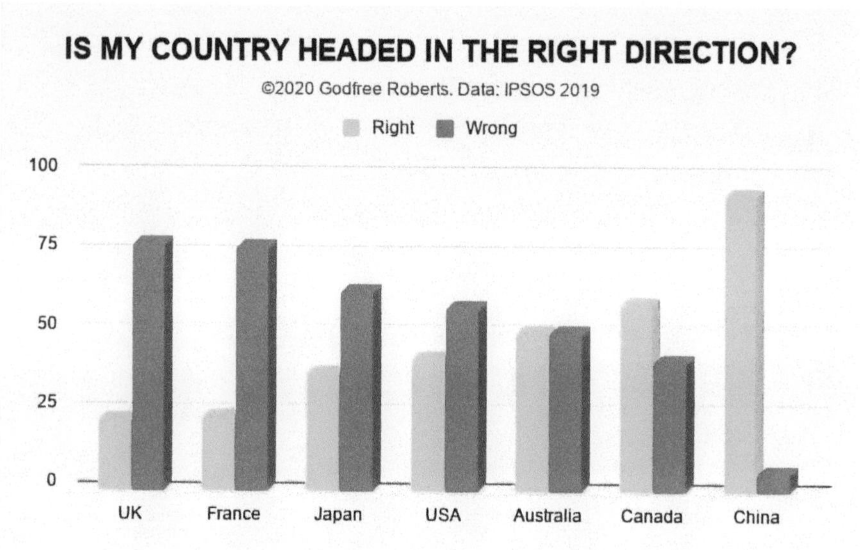

Imagine that our country was going where we wanted to go.

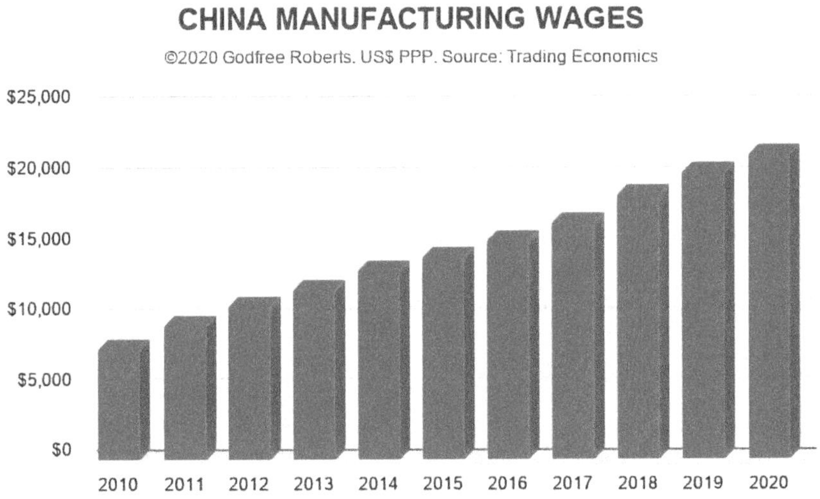

If our wages had grown, instead of stagnating, for the past forty years?

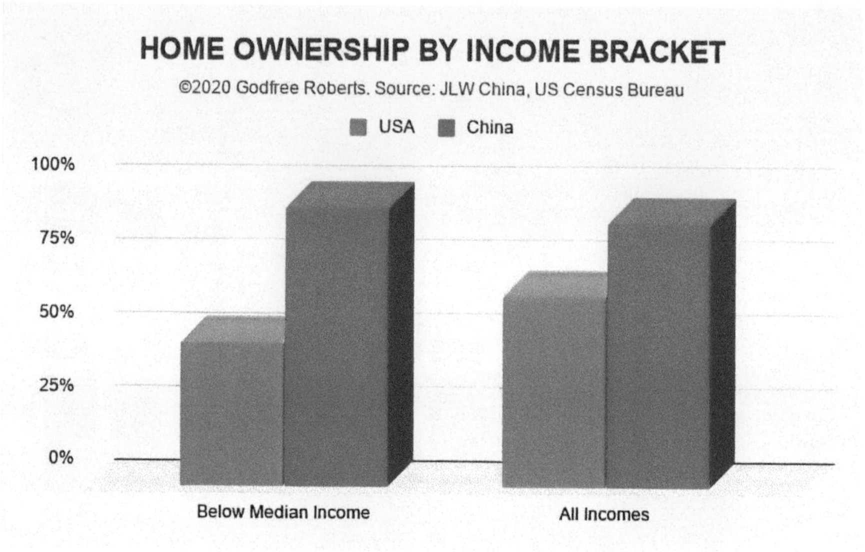

If we could all sleep in our own homes tonight and nobody slept in the streets?

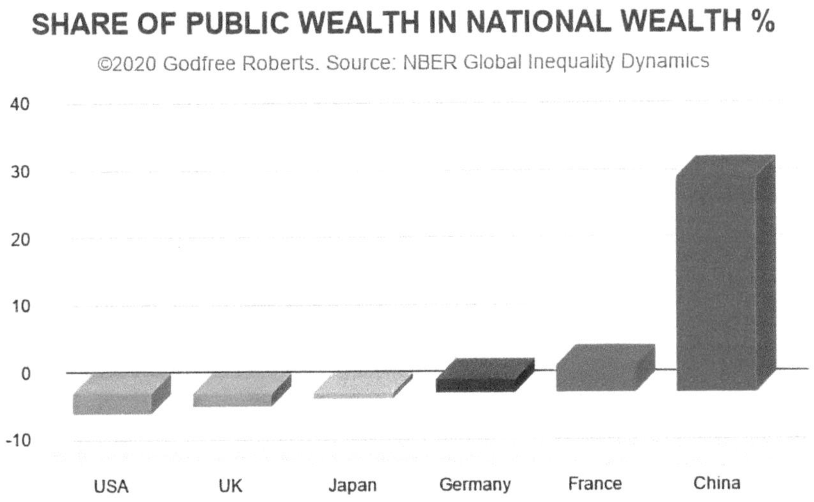

If, together, we owned all the land, the banks and insurance companies, the TV stations, utilities, and infrastructure.

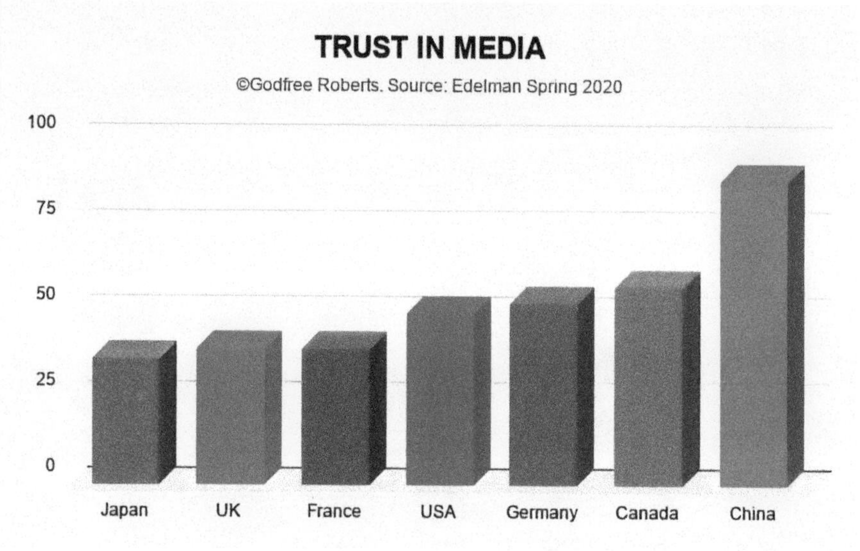

Finally, how would we feel if we trusted our media?

Pollsters have spent decades in China gathering those statistics, skeptics have audited them, and millions of visitors have verified them, but we struggle to believe them. This book explains why we should.

PART II

TALENT AT THE TOP

CHAPTER 2

A Little History

If rulers' own behavior is ethical, what difficulty will they have in governing? If their own conduct is improper, how can they demand lawfulness from their citizens? Confucius, *Analects.*

***

Governing is difficult, and governing *well* requires intelligent, honest, competent officials yet, in our political tradition–which dates to Ancient Rome–governance takes a back seat to politics. We have always elected[2] selfish, shallow, irresponsible, glib con artists, then wondered why they make such a mess of things.

The Chinese tradition, equally ancient, takes the opposite approach. They weed out selfish, shallow, irresponsible, glib con artists and painstakingly select officials with track records of brilliant governance–and thereby hangs this book's tale.

***

Three thousand years ago, in the intensively agricultural Yellow River Valley, in an already ancient land the size of modern France, literate Shang people, who called themselves the 'Middle Kingdom,' used currency to trade in silks, jade, and exquisite bronzes. In one Shang State,

2 *The Sociopath Next Door by Martha Stout* 2006.

the Duke of Zhou, regent for a child prince, governed compassionately, extended the realm, taxed the rich, and enriched the poor. When the young monarch came of age, the Duke retired to compose music, revise the legal code, and edit the still-loved *Book of Poems*. His name remains a household word and his legacy, the Mandate of Heaven, is the bedrock of Chinese politics: governments earn the right to rule by improving people's lives.

Five centuries after the Duke's death, Confucius, a political scientist and sometime government official, provided a tripartite formula for success which governments still follow: treat the entire nation as your own family;[3] transform the family's dreams into concrete goals, and *only* appoint people like the Duke of Zhou to lead them towards those goals.

Confucius further proposed two stages of familial wellbeing. First, a *xiaokang*[4] society in which everyone has a home, plenty of food and clothes, education, medical care, old-age support, and sufficient leisure for arts and contemplation. Then build on that foundation a *dàtóng*[5] society so egalitarian and compassionate that no one needs to lock her outer doors at night. His vision of social health is radically democratic, since *xiaokang* and *dàtóng* can exist only if every member of the family prospers and none is left behind.

He advised political leaders to begin by setting a personal example, "Rulers who led their people to a *xiaokang* lifestyle were pillars of courtesy, sincerity, justice, and virtue. Those who were not lost power, and everyone regarded them as pests".

He also recommended replacing the aristocracy with virtuous officials, "Morally upright superiors relate to ordinary people like wind to grass; grass bends when the wind blows over it". Like Plato's Philosopher Kings[6], they would establish a chain of respect—from dutiful children to parents, through grandparents, clan heads, upright officials, to the Emperor himself. Citizens, by gladly emulating their example, would

---

3 Perfect strangers still address one another as "aunty," "uncle," "sister," and "grandfather."

4 Chinese translators call it 'a moderately prosperous society' and we call it 'the Chinese Dream'.

5 From *Datong Shu*, Book on the Great Community, a commentary by Kang Youwei, which Mao memorized in its entirety.

6 "Until kings are philosophers or philosophers are kings, neither cities nor the human race will ever cease from ill, nor will our ideal polity ever come into being". Plato. *The Republic.*

vastly simplify law enforcement. "I have yet to see anyone create disorder who is respectful of superiors".

But rulers of the day were comfortable with the chain of command, and nobles rejected meritocracy[7] and Confucius, convinced that he had failed, died. For three centuries, corrupt eunuchs, scheming regents, dowager empresses, usurpers, concubines, wicked uncles, and rebellious generals continued their massacres, kidnappings, beheadings, infant stranglings, sibling drownings, poisonings, torturing, dismemberment, taxing, warring, and oppression while Confucius' disciples persistently advocated his plan until, in 188 BC, they persuaded Emperor Wen of Han[8] to stop imprisoning parents, wives, and siblings of common criminals.

Encouraged by the popularity of this policy and intrigued by the advantages of meritocracy, he began examining the literacy and moral maturity of nobles seeking high office, lowering taxes, abolishing *corvée* labor, and giving monthly pensions to widows, orphans, and retirees. When his mother fell ill he nursed her for three years, tasting her soups and medicines himself. If things went awry, Emperor Wen wrote Letters of Public Apology acknowledging his role as the people's servant. As Confucius had predicted, peace and prosperity prevailed.

Today, Chinese children know Emperor Wen as one of Twenty-Four Filial Exemplars, their parents measure every government against his, and modern officials still write Letters of Public Apology when things go astray–because they, too, studied Emperor Wen at school.

When the Emperor's grandson tried to extend Wen's reforms, his grandmother, Grand Empress Dowager Dou, sidelined him and banished the reformists. But the young man–the future Emperor Wu of Han (157 BC–87 BC)–secretly recruited scholars of humble birth to enter the civil service, used his limited influence to help them win promotions to

7 Britain's upper House of Parliament is reserved for the nobility, and Baroness Ursula Gertrud von der Leyen recently followed Count van Rompuy as President of the European Council.

8 (203 BC – July 6 157 BC) was the fifth emperor of the Han dynasty of ancient China. His reign brought much needed political stability that laid the groundwork for prosperity under his grandson, Emperor Wu.

mid-level positions and, upon the death of the Empress Dowager, called for proposals to renew the empire.

A Confucian scholar-official, Dong Zhongshu, responded by outlining a beguiling 'new broom' scheme that placed the Emperor at the center of the universe, controlling the World through sacred rituals[9] and, lest they imply imperial negligence, promised that officials would take responsibility for earthquakes, floods, comets, and famines. Intrigued, the young Emperor asked who would administer the scheme. Dong replied, "Your Highness, since not one man in the entire empire is currently qualified to respond to your call, I beg You to build an academy and appoint enlightened teachers to nurture, test, and goad young men to the limits of their ability. Do so, and you will recruit the flower of the empire's youth".

Emperor Wu established the Imperial College of Confucian Studies, banned competing ideologies, dismissed non-Confucian officials, burned their books, and required every child to study Confucius daily, as they still do. In 140 BC, he made Confucianism the imperial doctrine, established competitive civil service examinations, personally examined aspiring scholars, and commanded that examinations become the sole avenue to social advancement, as they still are.

While his selfless officials inspired and enriched the masses, the Emperor expanded the empire, centralized its administration, and created the Chinese script, the oldest writing system still in use. He fixed the cart axles' length to fit his extensive road network, dug canals between provinces to reduce freight costs, standardized weights, measures, and coinage, unified provincial walls into the Great Wall of China, and commissioned a tomb that is still guarded by his terra-cotta warriors.

Families sent promising offspring to Confucian cram schools, the Ivy League of their day, and, within a century, thirty thousand had enrolled at the Imperial College where, as a form of meditation, they memorized the Master's teaching on compassionate service until it permeated their feelings, thoughts, and dreams. Selected by increasingly competitive

9 *Inevitable Treason: Dong Zhongshu's Theory of Historical Cycles and Early Attempts to Invalidate the Han Mandate.* By Gary Arbuckle. Journal of the American Oriental Society Vol. 115, No. 4 (Oct-Dec. 1995)

examinations at the local, provincial, and imperial levels–and forbidden to work within five hundred miles of their hometowns–they laid the foundation for a governance system that is again the envy of the World.[10]

Centuries later, in 600 AD, Emperor Yang of Sui opened the imperial examination to peasants and instructed assessors—from whom candidates' identities were concealed—to find men with intellectual depth and moral maturity. To emphasize the importance of official integrity, he said, they should execute cheaters. Applicants answered questions on the economy, analyzed government policies, and composed original essays to demonstrate their brushwork, literacy, creativity, and knowledge of the World. The Emperor queried top candidates and listened as they quoted from memory governance case studies, extensive passages from the *Analects* and poetry, as modern applicants still do. Advancement by examination was class-blind (as it still is) because, said Imperial Censor Wang Ji, "If selection by examination is not strict, the powerful will struggle to be foremost, and orphans and the poor will have difficulty advancing".

The demand for literacy was so powerful that, in 1000 AD, Song Dynasty officials distributed millions of Confucian catechisms–the Little Red Books of their day–and delivered uplifting lectures on their content. A court official, Ouyang Xiu, reported how successful scholars became national celebrities, their academic feats memorialized in family books and their homecomings semi-hysterical (as they still are[11]), "When a scholar rides in a high carriage drawn by four horses, flag-bearers running ahead with a mounted escort bringing up the rear, people gather on both sides of the road to watch and sigh. Ordinary men and foolish women rush forward in excitement and humbly prostrate themselves in the dust stirred up by his carriage. This is a scholar's joy. This is when his ambition is fulfilled". When, during Ouyang's lifetime, the invention of paper and moveable type made the Confucian Classics widely available, literacy became a national obsession and remains so to this day. Though sons of the elite still benefited from their famous names and private

10 This is why the British call their senior civil servants 'Mandarins.'

11 President Xi dampened the hysteria in 2014 by observing that it over-glorified young graduates and ignored the sacrifices their parents, teachers, and society had made for them.

tutors, poor but brilliant young men gradually erased the distinction between government and governed. During Europe's Dark Ages, Chinese civilization reached its zenith and officials' moral authority far exceeded that of Rome's Popes.

The poor men who ascended on talent were the Emperor's men entirely. They could neither own land, serve in their home provinces, nor have relatives in the same government branch–prohibitions that still hold. For centuries, they competed for promotion by building public works–like the thousand-mile Grand Canal–to enrich the nation, honor the Emperor, and sustain the World's most formidable State. Dynasties rose and fell while loyal, intelligent, entrepreneurial, disciplined–often courageous–men served in remote regions, far from family and friends, frequently under terrible conditions until, by 1000 AD, one scholar-official for every eight thousand citizens[12] sustained the most harmonious, advanced, and prosperous nation on earth. By 1200 AD, of two-hundred seventy-nine senior officials whose families we know,[13] forty-four percent had forebears in government. By 2020 it was twelve percent and all, high or low, then or now, graduates of the most demanding education system the World has known.

---

12 Today, there is one for every twenty thousand, and they deliver far more social goods.

13 *China's Meritocratic Examinations and the Ideal of Virtuous Talents*. Xiao, H., & Li, C. (2013). In D. Bell & C. Li (Eds.), Cambridge.

CHAPTER 3

Education

When the people have full bellies and warm clothes on their backs, they degenerate almost to the level of brutes if they are allowed to lead idle lives without education and discipline. This gave the Sage King further cause for concern, so he appointed Hsieh as the Minister of Education. His duty was to teach the people human relationships: love between father and son, duty between ruler and subject, distinction between husband and wife, precedence of the old over the young, trust between friends.[14]

***

Between 1000 AD and 1911, seven hundred top *keju*[15] scorers won immortality as *zhuàngyuán*, 'the name at the top of the list.' Just as European nobility trace their lineage to great warriors, Chinese families trace theirs to *zhuàngyuán*, immortalize their feats in Family Books, and name landmarks for them. Selected for their academic brilliance, administrative competence, and moral probity, they formed a *just hierarchy*[16] at the pinnacle of Chinese society. Surpassingly intelligent, competent, honest, and self-sacrificing, the greatest are so revered that millions still

14 Mencius. Ed. and trans. D.C. Lau. Hong Kong: The Chinese University Press. 2003

15 Imperial Examination

16 Just (deserved) hierarchies are earned by meritorious service, while unjust hierarchies are established by birth or trickery and sustained by violence. *Just Hierarchy: Why Social Hierarchies Matter in China and the Rest of the World.* By Daniel A. Bell and Wang Pei. Princeton. 2020.

burn incense at their shrines, and parents still dream that their children will join their ranks.

Examinations were abandoned with the fall of the Manchu Dynasty and not until Mao introduced the *gaokao* in 1952 were national examinations held to select students for the handful of university places then available. Today, ten million youngsters compete for eight million positions at three thousand universities. The fiercest competition focuses on one-hundred-fifty top universities whose collective admission rate is under three percent. Even gaining admission, as Puzhong Yao[17] discovered, requires near-genius ability:

> It was the summer of 2000. I was 15, and I had just finished my high school entrance exam. I had made considerable improvements from where I started in first grade, when I had the second-worst grades in the class and had to sit at a desk perpendicular to the blackboard so that the teacher could keep a close eye on me. I had managed to become an average student in an average school. My parents, by then, had concluded that I was not going anywhere promising in China and were ready to send me abroad for high school. Contrary to all expectations, however, I got the best mark in my class and my school, ranking me among the top ten of more than 100,000 students in the whole city. Though my teacher and I both assumed the score was wrong when we first heard it, I got into the best class in the best school in my city and thus began the most painful year of my life.
>
> My newfound confidence was quickly crushed when I saw how talented my new classmates were. In the first class, our math teacher announced that she would start from chapter four of the textbook as she assumed, correctly, that most of us were familiar with the first three chapters and would find it boring to repeat. Most of the class had been participating in various competitions in middle school and had become familiar with a large part of

17 Excerpted from 'The Western Elite from a Chinese Perspective' by Puzhong Yao American Affairs. Winter 2017 / Vol I, No 4. More stories of his studies and the US at http://ajourneytothewest.co.uk/

the high school syllabus already and had grown to know each other from those years of competitions together. And here I was, someone who didn't know anything or anyone, surrounded by people who knew more to begin with, who were much smarter, and who worked just as hard as I did. What chance did I have?

During that year, I tried very hard to catch up: I gave up everything else and even moved close to the school to save time on the commute, but to no avail. Over time, going to school and competing while knowing I was sure to lose became torture. Yet I had to do it every day. At the end-of-year exam, I scored second from the Bottom of the class—the same place I began in first grade. But this time, it was much harder to accept, after the glory I had enjoyed just one year earlier and the enormous amount of effort I had put into studying this year. Finally, I threw in the towel and asked my parents to send me abroad. Anywhere on this earth would surely be better.

So I came to the UK in 2001, when I was 16 years old. Much to my surprise, I found the UK's exam-focused educational system very similar to China's. What is more, in both countries, going to the 'right schools' and getting the 'right job' are seen as very important by a large group of eager parents. As a result, scoring well on exams and doing well in school interviews—or even the play session for the nursery or pre-prep school—becomes the most important thing in the World. Even at university, the undergraduate degree from the University of Cambridge depends solely on an exam at the end of the final year.

On the other hand, although the UK's university system is considered superior to China's, with a population that is only one-twentieth the size of my native country, competition, while tough, is less intimidating. For example, about one in ten applicants gets into Oxbridge in the UK, and Stanford and Harvard accept about one in twenty-five applicants. But in Hebei, my Province in China, only one in fifteen hundred applicants gets into Peking or Tsinghua University.

Still, I found it hard to believe how much easier everything became. I scored first nationwide in the GCSE (high school) math exam, and my photo was printed in a national newspaper. I was admitted into Trinity College, University of Cambridge, once the home of Sir Isaac Newton, Francis Bacon, and Prince Charles, where I studied economics, a field that has become increasingly mathematical since the 1970s. My British classmates' behavior demonstrated an even greater herd mentality than what is often mocked in American MBAs. For example, out of the thirteen economists in my year at Trinity, twelve would join investment banks, and five of us went to work for Goldman Sachs.

Who can blame him for fleeing? The *gaokao,* which grants access to undergraduate study, is the culmination of a twelve-year educational marathon and the most significant affair in Chinese life. On *gaokao* day, road and air traffic are diverted and millions of relatives besiege school gates. Inside the examination room, personality, charm, community service, interview preparation, and athletic accomplishment count for nothing. All that matters is answering questions like these:

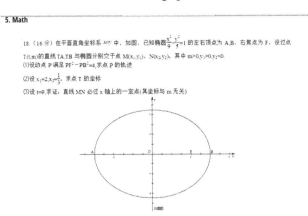

5. Math

18.（16分）在平面直角坐标系 xoy 中，如图，已知椭圆 $\frac{x^2}{9}+\frac{y^2}{5}=1$ 的左右顶点为 A,B，右焦点为 F，设过点 T(t,m)的直线 TA,TB 与椭圆分别交于点 $M(x_1,y_1)$，$N(x_2,y_2)$，其中 $m>0,y_1>0,y_2<0$.

(1)设动点 P 满足 $PF^2-PB^2=4$,求点 P 的轨迹

(2)设 $x_1=2,x_2=\frac{1}{3}$，求点 T 的坐标

(3)设 t=9,求证：直线 MN 必过 x 轴上的一定点(其坐标与 m 无关)

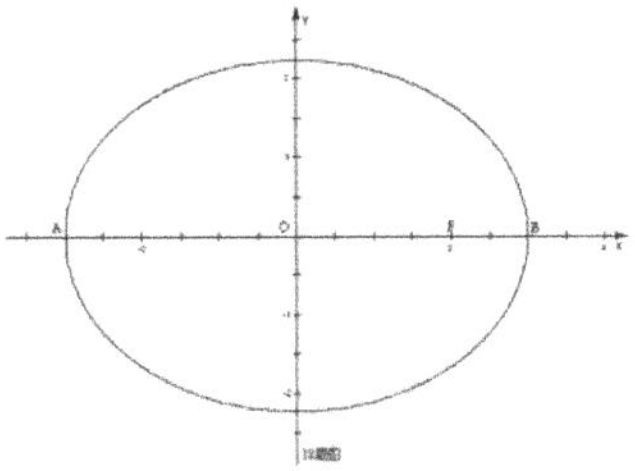

Given an ellipse $x^2/9+y^2/5=1$ whose vertices are A and B and right focus F.Suppose that line TA and line TB which pass through T(t,m) intersect the ellipse at $M(x_1,y_1)$ and $N(x_2,y_2)$ individually.($m>0,y_1>0,y_2<0$)

1) Moving point P satisfies equation $PF^2-PB^2=4$,find the track of P.

2) Assume that $x_1=2,x_2=1/3$,find the cooordinates of T

3) Assume that t=9,prove that line MN must passes through a definite point on the x axis(whose coordinates are independant of m)

— 2010 Jiangsu *Gaokao*

6. Writing

Description: Some men see things as they are and say why? I dream things that never were and say, "Why not?" Write an 800-word essay about your thoughts on these words of George Bernard Shaw.

7. Reasoning

Description: During WWII, US and British military forces researched the distribution of bullet holes on battered combat aircraft to upgrade their protective capability. Most scientists agreed that the upgrade should focus on areas with the most bullet holes, but Ward, a statistician, prevailed over them, noting that attention should be paid to the parts with fewer bullet holes since if those parts were damaged, the planes would have a smaller chance of returning home. However, his statistics were ignored. Later investigation proved Ward's theories were, in fact, correct. Please write an essay based on this information.

When the Education Ministry proposed limiting homework, *jianfu*, parents objected, "The government used to educate our children, but now they don't want to shoulder the responsibility, so they're throwing it back onto us!" They insisted that their children were perfectly capable of handling heavier workloads and waxed nostalgic for 'the nineties when the state supported students working day and night,' and Charlene Tan[18] questioned educators about this. One headmaster explained that many parents who had missed higher education "Put all their hopes in their child and devoted all their energies to the child because the child's learning, school promotion, and choice of career determine the fate of the entire family". Said another, "As long as a child is willing to learn, parents are willing to spend up to seventy percent of the family budget helping them".

18 Learning from Shanghai: Lessons on Achieving Educational Success. by Charlene Tan. 2013

Says Xiong Xuan'an, who was the *zhuàngyuán* in 2017, "People like me are from middle-class families. We don't have to worry about food or clothes. Our parents are educated. We were born in big cities like Beijing. We simply got better educational resources than the rest. Students from other places and rural areas are not able to get these benefits. It made my learning path easier, and the top scorers nowadays, generally speaking, come from upper-class families and are good at studying".

Meanwhile, finding that children in impoverished Guizhou Province were coming to school on empty stomachs, the Ministry built canteens and provided funds to buy produce directly from poor local farmers, with which to prepare fifteen million free lunches. It added monthly stipends for two million poor[19] students and focused on building their confidence in education as a way to lift their families out of poverty. Provincial administrators called on expert advice from teachers like Zhang Yan, a star principal in Zunyi City, "I've focused my plan on coaching teachers in poverty-stricken areas rather than giving lectures at rural schools". Respect for teachers is high: in public, people bow and address them as *laoshi,* a title implying a status higher than our 'professor'.

The Province relocated two million poor people from inhospitable, mountainous regions into new urban homes and enrolled their 130,000 children in 1,600 nearby schools. By 2021, it will complete three hundred nurseries and junior high schools and relocate a further fifty-thousand children. The relocated children, who are already testing as well as average EU children, are taking artificial intelligence courses.

As part of the campaign to improve national equality by 2035 the Education Ministry, over urban parents' objections, pushed city schools to admit migrant children to their local *gaokao* exams and provide university places for them. By 2019, eighty percent of migrant children were enrolled in city schools, and ninety percent were receiving financial support that will continue through university.

Though the Ministry has doubled support for rural education since 2015, children from underdeveloped areas were still struggling to win places in major universities so, in 2018, country schools began raising

19 Their families are officially enrolled in the government's anti-poverty campaign.

teachers' pay to match local officials, limiting primary class size to forty-five and employing at least ten senior music, fine arts, and physical education teachers for every thousand children. The Ministry gave them scholarships and favorable entry policies to seventy-five national universities and in 2019, recruited promising city teachers to relocate to impoverished areas of Anhui, Henan, Shaanxi, and Gansu Provinces. It promoted them to Chief Teachers at rural schools, encouraging them to explore their own ideas for lifting instructional quality. By 2020, the rural distance from national academic averages had narrowed says Andreas Schleicher, head of the OECD's educational testing, "Even in rural areas and in disadvantaged environments, you see a remarkable performance".

***

The Education Ministry is responsible for half a million schools, fifteen million teachers, and two-hundred sixty-million schoolchildren who speak thirty-five languages. Fifty million are disadvantaged. In 1979, to leverage its meager budget, the Ministry offered urbanites a pact: space your children, and we will invest the savings in better schooling. Throughout the 1980s, media urged couples to have 'later, longer, fewer, better' children and the Urban Family Planning Program, the so-called 'one-child policy,' saw parents and grandparents focus their time and resources on educating a generation of little princes and princesses.

Responding to this influx of resources, Shanghai teachers pledged, "There are no students who cannot be taught well, only teachers who cannot teach well". They rethought, retested, and rewrote their textbooks and shared their discoveries in late-night faculty sessions and found that most failures stemmed from too-wide gaps in instructional sequences. They broke each lesson into smaller, carefully spaced, tightly coupled steps and permitted classes to advance only when every child demonstrated mastery of each step.

Finding that their approach required meticulous preparation and more skillful class management, the Shanghai Education Department limited them to fifteen hours classroom instruction each week, so they could spend time observing exemplary instructors, sharing observations with colleagues, experimenting, refining lesson plans, and publishing their findings in education journals.

When they apply for a promotion, the Education Department invites professors of education, master teachers from across the city, parents, and citizens to observe their 'public lesson.' Only Senior Teachers–curriculum innovators with outstanding test results who are expert child counselors and have led research–can apply for administrative roles and, to underline the importance of their work, the city provides its two thousand school principals with limousines, personal drivers, and regular sabbaticals abroad.

In 2009, Shanghai participated in PISA, the international test of fifteen-year-old math, science, and reading conducted by the Organization for Economic Cooperation and Development. The OECD reported[20], "Mathematics scores for the top performer, Shanghai, indicate an equivalent to over two years of formal schooling ahead of those observed in Massachusetts, a strong-performing US State".

When Shanghai drew further ahead in the 2012[21], critics accused the city of cheating, of rote learning, of excluding disadvantaged children, and of subjecting pupils to inhumane pressure, but the OECD responded[22], "Only two percent of American and three percent of European fifteen-year-olds reach the highest level of math performance, demonstrating that they can conceptualize, generalize, and use math based on their investigations and apply their knowledge in novel contexts. In Shanghai, it's over thirty percent... We've tested[23] twelve Chinese provinces and even in some impoverished areas found performance close to the OECD world average".

By 2015, even poor Chinese children were outperforming Western youngsters in tasks like managing bank accounts, understanding financial risks and responsibilities, estimating income tax and discerning fraud,

---

20 Shanghai tops global state school rankings, Chris Cook, FT, December 8, 2010.

21 Programme for International Student Assessment (PISA) Results. 2012. "Among the 34 OECD countries, the United States performed below average in mathematics in 2012 and is ranked 27th. Performance in reading and science are both close to the OECD average".

22 China shines in PISA exams

23 Are the Chinese cheating in PISA, or are we cheating ourselves? OECD Education Today. December 10, 2013

yet they used rote[24] memorization less than Western children. Their disposition improved with subject mastery and, when the OECD asked[25] if they felt happy at school, eighty-six percent of children agreed,[26] as did seventy-nine percent of their American cousins.

One US educator[27] observed, "A couple of decades ago, Shanghai's school system was plagued by the same problems we're facing. There were significant disparities between the achievement levels of native children and the children of migrant families, and overall educational levels were low. Today, the best international measures show that Shanghai has the highest levels of educational excellence and equity in the World, and their fifteen-year-olds are three grade levels ahead of kids in Massachusetts, our highest performing state". And Shanghai's schools rank only fifth nationally in *gaokao* results.

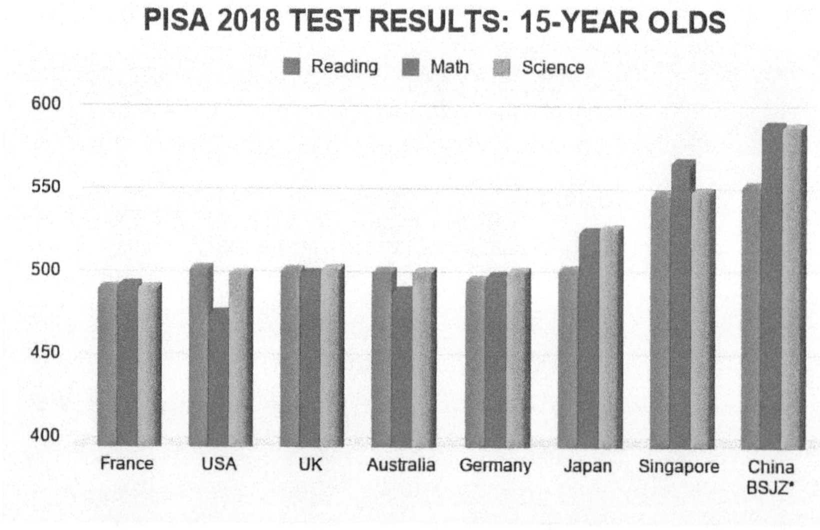

In 2006, just nine Chinese universities ranked among the World's top five hundred, and none reached the top one hundred. Twelve years later, there were sixty-two in the top five hundred, three in the top ten,

24 Lessons from PISA outcomes. Andreas Schleicher, OECD Observer No 297 Q4 2013
25 Ready to Learn: Students' Engagement, Drive, and Self-Beliefs. Vol. II OECD 2013. Ch. 1
26 Seventy-nine percent of American youngsters agreed.
27 Wendy Kopp, founder of Teach for America, to graduates. May 1, 2014

and one, Tsinghua, ranked first in engineering and computer science. By 2020, forty-six percent of eighteen-year-olds were at university[28] and ethnic minorities, which comprise nine percent of the population, occupied nine percent of undergraduate positions.

***

Though we eagerly compare heritable traits like height, appearance, and athletic ability, we rarely compare intelligence, yet we boast that America's Ashkenazi Jews, one percent of the population, have won forty percent of our Nobel Prizes. Chinese women are unambivalent. For millennia, they have refused to marry unintelligent men, 'dry branches', and thus culled their DNA from the gene pool. So ancient is this process that Ron Unz[29] found Chinese intelligence almost immune to socio-economic factors. Healthy Swiss are fifty times richer and receive twice the schooling of ill-nourished rural Chinese children who have carried a heavy disease burden for generations, yet Chinese IQs are consistently higher. "The reported Chinese PISA scores are far above those of the United States and nearly every European country, many of which are almost totally urbanized and have incomes ten times that of China. It is almost unimaginable that any non-East Asian population of rural villagers with annual incomes in the $1,000 range would have tested IQs very close to 100 [the US median]. We would certainly expect Chinese numbers to rise further as the country continues to develop. Still, my point is that East Asian IQs seem to possess a uniquely high floor compared with those of any other population".

What does that mean in practice?

Seventy percent of us have IQs between 85-115: we are smart enough to lead happy, productive lives. Five percent of us–those with IQs are above 125–are smart enough for medical school, but only one of us out of two hundred, with an IQ of 140, can handle a Ph.D. in theoretical

28 The figure in the US is forty-one percent.

29 The East Asian Exception to Socio-Economic IQ Influences. Ron Unz. The American Conservative, July 18, 2012

physics. And one in ten thousand have 160 IQs and can do groundbreaking work in any discipline.

The US, with a national average IQ of 100, has thirty-six thousand of these super-geniuses while China, with four times more people and a national IQ of 105, has three hundred thousand[30]. Anatoly Karlin predicts[31] that a combination of the Flynn effect[32], poverty elimination and improved rural education and nutrition will lift the national IQ average to Shanghai's 108, thus doubling the pool of super-geniuses. Since virtually all Chinese super-geniuses work for the government, it is not surprising that Henry Kissinger[33] concluded, "The Chinese are smarter than us".

Better than IQ for predicting[34] academic success is the scope of children's working memory[35], where Chinese children have another advantage. Basic literacy in Chinese demands a working memory capable of handling at least three thousand characters, and mastery requires the use of contextual variables to extract their meaning from millions of possible combinations. The implications of this become clear if we compare our old reading primer, *Fun with Dick and Jane*, with theirs. *The Three Character Classic* teaches the three thousand basic characters along with Confucian history, filial piety, public morality and, of course, the importance of study–and grandparents[36] still delight to hear three-year-olds recite it from memory.

I have reproduced it here in its entirety, but to emphasize the culture's

---

30 Because IQ is distributed logarithmically, and China has four times more people.

31 Through A Glass Ceiling Darkly: Racial IQ Disparities and the Wealth of Nations ANATOLY KARLIN • APRIL 16, 2012

32 The Flynn Effect is the substantial, sustained increase in intelligence test scores measured across the World in the 20th century: when the new test subjects take the older tests, in almost every case, their average scores are significantly above the earlier norm of 100.

33 Nixon's China Game. PBS. January 31, 2000

34 "Children's working memory skills at five years of age were the best predictor of reading, spelling, and math outcomes six years later. By contrast, IQ accounted for a smaller portion of unique variance to reading and math skills and was not a significant predictor of spelling performance". Investigating the predictive roles of working memory and IQ in academic attainment. Alloway TP, Alloway RG. J Exp Child Psychol. 2010 May;106(1):20-9.

35 Analogous to computer RAM; working memory is the part of short-term memory devoted to immediate conscious perceptual and linguistic processing.

36 Google 'Baby Genius Recites San Zi Jing'

approach to literacy, moral education and, above all, memory-training. Millions of little children can recite this from memory:

人之初，性本善。
Men at their birth are naturally good.
性相近，习相远。
Their natures are much the same; their habits become widely different.
苟不教，性乃迁。
If foolishly there is no teaching, the nature will deteriorate.
教之道，贵以专。
The right way in teaching is to attach the utmost importance to thoroughness.
昔孟母，择邻处。
Of old, the mother of Mencius chose a neighborhood;
子不学，断机杼。
and when her child would not learn, she broke the shuttle from the loom.
窦燕山，有义方。
Tou of the Swallow Hills had the right method.
教五子，名俱扬。
He taught five sons, each of whom raised the family reputation.
养不教，父之过。
To feed without teaching is the father's fault.
教不严，师之惰。
To teach without severity is the teacher's laziness.
子不学，非所宜。
If the child does not learn, this is not as it should be.
幼不学，老何为。
If he does not learn while young, what will he be when old?
玉不琢，不成器。
If jade is not polished, it cannot become a thing of use.
人不学，不知义。
If a man does not learn, he cannot know his duty towards his neighbor.
为人子，方少时。
He who is the son of a man when he is young

亲师友，习礼仪。
should attach himself to his teachers and friends, and practice ceremonial usages.
香九龄，能温席。
Xiāng, at nine years of age, would warm his parents' bed.
孝于亲，所当执。
Filial piety towards parents is that to which we should hold fast.
融四岁，能让梨。
Jung, at four years of age, could yield the bigger pears.
弟于长，宜先知。
To behave as a younger brother towards elders is one of the first things to know.
首孝弟，次见闻。
Begin with filial piety and fraternal love, then see and hear.
知某数，识某文。
Learn to count and learn to read.
一而十，十而百。
Units and tens, then tens and hundreds,
百而千，千而万。
hundreds and thousands, thousands and tens of thousands.
三才者，天地人。
The Three Forces are Heaven, Earth, and Man.
三光者，日月星。
The Three Luminaries are the sun, the moon, and the stars.
三纲者，君臣义。
The Three Bonds are the obligation between sovereign and subject,
父子亲，夫妇顺。
the love between father and child and the harmony between husband and wife.
曰春夏，曰秋冬。
We speak of spring and summer; we speak of autumn and winter.
此四时，运不穷。
These four seasons revolve without ceasing.
曰南北，曰西东。
We speak of north and south; we speak of east and west.

此四方，应乎中。

These four points respond to the requirements of the centre.

曰水火，木金土。

We speak of water, fire, wood, metal, and earth.

此五行，本乎数。

These five elements have their origin in number.

曰仁义，礼智信。

We speak of charity of heart and of duty towards one's neighbor, of propriety, of wisdom, and of truth.

此五常，不容紊。

These five virtues admit to no compromise.

稻粱菽，麦黍稷。

Rice, spiked millet, pulse, wheat, glutinous millet, and common millet.

此六谷，人所食。

These six grains are those which men eat.

马牛羊，鸡犬豕。

The horse, the ox, the sheep, the fowl, the dog, the pig.

此六畜，人所饲。

These six animals are those which men keep.

惟牛犬，功最著。

Especially of the ox and dog is the merit most conspicuous,

能耕田，能守户。

one can plough the fields, the other can guard the house.

昧天良，屠市肆。

It is to obscure your natural goodness of disposition to kill them and expose them for sale.

戒物食，免罪处。

Beware of eating them, and so avoid being punished.

曰喜怒，曰哀惧。

We speak of joy, of anger, we speak of pity, of fear,

爱恶欲，七情具。

of love, of hate, and of desire. These are the seven passions.

匏土革，木石金。

The gourd, earthenware, skin, wood, stone, metal,

与丝竹，乃八音。
silk, and bamboo,
yield the eight musical sounds.
高曾祖，父而身。
Great great grandfather, great grandfather, grandfather, father and self,
身而子，子而孙。
self and son, son and grandson,
自子孙，至元曾。
from son and grandson, on to great grandson and great great grandson.
乃九族，而之伦。
These are the nine agnates, constituting the kinships of man.
父子恩，夫妇从。
Affection between father and child, harmony between husband and wife,
兄则友，弟则恭。
friendliness on the part of elder brothers, respectfulness on the part of younger brothers,
长幼序，友与朋。
precedence between elders and youngsters, as between friend and friend,
君则敬，臣则忠。
respect on the part of the sovereign, loyalty on the part of the subject.
此十义，人所同。
These ten obligations are common to all men.
凡训蒙，须讲究。
In the education of the young, there should be explanation and elucidation,
详训诂，名句读。
careful teaching of the interpretations of commentators, and due attention to paragraphs and sentences.
为学者，必有初。
Those who are learners must have a beginning.
小学终，至四书。
The "Little Learning" finished, they proceed to the "Four Books".
论语者，二十篇。
There is the Lun Yü, in twenty sections.

群弟子，记善言。

In this, the various disciples have recorded the wise sayings of Confucius.

孟子者，七篇止。

The works of Mencius are comprised in seven sections.

讲道德，说仁义。

These explain the W Y and the exemplification thereof and expound charity and duty toward one's neighbor.

作中庸，子思笔。

The "Chung Yung" was written by the pen of Tzu-ssu;

中不偏，庸不易。

"Chung" (the middle) being that which does not lean towards any side, "Yung" (the course) being that which cannot be changed.

作大学，乃曾子。

He who wrote "The Great Learning" was the philosopher Tsêng.

自修齐，至平治。

Beginning with cultivation of the individual and ordering of the family, it goes on to government of one's own State and tranquilization of the Empire.

孝经通，四书熟。

When the "Classic of Filial Piety" is mastered, and the "Four Books" are known by heart.

如六经，始可读。

The next step is the "Six Classics", which may now be studied.

诗书易，礼春秋。

The "Books of Poetry", of "History", and of "Changes", the "Rites of the Chou Dynasty", the "Book of Rites", and the "Spring and Autumn Annals",

号六经，当讲求。

are called the Six Classics, which should be carefully explained and analyzed.

有连山，有归藏。

There is the "Lien shan" system, there is the "Kuei tsang",

有周易，三易详。

and there is the system of Changes of the Chou Dynasty; such are the three systems which elucidate the Changes.

有典谟，有训诰。

There are the Regulations, the Counsels, the Instructions, the Announcements,

有誓命，书之奥。

the Oaths, the Charges; these are the profundities of the Book of History.

我周公，作周礼。

Our Duke of Chou drew up the Ritual of the Chou Dynasty,

著六官，存治体。

in which he set forth the duties of the six classes of officials, and thus gave a settled form to the government.

大小戴，注礼记。

The Elder and the Younger Tai wrote commentaries on the Book of Rites.

述圣言，礼乐备。

They published the holy words, and Ceremonies and Music were set in order.

曰国风，曰雅颂。

We speak of the "Kuo feng", we speak of the "Ya" and of the "Sung".

号四诗，当讽咏。

These are the four sections of the Book of Poetry, which should be hummed over and over.

诗既亡，春秋作。

When odes ceased to be made, the "Spring and Autumn Annals" were produced.

寓褒贬，别善恶。

These "Annals" contain praise and blame, and distinguish the good from the bad.

三传者，有公羊。

The three commentaries upon the above, include that of Kung-Yang,

有左氏，有穀梁。

that of Tso, and that of Ku-Liang.

经既明，方读子。

When the classics are understood, then the writings of the various philosophers should be read.

撮其要，记其事。

Pick out the important points in each and take a note of all facts.

五子者，有荀杨。
The five chief philosophers are Hsün, Yang,
文中子，及老庄。
Wên Chung Tzu, Lao Tzu, and Chuang Tzu.
经子通，读诸史。
When the Classics and the Philosophers are mastered, the various histories should then be read,
考世系，知终始。
and the genealogical connections should be examined, so that the end of one dynasty and the beginning of the next may be known.
自羲农，至黄帝。
From Fu Hsi and Shên Nung on to the Yellow emperor,
号三皇，居上世。
these are called the Three Rulers, who lived in the early ages.
唐有虞，号二帝。
T'ang and Yu-Yü are called the Two emperors.
相揖逊，称盛世。
They abdicated, one after the other, and theirs was called the Golden Age.
夏有禹，商有汤。
The Hsia dynasty had Yü; and the Shang dynasty had T'ang;
周文武，称三王。
the Chou dynasty had Wên and Wu; these are called the Three Kings.
夏传子，家天下。
Under the Hsia dynasty the throne was transmitted from father to son, making a family possession of the empire.
四百载，迁夏社。
After four hundred years, the Imperial sacrifice passed from the House of Hsia.
汤伐夏，国号商。
T'ang the completer destroyed the Hsia Dynasty and the dynastic title became Shang.
六百载，至纣亡。
The line lasted for six hundred years, ending with Chou Hsin.
周武王，始诛纣。
King Wu of the Chou Dynasty finally slew Chou Hsin.

八百载，最长久。

His own line lasted for eight hundred years; the longest dynasty of all.

周辙东，王纲堕。

When the Chous made tracks eastwards, the feudal bond was slackened;

逞干戈，尚游说。

the arbitrament of spear and shields prevailed; and peripatetic politicians were held in high esteem.

始春秋，终战国。

This period began with the Spring and Autumn Epoch and ended with that of the Warring States.

五霸强，七雄出。

Next, the Five Chieftains domineered, and the Seven Martial States came to the front.

嬴秦氏，始兼并。

Then the House of Ch'in, descended from the Ying clan, finally united all the States under one sway.

传二世，楚汉争。

The throne was transmitted to Erh Shih, upon which followed the struggle between the Ch'u and the Han States.

高祖兴，汉业建。

Then Kao Tsu arose, and the House of Han was established.

至孝平，王莽篡。

When we come to the reign of Hsiao P'ing, Wang Mang usurped the throne.

光武兴，为东汉。

Then Kuang Wu arose and founded the Eastern Han Dynasty.

四百年，终于献。

It lasted four hundred years and ended with the emperor Hsien.

魏蜀吴，争汉鼎。

Wei, Shu, and Wu fought for the sovereignty of the Hans.

号三国，迄两晋。

They were called the Three Kingdoms and existed until the Two Chin Dynasties.

宋齐继，梁陈承。
Then followed the Sung and the Ch'i dynasties, and after them the Liang and Ch'ên dynasties.
为南朝，都金陵。
These are the southern dynasties, with their capital at Nanking.
北元魏，分东西。
The northern dynasties are the Wei dynasty of the Yüan family, which split into Eastern and Western Wei,
宇文周，兴高齐。
the Chou dynasty of the Yü-wen family, with the Ch'i dynasty of the Kao family.
迨至隋，一土宇。
At length, under the Sui dynasty, the empire was united under one ruler.
不再传，失统绪。
The throne was not transmitted twice, succession to power being lost.
唐高祖，起义师。
The first emperor of the T'ang dynasty raised volunteer troops.
除隋乱，创国基。
He put an end to the disorder of the House of Sui and established the foundations of his line.
二十传，三百载。
Twenty times the throne was transmitted in a period of three hundred years.
梁灭之，国乃改。
The Liang State destroyed it, and the dynastic title was changed.
梁唐晋，及汉周。
The Liang, the T'ang, the Chin, the Han, and the Chou,
称五代，皆有由。
are called the Five Dynasties, and there was a reason for the establishment of each.
炎宋兴，受周禅。
Then the fire-led House of Sung arose and received the resignation of the house of Chou.

十八传，南北混。
Eighteen times the throne was transmitted, and then the North and the South were reunited.
辽与金，帝号纷。
Under the Liao and the Chin dynasties, there was confusion of Imperial titles,
逮灭辽，宋犹存。
when the Liao dynasty was destroyed, the Sung dynasty still remained.
至元兴，金绪歇。
When the Yüan dynasty arose, the line of the Chin Tartars came to an end,
有宋世，一同灭。
and the House of Sung was destroyed together with it.
并中国，兼戎翟。
It united the Middle Kingdom and attached to the empire the tribes of the north and west.
明太祖，久亲师。
The founder of the Ming dynasty was for a long time engaged in warfare.
传建文，方四祀。
He transmitted the throne to Chien Wên only four years,
迁北京，永乐嗣。
when the capital was transferred to Peking, and Yung Lo succeeded the latter.
逮崇祯，煤山逝。
At length, Ch'ung Chêng died on the Coal Hill.
辽于金，皆称帝。
The Liao Tartars and the Chin Tartars all took the Imperial title.
元灭金，绝宋世。
The Yüans (Mongols) destroyed the Chin Tartars and put an end to the House of Sung.
莅中国，兼戎翟。
They governed the Middle Kingdom, and also the wild tribes of the north and west;
九十年，国祚废。
after ninety years their mandate was exhausted.

太祖兴，国大明。

Then T'ai Tsu arose, his dynasty being known as Ta Ming.

号洪武，都金陵。

He took as his year-title Hung Wu and fixed his capital at Chin-ling (Nanking).

逮成祖，迁燕京。

At length, under the emperor Ch'êng Tsu, a move was made to Swallow City (Peking).

十七世，至崇祯。

There were seventeen reigns in all, down to and including Ch'ung Chêng.

权奄肆，寇如林。

The hold on the people was relaxed, and rebels sprang up thick as forests.

至李闯，神器终。

Then came Li Ch'uang, and the Imperial regalia were destroyed.

清太祖，应景命。

The founder of the Ch'ing or Pure dynasty responded to the glorious summons;

靖四方，克大定。

he tranquilized the four quarters (N,S,E,W), and achieved the final settlement of the empire.

廿二史，全在兹。

The Twenty-two Dynastic Histories are all embraced in the above.

载治乱，知兴衰。

They contain examples of good and bad government, whence may be learnt the principles of prosperity and decay.

读史书，考实录。

Ye who read history must study the State Annals,

通古今，若亲目。

whereby you will understand ancient and modern events, as though having seen them with your own eyes.

口而诵，心而惟。

Recite them with the mouth and ponder over them in your hearts.

朝于斯，夕于斯。

Do this in the morning; do this in the evening.

昔仲尼，师项橐。
Of old, Confucius took Hasiang T'o for his teacher.
古圣贤，尚勤学。
The inspired men and sages of old studied diligently nevertheless.
赵中令，读鲁论。
Chao, President of the Council, studied the Lu text of the "Lun Yü".
彼既仕，学且勤。
He, when already an official, studied, and moreover with diligence.
披蒲编，削竹简。
One opened out rushes and plaited them together; another scraped tablets of bamboo.
彼无书，且知勉。
These men had no books, but they knew how to make an effort.
头悬梁，锥刺股。
One tied his head to the beam above him; another pricked his thigh with an awl.
彼不教，自勤苦。
They were not taught, but toiled hard of their own accord.
如囊萤，如映雪。
Then we have one who put fireflies in a bag, and again another who used the white glare from snow.
家虽贫，学不缀。
Although their families were poor, these men studied unceasingly.
如负薪，如挂角。
Again, there was one who carried fuel, and another who used horns as pegs.
身虽劳，犹苦卓。
Although they toiled with their bodies, they were nevertheless remarkable for their application.
苏老泉，二十七。
Su Lao-ch'üan, at the age of twenty-seven,
始发愤，读书籍。
at last began to show his energy and devote himself to the study of books.
彼既老，犹悔迟。
Then, when already past the age, he deeply regretted his delay.

尔小生，宜早思。
You little boys should take thought betimes.
若梁灏，八十二。
Then there was Liang Hao, who at the age of eighty-two,
对大廷，魁多士。
made his replies in the great hall and came out first among many scholars.
彼既成，众称异。
When thus late he had succeeded, all men pronounced him a prodigy.
尔小生，宜立志。
You little boys should make up your minds to work.
莹八岁，能咏诗。
Jung at eight years of age, could compose poetry.
泌七岁，能赋棋。
Pi, at seven years of age, could make an epigram on "wei-ch'i".
彼颖悟，人称奇。
These youths were quick of apprehension, and people declared them to be prodigies.
尔幼学，当效之。
You young learners ought to imitate them.
蔡文姬，能辨琴。
Ts'ai Wên-chi was able to judge from the sound of a psaltery.
谢道韫，能咏吟。
Hsieh Tao-yün was able to compose verses.
彼女子，且聪敏。
They were only girls, yet they were quick and clever.
尔男子，当自警。
You boys ought to rouse yourselves.
唐刘晏，方七岁。
Liu Yen of the T'ang dynasty, when only seven years of age,
举神童，作正字。
was ranked as an"inspired child" and was appointed a Corrector of Texts.
彼虽幼，身己仕。
He, although a child, was already in an official post.
尔幼学，勉而致。
You young learners strive to bring about a like result.

有为者，亦若是。
Those who work will also succeed as he did.
犬守夜，鸡司晨。
The dog keeps guard by night; the cock proclaims the dawn.
苟不学，曷为人。
If foolishly you do not study, how can you become men?
蚕吐丝，蜂酿蜜。
The silkworm produces silk, the bee makes honey.
人不学，不如物。
If man does not learn, he is not equal to the brutes.
幼而学，壮而行。
Learn while young, and when grown up apply what you have learnt;
上致君，下泽民。
influencing the sovereign above; benefiting the people below.
扬名声，显父母。
Make a name for yourselves, and glorify your father and mother,
光于前，裕于后。
shed lustre on your ancestors, enrich your posterity.
人遗子，金满赢。
Men bequeath to their children coffers of gold;
我教子，惟一经。
But I teach you children only this book.
勤有功，戏无益。
Diligence has its reward; play has no advantages,
戒之哉，宜勉力。
Oh, be on your guard and put forth all your strength.

CHAPTER 4

Leadership

The art of governance lies in attracting men of moral integrity, the kind who are only drawn to rulers who demonstrate moral integrity in their own lives. And how do rulers demonstrate moral integrity? By doing their duty and practicing compassion. Confucius. *The Doctrine of the Mean.*

***

As has been the case since the birth of Christ, China is governed by a Confucian *just hierarchy* that is designed to weed out sociopaths and recruit able, compassionate people willing to sacrifice their lives in service to the people.

So it is not surprising that, instead of viewing the State as intrusive, untrustworthy, and threatening, the Chinese see themselves belonging to a family-state and view their politicians as family patriarchs. Under such leadership, they value collective over individual well-being, the future over the present, pragmatism above ideology, and outcomes over promises–a value system that provides social cohesion and has made China the richest, strongest nation on earth for most of its existence.

***

Today, in place of the Emperor, morally outstanding people guide the nation's destiny. They are ninety-three million Communist Party members whose code of conduct resembles Rotary International's: service, integrity, world understanding, goodwill, and peace. They have sworn[37] "To bear the peoples' hardships first and enjoy their comforts last," despite the fact that membership in the Party is no more profitable[38] than in Rotary International's, and admission is more restrictive.

During the three-year application process, candidates explain their motives for applying; attend weekly classes in Party history and ideology; volunteer for local chores; list their shortcomings; detail their families' personal, financial, and political information; earn recommendations from two Party members; and supply character references from two non-relatives who guarantee their moral integrity for life.

Most university graduates apply, but only one-tenth gain admission. "I was very excited," said Allen Lin[39], a twenty-three-year-old college senior who credits his admission to his high grades, service to student government, and assistance to classmates. "Joining the Party is not easy–of the forty students in my class, only five were admitted". "It took me two years," said another graduate, "There were seventy-eight people and my party branch only recruited three. I wanted to join because it is really rare, a small group of people, and because I have a deep faith in the Party". Yet the People's Daily regularly laments[40] the shortage of youthful altruists and quoted one disillusioned applicant, "Many student members have little rigor and only a very shallow understanding of Party discipline. I was taught when I was young that the Party represents justice and that cadres are more dedicated in their jobs, but I found that students join because they want to work for a state-owned company or become an official".

Forty percent are women, one-third are 'exemplary farmers, herdsmen, and fishermen,' one quarter is white-collar workers, one-sixth

37 From *Advice to Officials*, by an eleventh-century chancellor, Fan Zhongyan, a famous altruist.

38 Economic Returns to Communist Party Membership: Evidence from Urban Chinese Twins. Hongbin Li, Pak Wai, Liu Junsen, Zhang Ning Ma. The Economic Journal. Vol. 117.

39 Membership in the Communist Party of China: Who is Being Admitted and How? | JSTOR Daily. By: R.W. McMorrow December 19, 2015

40 Chinese students flock to join the Communist Party. The Telegraph.Malcolm Moore, August 9, 2013.

retirees, one-eighth civil servants, one-tenth are ethnic minorities[41]. Between them, members contribute a billion dollars in annual dues and billions of volunteer hours, usually conducting surveys on rainy Sunday afternoons. They declare their membership on job applications because private firms appreciate the Party's thorough vetting. Though one-tenth will become officials, professors, generals, CEOs, or celebrities, most will simply mobilize support for new policies or volunteer in emergencies.

Their ability to mobilize is impressive. In 2000, China's application to join the World Trade Organization triggered public demonstrations since membership would disadvantage agriculture[42], undermine cherished industrial policies[43], and destroy eleven million jobs.

For the first time, the Party invited exemplary capitalists to join[44] its ranks and taught them the Five Unifiers: unified understanding so that everyone knows why China needs the WTO; unified policy so that everyone understands the local problems WTO membership cause; unified planning to coordinate different interests in applying WTO provisions nationally; unified direction so that leaders take direction from the next unit above; unified action so that, once consensus is reached, everyone at every level simultaneously applies their energy to solving WTO-related problems. The capitalists committed to hiring displaced workers, which swayed popular opinion, and China joined the WTO.

The Party is equally impressive in local emergencies. One night in 2010, a Shanghai high-rise fire killed fifty-eight people. Before dawn, members had coordinated twenty-five fire stations, a hundred fire trucks, and a thousand firefighters along with police, hospitals, finance, insurance, housing, donations, counseling, criminal investigators, and schools. Forty-eight hours later, state-owned insurers compensated families for lost property and wrote $250,000 checks for each death. Ten days later, Shanghai mayor Han Zheng confessed, "Our poor supervision of the construction industry caused the fire". He implemented new building

41 Ethnic minorities make up a twelfth of China's population.

42 WTO rules prohibit them from subsidizing domestic food production, even for local consumption.

43 Policies that advanced countries themselves used during their development phases.

44 There are currently thirty-one billionaires in the 3,000-member NPC.

codes, fired or demoted thirty officials, and indicted twenty-two, most of whom went to prison, two for sixteen years. The contrast with London's Grenfell Tower fire is stark[45].

The Party's principle responsibility, however, is the nation's future. Its 2015 report[46], abbreviated here, reveals priorities rarely discussed in the West [emphasis added]:

1. **Sustainability Led by Science and Technology**: the overriding mission of early-stage socialism is liberating and developing the forces of production. Socialism requires a minimal foundation of material and technological development, so science and technology's determining effect needs to be fully understood. We should recognize the strategic importance of science and technology in allocating scarce resources.

45 The first responders to the 2020 Coronavirus epidemic from outside Wuhan were 48,000 Party volunteers–mostly health specialists.

46 Bulletin of a conference on China's economy from the Communist Party Central Committee, December 2015. Quoted in <u>*A Theory of China's Miracle*</u> by Cheng Enfu and Ding Xiaoqin.

2. **Orienting Production to Improving Ordinary People's Livelihood**: the principal contradiction in socialism at its earliest stage is between people's increasing material and cultural needs and the backwardness of social production. This can only be overcome by the speedy, steady development of productive capacities–socialism's primary task in its initial phases. Improving people's livelihoods is an endless task, and new challenges continuously emerge... We should realistically assess the effects of our actions on living standards and ensure that public services create a reliable social safety net. Our objective must be a society in which all people contribute to the satisfaction of human needs to the extent they are able while enjoying access to the material, social, and spiritual resources they need for the full development of their human potential in accord with the needs of sustainability[47].
3. **Public Ownership Takes Precedence in National Property Rights**: The institutional guarantee for all Chinese people is that they will share the fruits of development... This principle highlights a fundamental difference between the socialist economy and the modern capitalist economic system, in which private ownership is dominant. We should learn from past errors of state-sector reform that allowed a narrow elite to amass huge fortunes by misdirecting funds. The collective and cooperative model of Chinese village economies needs further investment. New policies must be introduced to enhance the vitality, competitiveness, and risk management of the public economy[48].
4. **The Primacy of Labor in the Distribution of Wealth**. In any capitalist economy, wage laborers are paid only for their labor power expenditure–not for the value of the commodities they produce. Under these conditions, the specific wage a worker earns is associated with their position and performance... The distribution of wealth in our Chinese socialist economy must be

47 Everyone now has a home, an income, plenty of food and clothes, education, safe streets, health insurance, and old-age care.

48 Inequality has fallen each year. Public ownership is the highest in the World.

guided by the needs of labor, not capital. We must strive against exploitation and polarization, bridge the income gap, and increase income for all citizens coincident with economic growth and labor productivity. It is vital to establish a sound, scientific mechanism for determining wage levels and a means for regular wage increases[49].

5. **Market Principles Steered by the State**. The anarchic character of the capitalist market combined with individual capitalists' drive to innovate to reduce labor costs leads to periodic crises of overproduction in which workers suffer most... The government's responsibility is keeping macroeconomic policy steady, strengthening public services, guaranteeing fair competition, reinforcing market supervision, promoting collective prosperity, and rectifying–or compensating for–market failures.
6. **Speedy Development with High Performance**: A low growth rate with insufficient resource use inhibits full employment, wealth accumulation, and public welfare. A higher growth rate with extensive rather than intensive resource utilization is equally detrimental to ecological sustainability and distributive justice. We need a dialectical analysis[50] of indices based on the gross domestic product, GDP.
7. **Balanced Development with Structural Coordination**: We must abandon the persistent misconception that, if we eliminate economic surplus caused by administrative intervention, excess production capacity, and product surplus formed by marketization can be balanced automatically without government intervention. This neoliberal fallacy and its consequences explain the large structural excess capacity in the economy and go against the spirit of Chinese socialism.
8. **Economic Sovereignty and Openness**: A final principle is to open the economy to trade and investment because it is beneficial to economic growth at home and abroad, optimizing the

49 Real wages continue to double every decade.

50 Dialectical analyses probe the significance and limitations of ideas and values. If a dialectical analysis is sound, conclusions will be, too.

> allocation of resources and improving interactions between industry and technology. However, developing countries should devote particular care to their strategies and tactics when opening up to developed countries, given the risks and uncertainties inherent in such an unequal relationship.

Critics may carp about its pervasive presence, but the Party keeps its promises. By 2021, the centennial of its founding, everyone in China's lowest income bracket will own a home and have a guaranteed income, plenty of food and clothes, safe streets, health insurance, a pension and old age career. Their children will graduate high school three years ahead of ours and live longer healthier lives.

***

In addition to the moral uprightness required for Party membership, government officials must demonstrate extraordinary intelligence, competence, and self-discipline. They earn their positions in a relentless competition that begins in primary school and ends when–out of eight million annual university graduates–the brightest apply for the civil service. The top thirty thousand scorers spend weeks in interviews to demonstrate their capacity to learn and solve problems using logic, intuition, creativity, experience, and wisdom. The twenty-seven thousand who succeed (most with IQs above 140) will earn their first promotions after they have lived in poverty-stricken villages and raised local incomes by fifty percent.

Why the Communist Party Sent Me to the Desert

by Heng Xiao[51]

My adventure began with a phone call late one summer night. It was my boss, the deputy director of the state-funded Institute of International Studies. He had some unexpected news. The personnel department of our Academy had selected me as a candidate for its Grassroots Service Program (GSP) in one of China's most underdeveloped provinces, located some 1,500 miles from where I was living in Beijing. Before hanging up, he gravely informed me that all of my peers had refused to join the program–leaving me with little choice but to accept the offer. What followed was an incredibly difficult decision for me. As a sophomore researcher, I had spent the past year doing staff work instead of academic research, and I feared I might have fallen behind my colleagues. After consulting my wife, we agreed that my boss's call was to inform me of my participation in the program, not to ask my opinion on the matter. I reluctantly called back and accepted his offer. In hindsight, most of us–the 17 researchers who accepted GSP posts–wished we had never received that call.

The GSP's Chinese name is *guazhi. Guazhi* means "to hang your position," in the way one hangs a coat, and it is a common phrase among China's state-sponsored entities, including research institutes like the one I was part of. It involves temporarily moving to a new position for at least a year, while your old job is guaranteed upon your return. At the time, it was common practice for young China Communist Party (CCP) members to take on this responsibility at some point. This temporary job sometimes has no relation at all to the cadre's previous field of work. For example, it would not be unusual for a researcher on US foreign policy to be asked to manage rural development in

51 *The Gobi Diaries*, Part 1, by Heng Xiao. http://www.sixthtone.com/news/623/gobi-diaries-1-why-communist-party-sent-me-desert

> the Gobi Desert. The *guazhi* program is based on the traditional Chinese belief that different experiences lead to real knowledge and make a man competent. In its most radical form during the Cultural Revolution, this traditional belief was manifested as the "Up to the Mountains and Down to the Countryside" movement. During the Cultural Revolution, universities and colleges in China were closed, and urban youth were sent to poor, remote rural areas to, in the words of Mao Zedong, "learn from ordinary people". Although far removed from the modern-day GSP, the intention is similar: namely, a notion that the most thorough education comes from diversified experiences…
>
> Local officials were waiting for us at the airport when we landed at our destination on December 1. After a short rest and a dinner full of animated speeches, we–the 17 exhausted researchers–were dispatched to our new homes by town officials. Upon getting in the car, I was told that I would be working almost 13 miles from the urban area. During our drive along the rugged country road, I had a good talk with one of my future colleagues, the town's Party committee's vice-secretary. At one point, he asked me a strange question, "Secretary, where will you live in the city? Will the municipal government rent you an apartment?" It seemed that my future colleagues did not even know I was required to live where I worked. I began to realize that there would be no bedroom, no bathroom, and no nice furniture waiting for me. It was immediately apparent upon arriving at the town hall that I had been right in my premonitions, which did not make me happy at all. There was no breakfast or dinner provided, and I wasn't allowed to cook in the office. There was no hot water and no heating at night, despite temperatures of minus 20 degrees Celsius. I later reflected that the outdoor toilet I had noticed upon entering was the least of my worries compared with the other problems. On the plus side, my office was bright.

As Heng Xiao rises–from section chief, deputy division chief, division chief, deputy director and director of general office, vice-minister,

minister, deputy-state leader to state leader–his demonstration of the Confucian virtues–compassion, righteousness, propriety, wisdom, and fidelity–will be increasingly scrutinized. Zhao Bing Bing[52], a mid-level official in Liaoning Province explained the process to Daniel Bell:

> I was promoted in 2004 through my department's internal competition (30 percent on written exam results, 30 percent on interviews and public speaking, 30 percent on public opinion of my work, and 10 percent on education, seniority, and my current position) and became the youngest deputy division chief. In 2009, Liaoning Province (pop. 44 million) announced an open selection of officials in the national media. Sixty candidates met the qualifications, the top five of whom were invited for further interviews. Based on their test scores (40 percent) and interview results (60 percent), the top three were then appraised. The Liaoning Province organizational department sent four appraisers who spent a whole day checking my previous records. Eighty of my colleagues were asked to vote–more than thirty of whom were asked to talk with the appraisers about my merits and shortcomings–and they submitted the appraisal result to the provincial Standing Committee of the CCP for review.
>
> In principle, the person who scored the highest and whose appraisals were not problematic would be promoted. However, because my university major, work experience, and previous performance were the best fit for the position, I was finally appointed department chief of the Liaoning Provincial Foreign Affairs Office even though my overall score was second-best [the government discriminates positively in promoting women–ed]. Before the official appointment, there was a seven-day public notice period during which anybody could report to the organization department concerns about my promotion. I didn't spend any money during my three promotions; all I did was study and work hard and do my best to be a good person.

---

52 Daniel Bell and Zhao Bing Bing, *The China Model.*

> In 2013, thanks to an exchange program, I worked temporarily in the CCP International Department. The temporary exchange system offers opportunities to learn about different issues in different regions and areas like government and SOEs. In a famous quote, Chairman Mao said, "Once the political lines have been clearly defined, the decisive factor will be the cadres [trained specialists]". So, the CCP highly values organizational construction and the selection and appointment of specialists. There is a special department managing this work, The Organization Department, established in 1924, and Mao was its first leader. The department is mainly responsible for the macro-management of the leaders and the staff (team building), including the management system, regulations and laws, human resource system reforms—planning, research, and direction, as well as proposing suggestions on the leadership change and the (re)appointment of cadres. Also, it has the responsibility of training and supervising cadres. The cadre selection criteria are: a person must have 'both ability and moral integrity and the latter should be prioritized'. The evaluation of moral integrity focuses mostly on loyalty to the Party, service to the people, self-discipline, and integrity. Based on different levels and positions, the emphases of evaluation are also different. For intermediate and senior officials, the focus is on their persistence in faith and ideals, political stance, and coordination with the central Party. High-level cadres are measured against great politicians, and, among them, experience in multiple positions is very important.

Though their perquisites–overseas education for offspring who flunk the *gaokao*—improve as they rise, salaries are niggardly: the President's salary is sixty-six thousand dollars[53]. The track records of the top one thousand politicians, available online, are impressive. Most began their careers in the late sixties as manual laborers in dirt-poor villages. After doubling the incomes of those they served, they were promoted to run

53 After deducting income tax, social insurance, occupational pension, and housing provident fund, enough to purchase a home and a car and support a family of five.

huge provinces, Fortune 500 companies,[54] Universities, and space programs. They spent sabbaticals on the leafy, lake-studded campus of The Academy of Governance, earned PhDs, met the World's leading thinkers, critiqued senior officials' policies, and studied at Harvard, Stanford, Oxford, Cambridge, or the University of Tokyo. Since that was the current President's path, let us take this opportunity to meet him.

54 China is home to more Fortune 500 companies than any country. Most are state-owned.

CHAPTER 5

Filial Son

The rule of virtue can be compared to the Pole Star, which commands the homage of the multitude of stars without leaving its place while around it, all rotate. Confucius, *Analects*

Xi Jinping, brother Xi Yuanping, father Xi Zhongxun, 1958

In the 1960s, Mao sent thousands of elite children to live in remote villages, hoping that some would gain insight into the peasants' plight. Many, repelled by what they found, fled back to their parents but one who stayed is now China's President, and his family was legendary before he was born.

When Japan's invasion interrupted seventeen-year-old Xi Zhongxun's schooling in 1933, he recruited an army, established a rebel area in Shaanxi Province, and became a general at nineteen. Captured in 1936, he escaped from a Nationalist prison. Sentenced to death by fellow Party members for his liberal views, he sat on death row until, miraculously, Mao Zedong arrived at the end of the Long March and pardoned him. He became a provincial governor at twenty-three–and his adventures were just beginning.

Zhongxun spent twelve years governing Shaanxi Province, occasionally leaving his desk to rescue beleaguered armies. A superb negotiator–Mao found his equal only in the *Romance of the Three Kingdoms*—he would ride alone into the hills and return weeks later with entire rebel armies trotting behind him. People who knew him admired his competence, compassion, and outspoken honesty, says Sidney Rittenberg, "Xi Zhongxun took me with him a number of times, traveling in the countryside among the villages and he knew whose baby was sick and whose grandpa had rheumatism and so forth. He would go to these homes and talk to them, and they loved him. He was always getting into trouble because of his plebeian style and democratic way of thinking. In my opinion, he was a very good man, probably the most democratic-minded member of the old Party leadership. I just hope that a lot of this rubbed off on the son".

During the Cultural Revolution, Zhongxun was jailed for seven years for his outspoken pragmatism, then rehabilitated and assigned to govern destitute Guangdong Province, whose local government was trying to stop people from fleeing to neighboring Hong Kong, where wages were one hundred times higher. He liberalized Guangdong's economy, stopped the exodus, and built China's first Special Enterprise Zone, which now attracts Hong Kongers seeking better pay.

His first son, Jinping, was born in Shaanxi in 1953 and grew up listening to his famous father's stories. "He talked about how he'd joined the revolution and said, 'You'll certainly make revolution someday,' and he'd explain what revolution is. We heard so much of this our ears grew calluses". Xi's high birth brought high visibility. During the Cultural Revolution, the twelve-year-old was arrested and paraded as an enemy of the people but, since the juvenile prison was full, he was sent to poverty-stricken Liangjiahe Village. As they parted, he told his tearful family, "If I didn't go, I'm not sure I'll survive".

Years later, he recalled, "Just after I arrived in the village, beggars started appearing and, as soon as they turned up, the dogs would be set on them. Back then, we students, sent down from the cities, believed beggars were bad elements and tramps. We didn't know the saying, 'In January there is still enough food, in February you will starve, and March and April you are half alive, half dead.' For six months, every family lived only on bark and herbs. Women and children were sent out to beg, and the food could go to those who were doing the spring plowing. You had to live in a village to understand it. When you think of the difference between what the central Government in Beijing knew and what was actually happening in the countryside, you have to shake your head". Liangjiahe's hardbitten farmers rated the city boy six on a ten-point scale, "Not even as high as the women," he said[55],

> I was very young when I was sent to the countryside. It was something I was forced to do. At the time, I didn't think far ahead and gave no thought to the importance of cooperation. While the villagers went up the slopes and worked every day, I did as I chose, and people got a poor impression of me. After a few months, they sent me back to Beijing, and I was placed in a study group. When I was released six months later, I thought hard about returning to the village and talked to my uncle, who had been active in revolutionary work in the 1940s. My uncle told me about his work back then and how important it is to co-operate with the people you live with. That settled it. I went

55 Following the Leader: Ruling China, from Deng Xiaoping to Xi Jinping. By David M. Lampton

> back to the village, got down to work, and learned to cooperate. Within a year, I was doing the same work as people in the village, living as they lived, and working hard. The hardship of working shocked me, though I could eventually carry a shoulder pole weighing a hundred pounds up a mountain road. People saw that I had changed.

Growing to manhood there, he experienced the reality of rural poverty, sleeping on brick beds in flea-infested cave homes, enduring hunger and cold, plowing, pulling grain carts, collecting human manure. The village had neither running water nor electricity, and kerosene lamps provided light for his studies. There was no school, but he was 'always reading books as thick as bricks,' villagers recall. He began leading small projects and constructed the County's first sewage system. "The pipe from the pond was blocked, and I unblocked it. To the great amusement of the villagers, excrement and urine flew all over my face". From plans sent by his mother, he built the County's first public toilet and a methane digester that lit Liangjiahe at night. Eventually, the County named him 'a model educated youth' (a prerequisite for university admission during the Cultural Revolution) and awarded him a motorcycle, but, he said, "We didn't even have a road to ride my motorbike on," and he exchanged it for a milling machine.

After applying several times he was admitted to the Communist Party in 1974 and launched his political career by winning election as Liangjiahe Village Party Secretary. The following year he was accepted by Tsinghua University and a dozen villagers walked the twenty miles to the railhead with him, "It was the second time I cried there. The first time was when I got the letter saying that my big sister had died. Experiencing such an abrupt change from Beijing to a place so destitute had affected me profoundly".

He returned to Beijing to greet his father who, released from years of solitary confinement and unable to recognize his grown sons, recited a familiar Tang Dynasty poem:

Returning to my home village after years of absence,
My brows have grayed though my accent is unchanged.
Children who meet me don't recognize me.
Laughing, they ask, what village do you come from?

After graduation, his father's old comrade-in-arms Geng Biao, now Minister of National Defense, made him his personal secretary and the young man spent three years in uniform, studying the vast military he would one day command. Friends and classmates were going into business or studying abroad but his father encouraged him to enter government. He left Beijing and began a thirty-year apprenticeship administering villages, townships, cities, counties, and provinces and picking up a Ph.D. (in rural marketization) along the way.

Effective, diligent, and versatile like his father, he left a trail of prosperity behind him. Posted to backward Zhengding County, Hebei Province in 1982, he demonstrated the paternal flair for economic development: learning that CCTV was scouting locations for a production of *The Dream of Red Mansions*, he persuaded the County to build real mansions instead of temporary sets. Fees from the show almost covered the construction cost and, after shooting ended, he turned the site into a tourist attraction that still hosts a million paying visitors each year and has been the backdrop for countless dramas. As governor of Fujian, he upgraded the province's Internet, networked its hospitals' medical records, and made online government transactions transparent. He established non-Party citizens' committees to supervise Party Committees–an innovation the nation subsequently adopted–and was the first governor to crack down on food contamination and create an environmental monitoring system. Today, pristine Fujian attracts environmentally-oriented startups.

Earnest and blunt to the point of rudeness, he was a creative initiator, a reliable sustainer, and a determined finisher, says US Treasury Secretary Hank Paulsen, "The kind of guy who knows how to get things over the goal line". Taiwanese businessman Li Shih-Wei[56] says he was

56 The Washington Post

tirelessly effective, "When we discussed my problems, he would listen closely, track the issue, and try to find solutions. His working efficiency was pretty high–quite rare among the officials we encountered there. Meetings were usually in the government cafeteria, not the fancy restaurants most officials chose. His lifestyle wasn't luxurious". Xi urged officials to meet people face to face and set an example by meeting seven hundred petitioners in forty-eight hours. A regular at farmers' markets, on fishing boats, and down in coal mines, Xi was celebrated as the first Party Secretary to visit every village in Zhengding County. He repeated the feat wherever he governed[57].

His only recorded outbursts were over corruption. According to one Zhejiang official, Xi 'kept his reputation wholesome and untainted by allegations of corruption' and, under a pen name, contributed hundreds of earnest opinion pieces to local dailies. In an essay on graft, he said, "Transparency is the best anti-corrosive. As long as we embrace democracy, follow proper procedures, and avoid 'black' casework, fighting corruption won't be just empty words. How important the people are in an official's mind will determine how important officials are in the peoples' minds. Officials should love the people in the way they love their parents, work for their benefit, and lead them to prosperity".

But competition for promotion was fierce, and, despite his famous name and strong track record, he finished last in the 1997 elections for the Party's two-hundred-member Central Committee. Ten years later, assigned to clean up notoriously corrupt Shanghai, he turned the governor's mansion into a veterans' home, promoted green, sustainable development, and pushed the city to become a financial center. Success drew relieved headlines[58] in the People's Daily, "Glad to Hear Some Good News from Shanghai at Long Last!" (Today, Shanghai's pension fund is in surplus and the city ranks second among the world's financial centers. Its courts are a preferred international venue, and its education system is world famous). In 2008 he coordinated the military, police, bureaucracy, localities, diplomacy, security, logistics, and media and produced

57 He became the first president to visit all of China's thirty-three provinces and regions.
58 How China's Leaders Think: The Inside Story of China's Past, Current and Future Leaders by Robert Lawrence Kuhn. 7-Jun-2011.

a flawless, corruption-free Olympic Games on time and under budget. The US Embassy[59] in Beijing was paying attention:

US EMBASSY C O N F I D E N T I AL

SECTION 01 OF 06 BEIJING 003128

SIPDIS. 2009 November 16, 12:20 (Monday)

SUBJECT: PORTRAIT OF VICE PRESIDENT XI JINPING: 'AMBITIOUS SURVIVOR OF THE CULTURAL REVOLUTION.

Unlike those in the social circles the professor ran in, Xi Jinping could not talk about women and movies and did not drink or do drugs. Xi was considered of only average intelligence, the professor said, and not as smart as the professor's peer group. Women thought Xi was 'boring'.

The professor never felt wholly relaxed around Xi, who seemed extremely 'driven'. Nevertheless, despite Xi's lack of popularity in the conventional sense and his 'cold and calculating' demeanor in those early years, the professor said, Xi was 'not cold-hearted'. He was still considered a 'good guy' in other ways. Xi was outwardly friendly, 'always knew the answers' to questions, and would 'always take care of you'. The professor surmised that Xi's newfound popularity today, which the professor found surprising, must stem in part from Xi's being 'generous and loyal'.

Xi also does not care about money and is not corrupt, the professor stated. Xi can afford to be incorruptible, the professor wryly noted, given that he was born with a silver spoon in his

59 Beijing Embassy Cable: 09BEIJING3128_a. Wikileaks.

> mouth. In the professor's view, Xi Jinping is supremely pragmatic, a realist, driven not by ideology but by a combination of ambition and 'self-protection'.
>
> Xi knows how very corrupt China is and is repulsed by the all-encompassing commercialization of Chinese society with its attendant *nouveau riche*, official corruption, loss of values, dignity, and self-respect, and such 'moral evils' as drugs and prostitution, the professor stated. The professor speculated that if Xi were to become the Party General Secretary, he would likely aggressively attempt to address these evils, perhaps at the expense of the new moneyed class.

When China's version of our Electoral College[60] appoints officials, it consults decades of their personal data. Is their Ph.D. relevant to problems that upcoming Five-Year Plans will address? How consistently have they met their local Five-Year Plan goals? Their moral character? Innovations? Personal sacrifices? Medical history? Data is everything, and the selection committee votes in multiple rounds to eliminate less favored contenders.

Xi's name rose to the top on the third ballot, and Congress confirmed his appointment in 2012 and, though his elevation brought prestige, it came with little personal power. He could neither choose nor dismiss his Prime Minister and Cabinet nor advance legislation without their unanimous support. Nor could he set his own agenda: the Five-Year Plan required him to eliminate poverty, end corruption, reform the military, pass a National Social Security bill, and double average wages and pensions before the end of his second term.

Asked how he felt about being President, he replied with typical candor, "People who have little experience with power–those who are far from it–tend to regard politics as mysterious and exciting. But I look past the superficialities, the power, the flowers, the glory, the applause. I

60 "The individual citizen has no federal constitutional right to vote for electors for the President of the United States". Chief Justice Rehnquist for US Supreme Court, Bush v. Gore, December 12, 2000.

see the detention houses, the fickleness of human relationships. I understand politics on a deeper level".

His reply to a Mexican journalist's question about China's intentions was equally blunt, "There are some well-fed foreigners who have nothing better to do than point fingers at our affairs. First, China does not export revolution; second, export poverty and hunger; third, cause trouble for you. What else is there to say?"

His speeches[61] are businesslike and his first presidential address was pure retail politics. "People expect better wages, higher quality medical care, more comfortable homes, and a more beautiful environment". He challenged Congress to involve more people in the legislative process, asked the Carter Center to expand popular participation in policy-making, and demanded a more significant role for the Constitution in state affairs. Promising to tackle corruption, he called on officials to lead by example, quoting Confucius, "He who rules by virtue is like the North Star, which maintains its place and the multitude of stars pay homage".

In the first phase of his anti-corruption campaign, he formed cross-jurisdictional squads to coordinate investigations, gave them independence, and prosecuted a hundred ministers, generals, executives, university chancellors, and CEOs–a practice called 'killing chickens to frighten the monkeys'. When investigators filed a million disciplinary cases, they found outdated, inconsistent law codes and judicial unpredictability, which undermined faith in the legal system. Xi ended local government interference in the courts, professionalized the legal workforce, abolished re-education through labor and, calling for transparent legal proceedings, persuaded the Supreme People's Court to broadcast its hearings live.

In 2015, he proposed an Internet Code of Conduct but the US vetoed the resolution and, before his planned visit to the US, imposed[62] sanctions on several Chinese companies for alleged IT attacks. Xi promptly altered his itinerary and invited America's technology CEOs

61 In a 2000 interview with the journalist Chen Peng, of *Chinese Times*

62 China Flexes Tech Muscles Before a State Visit, By Paul Mozur and Jane Perlez, NYT September 8, 2015

to dinner at Bill Gates' Seattle home, Forbes[63] reported, "Beijing is pushing back in an unorthodox way by organizing a technology forum in Seattle to demonstrate its sway over the American tech industry. The meeting is rankling the Obama administration by veering off the script agreed to for Xi's carefully stage-managed visit". Apple's Tim Cook described the reaction when Xi entered the room, "Did you feel the room shake?" The CEOs discussed the Internet Code of Conduct over dinner and, the following day told President Obama that they supported Xi's position. Obama capitulated, announcing, "The United States will neither conduct nor knowingly support cyber-enabled theft of intellectual property, including trade secrets or other confidential business information, with the intent of providing competitive advantages to companies or commercial sectors". The Diplomat[64] observed, "In his visit, President Xi Jinping brilliantly outmaneuvered the United States", and The New York Times opined[65], "Looking back at the trip, the most memorable moment–and maybe the most important–was watching $2.5 trillion of American corporate power pay homage to the Chinese President".

President Obama invited ASEAN[66] leaders to California in 2016[67] to outlaw China's actions in the South China Sea. But ASEAN leaders knew China had occupied the same features in the Sea since 1988 and, as The Diplomat[68] reported, "The joint statement issued after the US -ASEAN summit did not contain a specific reference to China's assertiveness in the South China Sea".

With corruption on the run, poverty banished, and the Reform and

63 China's Meeting with US Tech Giants May Be More Reunion Than Response To Threatened Cyber Sanctions, by Lisa Brownlee. Forbes, September 10, 2015.

64 China-US Cyber Agreements: Has Beijing Outmaneuvered Washington? By Greg Austin. The Diplomat, September 28, 2015

65 Xi Jinping's US Visit. By Jane Perlez. NYT. September 21, 2015

66 The Association of Southeast Asian Nations. Brunei, Burma (Myanmar), Cambodia, Timor-Leste, Indonesia, Laos, Malaysia, the Philippines, Singapore, Thailand, and Vietnam.

67 Sunnylands and America's Pivot to ASEANAsia Maritime Transparency Initiative. February 12, 2016

68 A US -ASEAN South China Sea Failure at Sunnylands? By Prashanth Parameswaran. The Diplomat. February 19, 2016

Opening era ending, Xi is painting a new vision[69] for his country that we will examine later.

It is too soon to pass judgement on him but Lee Kwan Yew[70], who knew both Jinping and his father, has done so, "I would put him in Nelson Mandela's class of persons. Someone with enormous emotional stability who does not allow his personal misfortunes or sufferings to affect his judgment. In a word, he is impressive".

69 Colleagues granted him 'core leader' status for this purpose. They amended the Constitution to align his ceremonial Presidential role with his duties as Party General Secretary and Military Commission Chairman–which carry no term limits.

70 One Man's View of the World – 2013. Lee Kuan Yew

CHAPTER 6

Beyond Our Comprehension: Mao Zedong

There is no end to learning from experience. People make mistakes when they're young, but do older people avoid mistakes? Confucius said everything he did conformed to objective laws by the time he was seventy. Personally, I don't believe it. That's just bullshit. Mao Zedong.

***

We cannot understand China without understanding Mao Zedong, for he was its greatest leader, and he set its current agenda for the next century.

Harvard's John King Fairbank[71] summarized a lifetime of studying Mao in these words, "The simple facts of his career seem incredible: in a vast land of 400 million people, at age 28, with a dozen others, to found a party and in the next fifty years to win power, organize, and remold the people and reshape the land–history records no greater achievement. Alexander, Caesar, Charlemagne, all the kings of Europe, Napoleon, Bismarck, Lenin–no predecessor can equal Mao Tse-tung's scope of accomplishment, for no other country was ever so ancient and so vast as China. Indeed, Mao's achievement is almost beyond our comprehension".

71 The United States and China. John King Fairbank.

***

After the First World War, the victorious Allies secretly transferred Germany's colony in China to Japan, and the resulting May 4 protests moved Mao Zedong to found the Communist Party but, long before he was a Communist, he was an individualist[72], "I disagree with the idea that the life of the individual derives from the life of the nation in the same way that the four limbs derive from the body. The life of a nation, including its politics and language, all began well after the human race had evolved. The individual came before the nation; the individual did not come from the nation. There is no higher value than that of an individual. There is no greater crime than to suppress the individual".

He criticized[73] old methods of education, old marriage customs, and using Confucius to justify subservience to Japanese occupation, and was precociously interested in public morality[74]. At seventeen, when a series of bad harvests in Hunan led to famine, desperate Hunanese organized under the slogan, "Eat rice without charge," and seized stores of rice from wealthier farmers, including Mao's father. Mao recalled that, while he could not sympathize with his father–who continued exporting rice despite the famine–he could not condone the violence of those who seized others' property.

Xiao San[75], his best friend in youth, vividly recalled him passing nights reading *Great Heroes of the World*, biographies of Wellington, Lincoln, Rousseau, Montesquieu, Gladstone, and Napoleon. Xiao says it was Washington who gripped his imagination, "We need great people like this. We ought to study them and find out how we can make China rich and strong, and so avoid becoming like Annam, Korea[76], and India ... China is very weak; she will grow strong, rich, and independent only after many years; but the important thing is that we must

72 Stuart Schram, *Mao's Road to Power: Revolutionary Writings, 1912-49.*
73 Mao Zedong. "On the New Stage" (1938)
74 Mao Zedong: A Life by Jonathan D. Spence. 2006
75 Mao and I Were Beggars. Primary Source Edition. Xiao-Yu. 1959. Syracuse University Press.
76 Then occupied by the Japanese.

learn these things. And it is not impossible. After six years of hard fighting, Washington defeated the British and began building up America". Throughout his life he held up Washington as his exemplar, and did so in 1932, to American journalist Edgar Snow[77].

> Inwardly, I often smiled at the extravagance of Mao's claims, which then seemed more naive than Gandhi's hopes of conquering the British by 'love power.' There he sat, with two pairs of cotton pants to his name, his army a minuscule band of poorly armed youths, facing a precarious existence in the most impoverished corner of the land. Yet he spoke as if his Party already had an irrevocable mandate over 'the workers and peasants' of all China, acted as if he believed it, and told the foreign powers just how a free China of the future 'could' and 'could not' co-operate with them. 'Every man is an impossibility until he is born,' said Emerson. Mao was real enough and yet still a kind of impossibility. For 'everything is impossible,' to finish the epigram, 'until we see a success' – and at that moment, Mao looked a failure… His step-by-step reasoning gradually took hold of me as 'just possible' reality. As his personal story unfolded, thoughtfully told, well organized, and dramatic, I began to see that it was a rich cross-section of a whole generation seen in the life of a man who had deeply analyzed and studied its meaning… Unconscious, inarticulate, China's needs might be in 'the vast majority of the people.' Still, if social revolution could provide the dynamics which can regenerate China, then in this profoundly historical sense, Mao Tse-tung may become a very great man.

Though outnumbered ten to one, commanding ragged, underfed troops, and lacking artillery, communications, airplanes, heavy equipment, reserves, and trained officers, he won most battles decisively. No armchair general, he stayed behind with a small force to attract the Nationalists as the Red Army withdrew unmolested from Yan'an. His

77 Red Star Over China. Edgar Snow, 1937.

bodyguard was killed while standing beside him, and a bomb that drenched him with a soldier's blood left him unscathed. "Death never seemed to want me," he shrugged.

Mao's *Four Nevers* urged flexibility, "Never be afraid to negotiate; never be afraid to retreat; never be afraid to change your plans; never be afraid to attack". His scattered armies lacked communications equipment, so he united them with a poem. By arranging sixteen characters into four rhyming verses, Mao taught battlefield tactics to millions of illiterate troops. They sang them as they marched: "When the enemy advances, we retreat; when he escapes, we harass; when he retreats, we pursue; when he is tired, we attack". Later, he explained, "Those sixteen characters are the basic directives for a counter-campaign against encirclement–and the phases of both the strategic defensive and the strategic offensive–as well as for strategic withdrawal and the strategic counteroffensive in a defensive operation. In a sense, all that came afterward was just an elaboration of those sixteen characters".

His invisible army, said Robert Payne,[78] "Played a cunning, furious, violent game, circling the Nationalists in the shadows, just out of reach, feinting, threatening, needling, then suddenly destroying them with blows from quarters so unexpected that entire armies sometimes collapsed in shock".

He taught his peasant warriors by reducing strategic principles to marching songs and won battles by maneuver and morale alone. Field Marshal Bernard Montgomery, who knew Mao, compared his campaigns to the best of Alexander's and Napoleon's and singled out his Battle of the Four Crossings for special praise. Under fire from four hundred thousand Nationalists, his thirty thousand troops crossed the Chishui River—an exhausting and terrifying maneuver—then, crossing it thrice more, attacked the Nationalists' flank and reversed the course of the war. Payne comments that Mao played the game so well because he wrote the rules,

78 Payne, Robert. Mao Tse-Tung, Ruler of Red China (pp.195-196). Read Books Ltd., Kindle Edition

> Mao's contribution to the strategical operations can always be detected. Mao is the surgeon, exploring the wound, insisting above all on the delicate probing, the discovery of the enemy's weakened nerve, the dangerous point where weakness is balanced by strength: at this point, he will order the attack. There follows a cunning interweaving among the enemy columns–as Mao describes his tactics, they have something of the inevitability of a dance. Finally, there is the withdrawal to the chosen terminus, which may be within the enemy lines, or deep in enemy territory, or safely within the territory, the Reds have circumscribed for themselves. The theory, as he relates the battles, seems to be pure Mao. Mao's notes on the actions, compiled with the help of Chu Teh, give an impression of illusory ease to the whole campaign. It is almost a dance or a game of skittles. As Mao said after one campaign, "We faced the enemy with poise and ease".

Amidst the fighting he opposed political violence, kept the peace among the leadership, and prescribed re-education for heterodox views. Hearing of Stalin's bloody purges in 1937, he established a rule which still holds, "Not a single person must die from internal political struggles". After capturing Chiang Kai-shek, the warlord whose agents had murdered Mao's wife and thrown his children onto the street, he treated him honorably, sent him back to his troops, and offered to place the PLA under American command.

***

By war's end, China was agrarian, backward, feudalistic, ignorant, and violent. Most of its four hundred million people could neither read nor write, life expectancy was thirty-five years, and fifty-million drug addicts roamed its cities. Peasants paid seventy percent of their produce in rent; women's feet were bound; desperate mothers sold their children for food; poor men, choosing slavery over starvation, sold themselves. The Japanese had massacred twenty-million people, and US Ambassador John Leighton Stuart reported that ten million starved to death in just three provinces. Hundreds of millions, their lives catastrophically dislocated by a century of war, needed vast quantities of food, clothing, and shelter merely to survive. Entering Beijing in 1949, the ordinarily self-assured Mao was anxious, "We don't know enough about managing a whole country! We'll be lucky if we don't get thrown out!"

Convinced that China needed foreign investment, Mao wrote[79] to President Roosevelt with a plea he repeated to Truman and Eisenhower, "China must industrialize, which can only be accomplished by free enterprise. Chinese and American interests fit together, economically and politically. America need not fear that we will not be co-operative. We cannot risk any conflict". When they ignored his requests, he was philosophical[80], "Some people refuse to understand why we do not fear capitalism, but, on the contrary, develop it as much as possible. Our answer is simple: we have to replace foreign imperialist and native feudalist oppression with capitalist development because that is the inevitable course of our economy, and because both the capitalist class and the proletariat benefit. What we don't need is not native capitalism, but foreign imperialism and native feudalism".

He published transcripts of Voice of America broadcasts because, he said, "Many people refuse to admit that contradictions still exist in a socialist society so, confronted with social contradictions they become timid and helpless. Contradictions arise continually and must be continually resolved. These contradictions among our people are the very forces that move society".

The scale and savagery of Japanese war crimes had aroused outrage abroad and at home, and demands for vengeance rose from a million throats, yet Mao forbade[81] retribution. He commuted[82] the death sentences of all but forty-six Japanese war criminals, pardoned and repatriated a million occupying troops, dissuaded Japan's puppet Chinese

79 *Mission to Yenan: American Liaison with the Chinese Communists, 1944-1947* by Carolle J. Carter

80 Portrait of a Revolutionary. Robert Payne. Abelard-Schuman. 1950.

81 Collected Works of Mao Tse-Tung (1917-1949), Volumes 1-2. January 1, 1978. Joint Publications Research Service, Arlington, VA

82 Collected Works of Mao Tse-Tung (1917-1949), Volumes 1-2. January 1, 1978. Joint Publications Research Service, Arlington, VA

emperor, Pu Yi, from committing suicide, edited his memoirs, and found a wife for the remorseful man.

His instructions[83] for establishing order were clear, "What harm is there in *not* executing people? Those amenable to labor reform should go and do labor reform so that rubbish can be transformed into something useful. Remember, people's heads are not like leeks. When you cut them off, they won't grow again. If you cut off a head wrongly, there is no way of rectifying the mistake even if you want to". William Sewell, then a Christian missionary in China, wrote[84]:

> We knew from the papers that, in some parts of China where Land Reform had already taken place, there had been angry scenes, and landlords had been beaten to death by the people or had killed themselves in fear. The government realized that they had greatly underestimated the passions of the people when they were aroused, but now the cadres[85] were wiser and were present to see that matters did not get out of control. After the people had spoken, the landlords were either handed over to the police for trial or allowed to remain free, according to circumstance. Only those proven responsible for a tenant's death combined with rape or for several deaths were legally liable for the death penalty.

His next challenge was bringing democracy[86] to a Confucian society, "What does democracy consist of? Upon what forces does it rely? How does it express itself? To some extent, of course, it expresses itself in the ballot box. It also expresses itself in the deliberations of the village councils, in the opinions seeping up through the ranks of the army, in the resolutions of county governments, in the overt signs of change which appear in the political atmosphere of the times. Without democracy, you have no understanding of what is happening down below; the general

83 Chairman Mao Talks to The People: Talks and Letters: 1956-1971 (The Pantheon Asia Library)

84 I stayed in China, – by William G Sewell 1966

85 Cadre: a small group of people specially trained for a particular purpose or profession: 'a small cadre of scientists.'

86 Mao Zedong. "On New Democracy" (1940)

situation will be unclear. Thus, you will find it difficult to avoid being subjectivist; it will be impossible to achieve unity of understanding and unity of action and achieve true centralism. Thus, the main task of the leader is to keep his ear to the ground".

Aware that Britain's agrarian and industrial revolutions had been bought at the cost of two centuries of misery and bloodshed, he completed both in twenty-five years, without bloodshed, and under stringent Western embargoes. He relieved farmers of annual payments of seventy billion tons of grain and distributed half the arable land, livestock, and implements to landless peasants.

China's landlords, the world's oldest hereditary class, retained enough land to earn a living but vanished from the pages of history which, Mao warned, created new inequalities. "As is clear to everyone, the spontaneous forces of capitalism have been growing in the countryside in recent years, with newly rich peasants springing up everywhere and many well-to-do middle peasants striving to become rich. On the other hand, many poor peasants are still living in poverty for lack of the means of production, some are falling into debt, and others are selling or renting out their land. If this tendency goes unchecked, polarization in the countryside will inevitably worsen".

Some of his colleagues were opposed to collectivization. Until China developed a strong industrial base and introduced mechanization, they said, collectivization was premature, dangerous, and utopian. Socialism and collectivization belonged in the distant future, after the countryside went through a capitalist transformation. Others, wishing only to stabilize the existing economy, rejected both capitalism and socialism, but Mao argued for basing agricultural collectivization on mechanization, not the other way around. No one family could afford–or economically use–a tractor, but a collective could do both, he said. Collectively, peasants could better resist natural disasters, manage their labor, adapt to new technologies and crop varieties, and purchase industrial products. When opponents pointed to peasants' inexperience, Mao argued that they could only gain experience by doing things themselves. He said China should do a better job of collectivization because it could learn from the USSR's mistakes.

By 1958, communications were still primitive, the government was still inexperienced, goal-setting was amateurish, and Beijing's capacity to coordinate national programs was crude, yet Mao was under relentless pressure. Hhe had doubled food production and halved the death rate, but the birthrate had doubled and he was racing to modernize the country while under foreign embargoes and threats of a nuclear attack. Though he had re-centralized state power, reunified the country, fashioned a modern nation-state, created a national market, and abolished landlord-tenant relations, he considered the changes cosmetic, "Dividing up the land and giving it to the peasants transforms the property of the feudal landlords into the individual property of the peasants–but this remains within the limits of a bourgeois revolution. To divide up the land is nothing remarkable. MacArthur did it in Japan. Napoleon divided up the land, too. Land reform can neither abolish capitalism nor lead to socialism".

As a matter of survival, he insisted, China must develop agriculture and industry simultaneously, "If, after working at it for fifty or sixty years, you are still unable to overtake the United States, what a sorry figure you will cut! You should be read off the face of the earth. To overtake the United States is not only possible but necessary and obligatory[87]. Otherwise, the Chinese nation will disappoint the world and not contribute to humanity… In building the country, we–unlike materialists who stress mechanization and modernization–must pay chief attention to revolutionizing the human spirit… In man, motivation derives from consciousness, which, in turn, comes from socialization. Motivation is the source of moral energies like dedication, devotion, determination, faith, frugality, diligence, and simplicity. Consciousness and inspiration reinforce each other and can be transformed, one into the other".

China could not afford to walk, he told them. Even to survive, it must take a giant leap. He discussed the challenges of managing through corrupt local officials and wrote directly to local production teams and even local work squads, warning against inflated claims:

---

87 "Strengthen Party Unity and Carry Forward Party Traditions" (1956). China's economy overtook America's fifty-eight years later.

> I want to address a problem with our agriculture. Please ignore top-down crop targets and stick to what is feasible. Thirty percent, even sixty percent higher yield than last year would be excellent, but what's the point of boasting about four hundred percent when that's merely impossible? As for dense planting, let old, middle-aged, and younger farmers discuss it and decide it within your production teams. Save your food! Preserve it well, build a reserve for future emergencies. We can't afford boasting or empty talk for at least ten years. Make high yields in small fields your immediate goal because mechanization will take at least ten years, so we must simply farm more acreage for the next three years. Plant on a larger scale. Set up research institutes for farming tools. Fertilizer is essential. Many lies are caused by pressure from superiors who boast and pressure those below them, and they're difficult to deal with. Speak the truth. Promise only the number you can deliver. Don't pretend you can 'do it with effort' when you actually can't. Just report how much the harvest really is. If the reality is not as low as I predict–if a real, high outcome makes me look like an out-of-touch conservative–I'll thank heaven and earth. – Mao Zedong, Chairman.

Innovative and enormously ambitious, his great leap would teach peasants industrial production while simultaneously overcoming famine and threats of foreign aggression. Communalized peasants and workers would share responsibilities. Communal childcare and communal kitchens would free women to join the workforce and, by distributing development throughout the countryside, they would make centralized, expensive, nationwide transportation infrastructure unnecessary. Peasants 'walking on two legs' would both farm *and* develop light industry while erecting dikes, building dams, and expanding irrigation. Increased agricultural productivity would free up labor for local manufacturing, and, in the absence of foreign capital, labor-intensive rural industries would meet local needs. Locally produced cement would build local dams that would water soil enriched with locally made fertilizer through locally made irrigation equipment.

After generations of semi-starvation the nation was giddily optimistic, and peasants presumed an unlimited supply of government-guaranteed food. Communal dining rooms provided such abundance that farmers said they had never eaten better in their lives. Families depleted their stores of grain and livestock, slaughtered domestic animals, and held feasts. According to one report[88], "Instead of transferring draft animals to the ownership of the collectives, peasants slaughtered them to keep the meat and hide ... estimates suggest that animal loss during the movement was almost ten million head. Grain output dropped by seven percent due to lower animal inputs and lower productivity".

When villages reported lower harvests at the end of the first year, their superiors blamed temporary setbacks or simple errors. If one region reported improved yields, neighbors felt pressured to make similar claims, especially since communal farming represented the pinnacle of Communist development. Rather than dampen revolutionary zeal, managers convinced themselves that they could make up shortfalls the next season and inflated their figures until reports lost touch with reality. "Some fields would have to be so thick with grain that farmers could walk on them," scoffed an agronomist. When inspectors reported the results of physical audits, their superiors, entranced by the prospect of Socialism in one generation, rejected their reports and continued diverting grain reserves to traditionally poor regions and newly urbanized industrial workers.

Nevertheless, coal, steel, textile, and electricity generation rose thirty percent, and infrastructure rose forty percent in three years, and peasants built thousands of dams, including nine of today's ten largest. One of them, the gigantic Xinfengjiang Reservoir, holds ten cubic meters of clean water for every Chinese and has generated billions of kilowatts of electricity, powered rural and urban development, played a vital role in flood control and irrigation, and still waters Guangdong and Hong Kong.

Says Maurice Meisner[89], "The higher yields obtained on individual family farms during later years would not have been possible without the

88 There Will Be Killing: Collectivization and Death of Draft Animals, Shuo Chen and Xiaohuan Lan.

89 Mao Zedong: A Political and Intellectual Portrait, 1st Edition. by Maurice Meisner 2007

vast irrigation and flood-control projects–dams, irrigation works, and river dikes–constructed by collectivized peasants in the 1950s and 1960s. By some key social and demographic indicators, China compared favorably even with middle-income countries whose per capita GDP was five times greater". Indeed, of all the industrial projects China would launch in the next fifteen years, two-thirds were founded during the Great Leap.

But a catastrophe overshadowed its achievements.

Mao had anticipated bureaucratic resistance, foreign embargoes, official corruption, and peasant reluctance but not that, as his grand experiment got underway, China would endure three years of the worst weather in a century. An El Nino cycle–which halved Canada's prairie wheat crop[90] and created New England's worst recorded drought–cut the cereal harvest by one-third. The spring harvest in the Southwest rice bowl was lost to drought and the Hunan region was flooded. From two hundred million tons in 1958, yields fell to one-hundred forty-three million in 1960. Writes Roderick MacFarquhar[91],

> Not surprisingly, given the drought, most of the flooding had been due to the typhoons, more of which had hit the Chinese mainland than in any of the previous 50 years–eleven between June and October. Each storm had lasted longer than usual, averaging ten hours, the longest stretching to 20. Moreover, nature had played an additional trick. The typhoon did not strike north-westwards as usual, but northwards, which added to their impact. There were no high mountains to ward them off, and less rain reached the rest of the country. In the aftermath of the drought and floods came insect pests and plant diseases.

After the disastrous harvest, the Party gathered in Lushan, and war

90 The US Geological Survey says the New England Drought began in 1960 in western Massachusetts; then, in 1962, eastern Massachusetts dried up. The drought was "such a rare event that we should ordinarily expect it to occur in this region only about once in a couple of centuries." The 1965 Drought, New England's Worst Ever. New England Historical Society. Updated 2019.

91 The Great Leap Forward 1958-1960, Volume 2 of The Origins of the Cultural Revolution, p. 322.

hero Peng Dehuai accused Mao's peasant supporters of 'petty-bourgeois fanaticism.' Mao protested, "At least thirty percent of them are actively on our side, another thirty percent are pessimists and landlords, while the rest are middle-of-the-roaders. How many people are thirty percent? It's 150 million people! They want to run communes and mess halls and do everything cooperatively. They are very enthusiastic and keen. How can you call them petty-bourgeois fanatics?"

Unmoved, his colleagues passed a resolution against "Impetuous actions, utopian dreams, and ignoring the necessary stages of social development which could only be achieved after the lapse of considerable time." A crestfallen Mao admitted, "We rushed into a great catastrophe. The communes were organized too quickly. The Great Leap has been a partial failure for which we have paid a high price. The chaos was on a grand scale, and I take responsibility for it… The transition to a *dàtóng* society might take longer than I had envisaged, perhaps as many as twenty Five-Year Plans, but the drive to attain it should never be abandoned".

Declining to stand for re-election he wandered around, as he said, "Like a mourner at my own funeral," but bore the rebuke philosophically, "If you can't handle being impeached by the Party, you are not Party material".

His successor, Liu Shaoqi, attributed seventy percent of the Great Leap's problems to human error and thirty percent to weather and canceled Mao's Five-Year Plan. Thenceforth, he said, policies should rely on material incentives and never on idealistic, unplanned mass mobilizations–a resolve he would break a decade later.

As the drought deepened, the Party drew on decades of experience feeding millions of men on the march and mounted the most comprehensive food relief program in history. Thanks to ration books and efficient distribution, everyone had something to eat every day but, at a time when life expectancy was fifty-eight years, constant hunger weakened older people who had grown up malnourished amidst cholera, tuberculosis, and war. Grandparents gave their meager rations to grandchildren, and, as harvests fell, death rates rose relentlessly, from twelve per thousand in 1958 to fifteen in 1959 and twenty-five in 1960, not falling back to fourteen until 1961. Mobo Gao says[92] the only suicide in the history of his village occurred during the Great Leap.

> A woman hanged herself because of family hardship. The Great Leap Forward years were the only time in anybody's memory that Gao villagers had to pick wild vegetables and grind rice husks into powder to make food. Throughout my twenty years in Gao village, I do not remember any particular time when my family had enough to eat … as a rural resident, life was always a matter of survival. However, the Great Leap Forward made life even more difficult. Our region was hit very hard by natural disasters for two consecutive years… But during the two years of natural disasters, we got relief grain from the Central Government, the provincial Government, Qingdao City, Shanghai City, and many other regions… Whenever and wherever one place had difficulties, people from different places helped. I remember many peasants told me that if it were not for the People's Government's help, many people would have starved amid disasters like the one in 1960. By contrast, in Northern Henan Province (where the grain shortage during the Great Leap Forward was supposed to have been severe), five million people starved to death in 1942. The government at that time had done nothing to help the local people.
>
> In the 1990s, I accompanied Ralph Thaxton, my graduate school advisor, to study (on a Guggenheim scholarship) the region's famine. When he said that he had come to study the famine, peasants thought that he was studying the famine of 1942-1943. During that 1942-1943 famine, not only did five million people starve, but many people had to sell their land, their houses, and their children before fleeing their hometowns. The local and national governments did nothing to help the people there. But nothing like that took place during the grain shortage of the Great Leap Forward.

92 Mobo Gao. *Gao Village*.

Mao's bodyguard, Li Yinqiao, described[93] how Mao's wife, Jiang Qing, and their cook prepared a family banquet when Mao's teenage daughter, Li Na, returned from boarding school. She was so hungry and ate so fast that Mao and Jiang put down their bowls and watched her devour every dish on the table until, by the end, the cook and Jiang Qing were sobbing, and Mao was wandering around the courtyard, speechless. Journalist Sidney Rittenberg said Party members were forbidden to stand in line to buy food. He recalled a woman who broke the rule, "They had this big meeting where she made a self-criticism, weeping, weeping, weeping, saying, 'I'm not a good communist, I put my children's health above the health of the masses.' Can you imagine that today, anything even remotely similar? Today it's 'get mine!'"

The harvest failures were widely known, and the US Government embargoed grain shipments to China and tasked the CIA[94] with reporting on its effectiveness:

> **April 4, 1961**: The Chinese Communist regime is now facing the most serious economic difficulties it has confronted since it concentrated its power over mainland China. As a result of economic mismanagement, and especially of two years of unfavorable weather, food production in 1960 was hardly larger than in 1957, at which time there were about 50 million fewer Chinese to feed. Widespread famine does not appear to be at hand. Still, in some provinces, many people are now on a bare subsistence diet, and the bitterest suffering lies immediately ahead, in the period before the July harvests. The dislocations caused by the 'Leap Forward' and the removal of Soviet technicians have disrupted China's industrialization program. These difficulties have sharply reduced the rate of economic growth during 1960 and have created a severe balance of payments problem. Public morale, especially in rural areas, is almost certainly at its lowest point since

93 Gao, Mobo. The Battle for China's Past: Mao and the Cultural Revolution (pp. 89-90). Pluto Press. Kindle Edition.

94 Prospects for Communist China. National Intelligence Estimate Number 13-4-62.

the Communists assumed power, and there have been some instances of open dissidence.

May 2, 1962: The future course of events in Communist China will be shaped largely by three highly unpredictable variables: the wisdom and realism of the leadership, the level of agricultural output, and the nature and extent of foreign economic relations. During the past few years, all three variables have worked against China. In 1958, the leadership adopted a series of ill-conceived and extremist economic and social programs; in 1959, there occurred the first of three years of bad crop weather; and in 1960, Soviet economic and technical cooperation was largely suspended. The combination of these three factors has brought economic chaos to the country. Malnutrition is widespread, foreign trade is down, and industrial production and development have dropped sharply. No quick recovery from the regime's economic troubles is in sight.

Ridiculing the Great Leap Forward as 'The Great Leap Backward,' Edgar Snow[95] confirmed the CIA's findings:

Were the 1960 calamities as severe as reported in Peking, 'the worst series of disasters since the nineteenth century,' as Chou En-lai told me? The weather was not the only cause of the disappointing harvest, but it was undoubtedly a major cause. With good weather, the crops would have been ample; without it, other adverse factors I have cited–some discontent in the communes, bureaucracy, transportation bottlenecks–weighed heavily. Merely from personal observations in 1960, I know that there was no rain in large areas of northern China for 200-300 days. I have mentioned unprecedented floods in central Manchuria where I was marooned in Shenyang for a week ...while eleven typhoons struck northeast China–the largest number in fifty years, and

95 Snow, Edgar. *Red Star Over China*, Victor Gollancz 1937. p.120

I saw the Yellow River reduced to a small stream. Throughout 1959-1962, many Western press editorials continued referring to 'mass starvation' in China and continued citing no supporting facts. As far as I know, no report by any non-Communist visitor to China provides an authentic instance of starvation during this period. Here I am not speaking of food shortages, or lack of surfeit, to which I have made frequent reference, but of people dying of hunger, which is what 'famine' connotes to most of us, and what I saw in the past.

Felix Greene[96], too, traveled throughout China in 1960:

With the establishment of the new Government in Peking in 1949, two things happened. First, starvation–death by hunger–ceased in China. There have been food shortages–and severe ones, but no starvation–a fact fully documented by Western observers. The truth is that the sufferings of the ordinary Chinese peasant from war, disorder, and famine have been immeasurably *less* in the last decade than in any other decade in the century.

During a visit to Yan'an in 1961, Field Marshall Bernard Montgomery, an expert on physical conditioning, even inspected public bathhouses. "Before coming here, some people told me China is having a famine, hundreds of thousands have starved to death, but here people's musculature is very good. I did not see signs of famine". Reginald Maudling, Britain's Colonial Secretary, summarized intelligence reports, "There was little evidence that Chinese refugees attempting to enter Hong Kong were suffering from malnutrition. Except for occasional signs of vitamin deficiency, those refugees seen by Mr. Hughes indicated that food rationing–to cope with three years of failing agricultural production and bungled corrective methods–has obviously served to ward off mass starvation".

Like all famines, this one cut fertility by fifty percent and, combined

96 *Curtain of Ignorance, Felix Greene*

with the entry of women into the workforce, migration of young villagers to cities further suppressed the birth rate. Yet the US National Institutes of Health[97] found that life expectancy under Mao "Ranks among the most rapid, sustained increases in documented global history. These survival gains appear to have been largest during the 1950s, with a sharp reversal during the 1959-61 Great Leap Famine, followed by substantial progress again during the early 1960s". Survival *gains*–not the population–suffered the reversal.

Historian Han Dongping, who lost two grandparents[98] during the Great Leap, later visited[99] the sites of the worst shortages, Shandong, and Henan Provinces. Yes, farmers told him, the abundance of 1958 had led to carelessness in harvesting, consuming, and storing food, for they had assumed that the communes relieved them of responsibility for their food security. "I interviewed numerous workers and farmers in Shandong and Henan and never met one who said that Mao was bad. I talked to a scholar in Anhui who grew up in rural areas and had done research there. He never met one farmer that said Mao was bad nor a farmer who said Deng [Mao's successor] was good". As historian Gwydion Williams dryly observed[100], "The peasants, heavily armed for the only time in history, took no action. Had their faith in Mao been shaken, would the survivors have shown the enthusiasm for his Cultural Revolution that they demonstrated from 1966 onwards?"

For all its chaos and disappointment, we must consider China's fate had there been no Great Leap, for it was the foundation of the country's current success. Without its forty-six thousand communally constructed reservoirs, the effects of later droughts would have been truly disastrous says agronomist William Hinton[101], "When I spent three weeks in

97 An exploration of China's mortality decline under Mao: A provincial analysis, 1950–80. https://www.ncbi.nlm.nih.gov/pmc/articles/PMC4331212/

98 Like all excess deaths in those years, they were over 60 years of age at a time when life expectancy was 58.

99 Farmers, Mao, and Discontent in China: From the Great Leap Forward to the Present. Dongping Han. Monthly Review. December 1, 2009

100 How Mao Modernised Chinese Thinking: Maoism As Normal Politics. by Gwydion M. Williams. Labour & Trade Union Review, 2010

101 Fanshen: A Documentary of Revolution in a Chinese Village, by William Hinton and Fred Magdoff. 1966

China in 1983 visiting several communes—which still existed then—I was told every time, 'We built our water conservation system during the Great Leap.'"

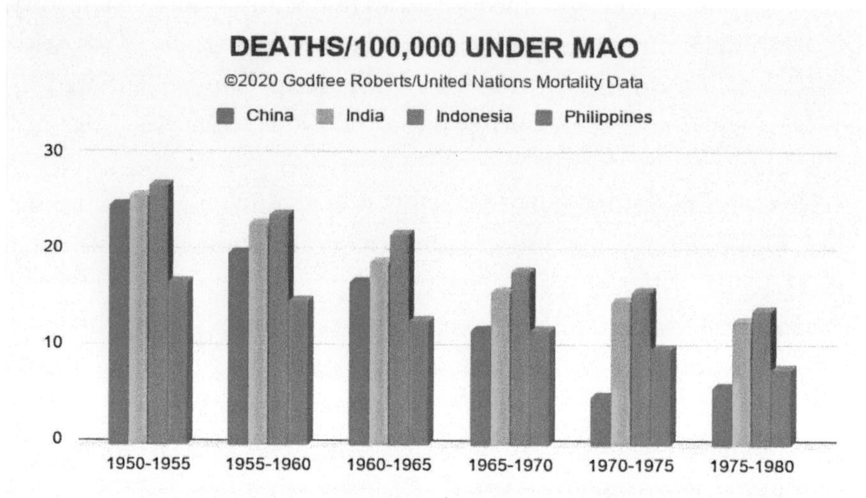

The Great Proletarian Cultural Revolution

There were two Reigns of Terror if we would but remember and consider it: the one wrought murder in hot passion, the other in heartless cold blood; the one lasted mere months, the other had lasted a thousand years; the one inflicted death upon ten thousand persons, the other upon hundred millions; but our shudders are all for the "horrors" of the minor Terror, the momentary Terror, so to speak; whereas, what is the horror of swift death by the ax, compared with lifelong death from hunger, cold, insult, cruelty, and heartbreak? What is swift death by lightning compared with death by slow fire at the stake? A city cemetery could contain the coffins filled by that brief Terror which we have all been so diligently taught to shiver at and mourn over; but all France could hardly contain the coffins filled by that older and real Terror–that unspeakably bitter and awful Terror which none of us has been taught to see in its vastness or pity as it deserves. Mark Twain, *The French Revolution.*

***

By 1966, China was a people's democratic dictatorship in name only. Land reform had channeled excess production from private landlords to the State. However, otherwise, little had changed: eighty-percent of people were still rural, semi-destitute, and illiterate, without access to basic needs, education, or medical care. In reality, scholarly and bureaucratic intellectuals who had always commanded vast influence and prestige in Chinese society[102]. Urban privilege, scholarly elitism, official impunity, corruption, and exploitation were undoing early gains, as William Hinton[103] explained, "Socialism must be regarded as a transition from Capitalism to Communism. As such, it bears within it many contradictions, many inequalities that cannot be done away with overnight or even in the course of years or decades. As long as these inequalities exist, they generate privilege, individualism, careerism, and bourgeois ideology. They can and do create new bourgeois individuals who gather as a new privileged elite and ultimately as a new exploiting class. Thus, Socialism can be peacefully transformed back into capitalism".

Few officials were socialists–let alone Communists. Though they embraced Mao's theory of class struggle, he knew they would desert him if it threatened their positions so, rather than condemn them as members of an exploitive bureaucracy, he purged[104] them. He had often warned them about peasant rebellions, "When frustrations burst forth in emotional storms in which hatreds, resentments, and a sense of hopeless desperation break social restraints in an overwhelming surge", he warned[105] officials, "If you alienate yourself from the people and fail to solve their problems, the peasants will wield their carrying-poles, the workers will demonstrate in the streets, and the students will create disturbances. Whenever such things happen, they must, in the first place, be taken as good things. That's how I see them, anyway".

He had no magic wand. If the peasants wanted freedom, they would have to learn how political forces work in society, the culture, and the world. Only through study and effort could they grasp the link between

102 He still held political and cultural power. Chungwu Kung, "The Cultural Revolution in Modern Chinese History," quoted in Victor Nee and James Peck (eds), China's Uninterrupted Revolution: From 1840 to the Present, NY. Pantheon, pp. 3-56.

103 Turning Point in China by William Hinton, Monthly Review Press, 1972.

104 Unlike Soviet 'purges', Mao's were non-violent. Officials usually returned to power after a period of penance and reflection.

105 Speech at the Second Plenary Session of the 8th Central Committee, November 15, 1956

their struggles and the wider world, "Democratic politics must rely on everyone running things, not just on a minority of people running things". Modernizing land ownership, infrastructure, agriculture, and industry were secondary. If working people were not politically mobilized around broader issues, they could not transform the economy, management, and labor.

A *cultural* revolution, he said, would spiritually revolutionize the people, especially the youth, and revitalize the Revolution's socialist goals while employing the rhetoric of class struggle. Through the power of ideology expressed in political slogans, he proposed to direct the peasants' energy outward to "Break the shackles of repression with study and convert thought into creative action".

To gain control of their lives, peasants must control intellectual capital so, having eliminated the barriers to land ownership, he would now destroy the obstacles to the ownership of knowledge, "Working men and women must have their own army of technical specialists and professors, teachers, scientists, journalists, writers, artists, and Marxist theorists... We call for a technical revolution that is also a cultural revolution, a revolution to do away with ignorance and stupidity. We can't do it without intellectuals, either. We can't do it just by relying only on uneducated people like ourselves".

His rhetoric was radical, but his revolution would be cultural, political, and ideological, and he prohibited the use of force or the disruption of economic production. His Great Proletarian Cultural Revolution, the only successful social uprising of the 1960s, would be a ten-year saga during which hundreds of millions of peasants would emancipate themselves from second-class citizenship. Theoretical study groups and working people's cultural activities would take place at 'universities of class struggle' where everyone could practice the Four Freedoms: speaking out freely; airing views fully; holding great debates, and writing big-character posters, and he promised that the government would turn their ideas into concrete programs and so consolidate their political power[106]. He would empower and educate hundreds of millions of underprivileged

106 Critique of Soviet Economics by Mao Tsetung. Translated by Moss Roberts. Monthly Review Press. 1977

people, raise their consciousness and, simultaneously, revolutionize agriculture and industry through radical cooperation.

When colleagues questioned the feasibility of such a transformation, he repeated Confucius' warning, "Regulations alone will not work. Men's minds must change. That's the importance of ideology, shaping the ideological environment in which all decisions are made, and of collective responsibility–people internalizing goals and engaging in vigorous political struggle. The class that controls material production simultaneously controls the means of mental production so that the ideas of those who lack the means of mental production are subject to it".

In the heat of July 1966, Mao, a consummate politician, dramatized the most auspicious omen in the *I Ching*: "It is favorable to cross great rivers; Heaven looks favorably upon your plans; it is the right time to dare great undertakings". He swam the Yangtze River signaling[107], "Cross the great river with me. Join me in this auspicious undertaking, the Cultural Revolution. Now. Together. In real life". The only national leader in history to overthrow his own government, he told horrified colleagues, "I firmly believe that a few months of chaos, *luan*, will be mostly for the good". (Forewarned, the Party published[108] 'Suggestions for the protection of cultural relics and books during the Cultural Revolution.' It protected cultural institutions and relics and even helped discover the Terracotta Army and Hunan's Mawangdui tombs).

Enlisting student Red Guards as catalysts, Mao admonished them, "When there is a debate, conduct it by reasoning, not by coercion or force. Anyone should be allowed to speak out, whoever he may be. So long as he is not hostile and does not make malicious attacks, it doesn't matter if he says something wrong. Leaders at all levels have to listen to others and encourage people to observe three principles: Say all you know, say

107 Mao's legacy defended, and famous swim decoded for clueless academics. Ramin Mazaheri. MR Online, April 17, 2018

108 Mobo Gao, The Battle for China's Past: Mao and the Cultural Revolution (London, Pluto Press, 2008), p. 21.

it without reserve, and don't blame the speaker but take his words as a warning". Journalist Wilfred Burchett[109] experienced *luan* first-hand:

> From the window of my hotel room on the morning after my arrival, I had witnessed an extraordinary scene–straight out of Peking opera–with the flat roof of the big department store in nearby Wang Fu Jing (formerly Morrison Street) as the stage. Two hostile groups, each with leaders waving poles with giant red flags, followed by hundreds of supporters with small flags, were fighting it out for possession of the roof. The crowds swayed back and forth, flags and banners were raised and lowered as instruments of combat, and it was all a tremendous visual pandemonium. I decided to go and have a look but retreated when confronted with the vast crowd which had spilled over into the spacious courtyard in front of the hotel and through which I would literally have to use my elbows to advance a few yards. The crowd was not hostile–curious would be a correct definition–but the atmosphere was such that I thought a misunderstood word or gesture might provoke an incident... The group which represented the management had succeeded in getting the combatants out of the shop and padlocking the doors. Not to be outdone, the contenders had returned with a massive chain and an even bigger padlock 'to protect the people's property' and locked the entrance with an appropriate *da tze pao* (big-character posters). Such posters covered every building from street level to the roofs wherever you looked or went in Peking (and viewed from the train windows from the frontier with Vietnam to that with North Korea, it was the same everywhere). The battle for control of the store had started the previous afternoon. Each of the factions, the East is Red and the Red Flag, had its supporters in the industrial area and the villages in the outskirts and had urged them to drop their work and come out to do battle–in

109 Wilfred Burchett, Memoirs of a Rebel Journalist. The Autobiography of Wilfred Burchett, edited by George Burchett and Nick Shimmin, UNSW Press, 2005. Chapter 38, Cursed Be the Peacemaker, pp 584-86

the very heart of Peking. The only battle was a verbal one, with the chief propagandists of each side, the Little Red Books of Mao's Thoughts in their hands, shouting appropriate phrases at each other and posing as the true champions of the Great Proletarian Cultural Revolution, the official designation for what was going on.

Adolescent zealotry soon threatened real chaos, as the CIA reported[110] insightfully:

> **December 1968**. While it would be too much to say that the Cultural Revolution has followed a precise master plan–there have been too many tactical adjustments and shifts along the way–it is clear that Mao envisaged two distinct phases from the start: destructive and constructive. The Red Guards were Mao's vanguard during the destructive phase but proved to be a woefully defective instrument during the constructive phase. Mao's disillusionment with the Red Guards became apparent after their dismal, self-seeking performance during the initial 'power-seizures' of early 1967 and was intensified by their indiscriminate internecine warfare during the following summer. Time and again, Mao ordered the young students to rectify themselves voluntarily. They did not do so, thereby confirming Mao's assessment of the negative qualities of China's intellectuals. As early as 1939, Mao had written that the sole criterion to judge whether or not a youth is revolutionary is if he is 'willing to integrate himself with the broad masses of workers and peasants and does so in practice'. The Red Guards had not been willing to do so. Thus, Mao replaced them with a new vanguard–the working class–when he decided that the time had come to start building and consolidating his new revolutionary order. He forcibly dispatched the young intellectuals to rural areas by the hundreds of thousands for further 'revolutionary purification'.

110 The Role of the Red Guards and Revolutionary Rebels in Mao's Cultural Revolution. CIA: POLO XXXIV) EO-12958. Dec.1968

Luan had served its purpose so, sending the youngsters back to school or down to the countryside, he turned to his own class, "The peasants are clear-sighted. Who is bad and who is not, who is the worst and who is not quite so vicious, who deserves severe punishment and who deserves to be let off lightly; the peasants keep clear accounts and very seldom has the punishment exceeded the crime". He charged them to narrow the Three Differences–between mental and manual work, workers and peasants, city and countryside–by establishing 'three-in-one production teams' of workers, technicians, and specialists to raise productivity through participative innovation[111]. Concern with technological balance brought forward the policy of 'walking on two legs,' or utilizing both advanced and simple or traditional technologies, and spreading technology and scientific know-how that people could master and apply: peasants learned and practiced seed-selection and seed-crossing, for example.

Highly industrialized areas sent half their revenues to the center, and less developed regions received subsidies. Skilled labor and technical expertise were transferred from more developed to less developed areas. By the early 1970s, Shanghai had supplied over half a million skilled workers to industry in the interior so that the least industrialized areas experienced the fastest growth. Dongping Han describes[112] the impact on a hundred thousand villages like his own:

> I grew up in Jimo, a Chinese village. In 1966, there were many illiterate people in my village. The Cultural Revolution weakened professionals' control of education and allowed workers and peasants to have more say in their children's education. Peasants were allowed to run their own village schools. A village would build its own primary school with local materials, hire its own teachers, and provide free access to all children in the village. Several villages would pool their resources to build a free middle school for all peasant children, and then the local commune

111 Economic Growth and Distribution in China. Nicholas Lardy (Cambridge: Cambridge University Press, 1978), pp.153-164.

112 The Socialist Legacy Underlies the Rise of Today's China in the World by Dongping Han. Remembering Socialist China, 1949-1976. Aspects of India's Economy

would open free high schools for them. There were 1,050 villages in Jimo County and every village set up a primary school. All rural children were able to go to school free.

Before the Cultural Revolution, there were only seven middle schools for Jimo County's 750,000 population. Now, the number of middle schools increased to 249, and all primary school graduates could attend them free of charge, without passing tests. In the previous seventeen years, only 1,500 people graduated from the only high school in Jimo County, and half went to college and never came back. Jimo was unable to train a single high school graduate for each village in the County. Now, every commune had three high schools. When I graduated from middle school in 1972, only 70 percent of my classmates could enter high school. When my younger sister graduated in 1973, all her classmates could go to high school. By the end of the Cultural Revolution, in 1976, there were 100 high school graduates in my village and 12,000 in my commune. The expansion of education during the Cultural Revolution years was unprecedented in Chinese history. It profoundly transformed the Chinese people and society. As people became more educated, they became more empowered in both political and economic activities.

Mao told high school graduates they would have to work at least two years in a factory, the countryside, or the army to earn college admission. The *gaokao* college entrance exam was suspended, and students–selected by fellow workers and peasants–returned to serve their communities after graduation. With education reform underway, Mao turned to peasants' health.

"Tell the Ministry of Public Health that it only works for fifteen percent of the population, and that fifteen percent is mainly composed of urban gentlemen, while the broad masses of the peasants get no medical treatment: they don't have any doctors, and they don't have any medicine. The Ministry is not a Ministry of Public Health for the people, so why not change its name to

> the Ministry of Urban Health, of Gentlemen's Health, or even to the Ministry of Urban Gentlemen's Health? The methods of medical examination and treatment currently used by hospitals are not at all appropriate for the countryside, and the way doctors are trained to benefit the cities exclusively, though five hundred million of us are peasants. Medical education must be reformed. It will be enough to give three years' training to graduates from higher primary schools who can then study and raise their proficiency through practice. If such barefoot doctors are sent to the countryside–even if they haven't much talent–they will be better than the current quacks and witch doctors, and the villagers can afford to keep them".

The Rural Cooperative Medical System trained Barefoot Doctors[113] who lived in their own villages and were always available to administer vaccinations, teach nutrition and childcare, demonstrate correct handling of pesticides, and introduce new sanitation methods. They cut infant and maternal mortality by half, and urban doctors, now required to tour the countryside, provided free treatment and trained promising medics at local hospitals. By the end of 1976, every village had a clinic, newborn survival soared, and the death rate had fallen by eighteen percent.

Mao turned next to democracy, "For democracy to work for everyone's benefit, everyone must be empowered. There can be no privileged class". He encouraged criticism of the elite through "big-character posters" and instructed villagers in political activism through the Little Red Book.

- Pay attention to uniting and working with comrades who differ with you. This should be borne in mind both in the localities and in the Army. It also applies to relations with people outside the PartyParty. We have come together from every corner of the country and should be good at uniting in our work not only with comrades who hold the same views as we do but also with those who have different opinions.

---

113 *A Barefoot Doctor's Manual. US National Institutes of Health.*

- Guard against arrogance. For anyone in a leading position, this is a matter of principle and an essential condition for maintaining unity. Even those who have made no serious mistakes and have achieved very great success in their work should not be arrogant.
- In our people's political life, how should right be distinguished from wrong in one's words and actions? Based on the principles of our Constitution, the will of the overwhelming majority of our people, and the common political positions which have been proclaimed on various occasions by our political parties and groups, we consider that broadly speaking, the criteria should be as follows: words and actions should help to unite, and not divide, the people of our various nationalities; they should be beneficial and not harmful, to socialist transformation and socialist construction; they should help to consolidate, not undermine or weaken, the people's democratic dictatorship; they should help to consolidate, and not undermine or weaken, democratic centralism; they should help to strengthen, and not discard or weaken, the leadership of the Communist Party; they should be beneficial, not harmful, to international socialist unity and the unity of the peace-loving people of the world.
- It is necessary to criticize people's shortcomings, but, in doing so, we must truly take the stand of the people and speak out of wholehearted eagerness to protect and educate them. To treat comrades like enemies is to take the stance of the enemy.

Shocking fellow officials, Mao encouraged peasants to elect village leaders who would work in the fields for three hundred days a year. County officials would labor for two-hundred days, live in ordinary houses, send their children to rural schools, bicycle to work, and 'make revolution' when the day's work was done.

To dramatize rural empowerment, he appointed Chen Yonggui, a peasant with a keen sense of political theater, Minister of Agriculture. Chen wore his field clothes when he greeted American plant geneticist and father of the Green Revolution; Sterling Wortman[114], who led a delegation on a tour of inspection, "The rice crop is really first-rate. There was just field after field that was as good as anything you can see. They're all being brought up to the level of skills of the best people. They all share the available inputs". Nobel agronomist Norman Borlaug agreed, "You had to look hard to find a bad field. Everything was green and nice everywhere we traveled. I felt the progress had been much more remarkable than I expected". Wortman's Green Revolution was then crushing Third World grain prices, destroying millions of small farms, ruining farming communities, and creating vast shantytowns of rural immigrants that persist to this day.

To save capital and create local jobs, teams of peasants, workers, and technicians built thousands of local fertilizer plants and farm machinery factories where peasants learned industrial skills without leaving their communities. Says Nicholas Lardy, "Socialism eliminates the barrier of private ownership. Innovations and knowledge become social property. One task of the planning system in China was to socialize such knowledge".

Industrial output rose fifty-eight percent, outpacing Germany's thirty-three percent and Japan's forty-four percent growth during their takeoffs. Social morality, damaged by a century of war, improved sharply. Rural participation in the arts rose. Short stories, poetry, paintings and sculpture, music, and dance flowered. In place of old court dramas, revolutionary works in opera and ballet—some now in the international canon—emphasized workers' and peasants' resistance to oppression. Mobo Gao describes[115] their impact,

> For the first time, the rural villagers organized theater troupes and put on performances that incorporated the contents and structure of the eight model Peking operas with local language and music. The villagers entertained themselves and learned how to read and write by getting into the texts and plays. And

114 US Crop Experts Praise China's Achievements in Growing Food. By Joseph Lelyveld. The New York Times, September 24, 1974

115 Gao, Mobo. The Battle for China's Past: Mao and the Cultural Revolution (p. 23).

> they organized sports meets and held matches with other villages. All these activities gave the villagers an opportunity to meet, communicate, fall in love. They gave them a sense of discipline and organization, creating a public sphere where meetings and communications went beyond the traditional household and village clans. This had never happened before and has never happened since.

Throughout the ten years of revolutionary upheaval, Mao drove inequality to the lowest level ever recorded and kept the economy growing more than six percent annually–twice America's rate. He mechanized agriculture with a twenty-fold increase in tractors; a thirty-five-fold increase in diesel engines; a sixteen-fold increase in electric motors; a seven-fold increase in mills; a fifty-fold increase in grinders, and a thirteen-fold increase in sprayers.

By the end, rural literacy was taken for granted and rural people, no longer 'peasants,' were as intolerant of oppression and corruption, as vocal about their priorities, as enthusiastic about voting, and as eager to voice complaints as their urban cousins. For the first time in history, they were full citizens who could point to the infrastructure they built, the agricultural advances they had made, and the problems they had solved.

Yet, though hundreds of millions of rural people benefited from the Cultural Revolution, many urbanites felt that, by destroying the hierarchy, Mao had destroyed the culture itself–a charge that resonated with elites worldwide. Many fled abroad and published semi-fictional books about their sufferings. Officials had struggled to maintain their sanity amid an administrative nightmare, others were subjected to public humiliation or years in prison while some, crushed by criticisms they could not comprehend, committed suicide. Few forgave Mao.

His successors, exhausted by *luan*, humiliation, and persecution, sought to discredit him and his revolution. Their revenge was swift, says Mobo Gao[116]:

---

116 Mobo Gao, The Battle for China's Past: Mao and the Cultural Revolution (London, Pluto Press, 2008), p. 21.

> Soon after Mao died, his vision of educating workers, peasants, and soldiers to be new leaders of the socialist society was denounced. The new 'reformers' charged that workers, peasants, and soldier-students were not suited for college education and lacked the cultural background to become the educated and charged that China had wasted ten precious years by not educating its brightest. In 1977, the college entrance examination was reinstated, and the Education Reform instituted during the Cultural Revolution was repudiated and abandoned. By 1980, the worker, peasant, and soldier university study program disappeared. Like all other newborn things in the Cultural Revolution, they vanished from China's red earth like falling stars. However, even though the education revolution was defeated, its glory continues to shine–just like the Paris Commune. The education revolution was a successful attempt by workers, peasants, and soldiers to occupy the sphere of ideology. It was an unprecedented milestone in human development on the long road to human emancipation.

Deng Xiaoping, the scion of an elite family, dissolved the communes, clinics, and schools and, despite fierce resistance, forced peasants back to small producers' status. His Reform and Opening, says Orville Schell[117], "Rammed Chinese society into reverse gear, stampeding the country into a form of unregulated capitalism that made the US and Europe seem almost socialist by comparison". A new generation of illiterate peasants, particularly women, emerged. Life expectancy fell as poverty, prostitution, drug trafficking and addiction, the sale of women and children, petty crime, organized crime, official corruption, pollution, racketeering, and profiteering returned.

By 1983, peasants unable to afford their children's tuition or medical care, teenagers who were forced out of school, and farmers who could not afford privately manufactured fertilizer created a severe crime wave. Deng executed thousands and crushed all signs of dissent and, seven

117 Mandate of Heaven: The Legacy of Tiananmen Square and the Next Generation. By Orville Schell

years later, in a hugely popular film, *The Herdsman*, a poor herder talks with an intellectual who had been a herder in Mao's time and later became a teacher, "You were one of us once; now us folk are all done for". Says Dongping Han[118],

> The Chinese government's official evaluation of the Cultural Revolution serves to underline the idea, currently very much in vogue worldwide, that efforts to achieve development and efforts to attain social equality are contradictory. The remarkable currency of this idea in China and internationally is due, at least in part, to the fact that such a view is so convenient to those threatened by efforts to attain social equality. This study of the history of Jimo County has challenged this idea. During the Cultural Revolution decade and in the two decades of market reform that followed, Jimo has experienced alternative paths, both of which have led to rural development. The difference in the paths was not between development and stagnation but rather between different kinds of development. The main conclusion I hope readers will draw from the experience of Jimo County during the Cultural Revolution decade is that measures to empower and educate people at the bottom of society can also serve the goal of economic development. It is not necessary to choose between pursuing social equality and pursuing economic development. The real choice is whether or not to pursue social equality.

Like all revolutions, the Cultural Revolution brought mixed blessings. For every tale of outrage, imprisonment, or suicide, there are a million from peasants who, despite government campaigns against 'Cultural Revolution nostalgia,' reunite each year to celebrate their emancipation. Mao had no doubts. Shortly before his death, someone asked about his proudest achievements, and Mao answered, "Winning the war, of course, and the Cultural Revolution".

If we attribute excess deaths to Mao, we must also credit him with

118 The Unknown Cultural Revolution: Life and Change in a Chinese Village. Dongping Han. 2008.

a billion excess lives and a nation transformed. When he stepped down in 1974, he had reunited, reimagined, reformed, and revitalized the largest, oldest civilization on earth, modernized it after a century of failed modernizations, and ended millennia of famine. Under the West's crushing, twenty-five-year embargo on food, finance, technology, and medical and agricultural equipment, and its exclusion of China from the family of nations, Mao worked a miracle. He banished invaders, bandits, and warlords; eliminated severe crime and drug addiction; doubled the population, life expectancy, and literacy; liberated its women and educated its girls; erased its disparities of wealth and land; built its infrastructure; grown its economy twice as fast as the West's; led four revolutions and succeeded in three; produced jet aircraft, locomotives, oceangoing ships, ICBMs, hydrogen bombs, and satellites, and left the country debt-free.

Today, ninety-eight percent of Chinese admire Mao. His image, like St. Christopher's, adorns taxis and stares down from the walls of offices, businesses, and restaurants, and upon Tiananmen Square. He destroyed the ancient myth of elite authority, altered China's consciousness and the peasants' destiny.

Today, despite official disapproval, ten million people visit his birthplace every year: more than all the people who visit all the world's shrines.

PART III

DATA IN THE MIDDLE

CHAPTER 7

Data-Driven Democracy

The People are supreme. The State is secondary, and the Ruler is least important. Only those who please the people can rule. Mencius[119].

***

For almost three thousand years, Roman governments like ours have maintained the *status quo* on behalf of the wealthy elites who have always controlled them. Though occasionally paying lip service to progress, they have rarely improved ordinary people's lives.

That was China's governance model for a thousand years, too, but then Confucius proposed a progressive model which, he claimed, held sway in a Golden Age. To retain legitimacy, compassionate governments promoted people's prosperity and society's harmony. Those that did not were deposed. There is nothing remarkable about this scheme. Idealists have proposed it since the dawn of time. What is remarkable is that the First Emperor adopted it wholeheartedly and set a pattern that persists to this day.

Mao refined the Confucian process by adding democratic oversight, surveys, and local experimentation on a scale so vast that today the process is an industry in itself. China's Academy of Social Sciences, CASS, with fifty research centers covering two-hundred sixty social disciplines

119 Confucius' most famous disciple, Mencius (372 BC - 289 BC).

and four-thousand full-time researchers, now uses questionnaires and grassroots forums to initiate and evaluate all legislation.

Teams tour the country, appear on TV, hold meetings, listen to local opinions and formulate proposals. Congress commissions scholars to evaluate and economists to budget their recommendations. Says a CASS planner[120], "Computers have made huge improvements in collecting and analyzing the information. Still, thousands of statisticians, actuaries, database experts and technicians with degrees in urban, rural, agricultural, environmental and economic planning invest thousands of hours interpreting and analyzing this vast trove of data, statistics and information. Needless to say, for a continent-sized country with over a billion citizens, it takes hundreds of thousands of people to develop a Five-Year Plan".

The country's Brains Trust, the State Council, publishes draft Plans and solicits feedback from employees, farmers, business people, entrepreneurs, officials and specialists, and feasibility reports from the twenty-seven levels of bureaucracy responsible for implementation. The Finance and Economics Committee analyzes Plan budgets and, after the State Council signs off. Congress votes. Then discussion is suspended and experimentation and data collection begin. The process resembles Proctor & Gamble more than Pericles of Athens, with solutions to problems test-marketed everywhere, says venture capitalist Robin Daverman:

> China is a giant trial portfolio with millions of trials everywhere: innovations in everything from healthcare to poverty reduction, education, energy, trade, and transportation are being trialed in different communities. Every one of China's 662 cities is experimenting: Shanghai with free trade zones, Guizhou with poverty reduction, twenty-three cities with education reforms, Northeastern provinces with SOE reform, pilot schools, pilot cities, pilot hospitals, pilot markets, pilot everything. Mayors and governors, the Primary Investigators, share their 'lab results' at the Central Party School and publish them in State-owned media, their 'scientific journals.'

120 Jeff J. Brown, *China Rising.*

> Significant policies usually begin as 'clinical trials' in small towns, where they generate test data. If the stats look right, they'll add test sites and do long-term followups. They test and tweak for 10-30 years, then ask the 3,000-member People's Congress to review the data and authorize national trials in three provinces. If those trials are successful, the State Council [China's Brains Trust] polishes the plan and takes it back to Congress for a final vote. It's very transparent, and if your data is better than mine, your bill gets passed, and mine doesn't. Congressional votes are nearly unanimous because reams of data back the legislation.
>
> This allows China to accomplish a great deal in a short time because your winning solution will be quickly propagated throughout the country. You'll be a front-page hero, invited to high-level meetings in Beijing and promoted. As you can imagine, the competition to solve problems is intense. Local governments have a great deal of freedom to try their own things as long as the local people support them. Various villages and small towns have tested everything from bare-knuckled liberalism to straight Communism.

Thousands of Trial Spots generate immense volumes of data[121], says author Jeff J. Brown[122], "My Beijing neighborhood committee and town hall are constantly putting up announcements, inviting groups of people–renters, homeowners, over seventies, women under forty, those with or without medical insurance, retirees–to answer surveys. The CPC is the world's biggest pollster for a reason: China's democratic 'dictatorship of the people' is highly engaged at the day-to-day, citizen-on-the-street level. I know, because I live in a middle class Chinese community and I question them all the time. I find their government much more

121 The Chinese Labor Dynamics Survey (Sun Yat-Sen University), the Chinese Family Panel Survey (Peking U), the Chinese General Social Survey (Renmin U), the Chinese Income Inequality Surveys (Beijing Normal U) and polls by Harvard University, Gallup, Edelman, World Values and Asian Barometer.

122 *44 Days Backpacking in China: The Middle Kingdom in the 21st Century, with the United States, Europe, and the Fate of the World in Its Looking Glass.* Jeff J. Brown. 2013

responsive and democratic than the dog-and-pony shows back home, and I mean that seriously".

One of the earliest Trial Spots began spontaneously in poverty-stricken Yiwu in 1978 when China first embraced market economics, and Huaichuan Rui[123] recalls his mother exchanging chicken feathers with an itinerant Yiwu trader to buy him candy. "Years later, after considerable research, I learnt that that Yiwu's 'exchanging candy for chicken feathers' dated to the sixteenth century!" Rui tells the story of Zhou Xiaoguang, now in her 60s, who had begun trading when she was sixteen years old, carrying small goods like embroidery needles from Yiwu to sell in neighboring provinces:

> Life was harsh. Information was unavailable, and communication tool was almost none except for telegraph and limited public telephone. We had to explore every potential market by traveling to the place. Train tickets were so difficult to get. Once getting on a train, we often slept under the seats of other passengers.... Once arriving at a place, we sought a popular location as a temporary market to sell goods and were frequently driven away by local officers. If the local demand was low, we moved to another place. In this way, we accumulated the most valuable market experience, which benefits us for life. At the end of 1978, Yiwu traders attempted to break through the policy restrictions on trade. They formed many temporary markets in Yiwu by simply placing their trading baskets together on the roads of villages and towns. This was the earliest market form of Yiwu.
>
> In 1982, Xie Gaohua became the Party Secretary of Yiwu County and recalled, "I am not a native of Yiwu. My mother was upset when I was appointed to Yiwu County, asking why I was allocated to such a poor county? But I felt strongly that my prime responsibility was eradicating the poverty of Yiwu". A woman trader, Feng Aiqian, was angry that she was frequently driven away by tax officers, so she came to the County Government

123 Yiwu: Historical transformation and contributing factors by Huaichuan Rui. Journal of History and Anthropology Vol. 29, September 20, 2018

building to seek justice. Xie says she reinforced his determination to allow local people to trade. "I asked her to calm down and explain why she should be supported. Ms. Feng stated that she had no job but four kids; she conducted small trading to supplement her family living and her behavior did not harm anyone. I was impressed and thought deeply about what she had told me. As central government did not switch the green light to trading by farmers, I went to rural areas to investigate the truth. I witnessed the hardship of local people and realized that trading was indeed a major income supplement to farmers. On my return I abruptly promoted the idea that, 'small commodity trading is Yiwu's major advantage' and supported market development. I offered to take full responsibility if provincial and central governments criticized this decision. I was determined to open the small commodity market even though I risked losing my official hat, *wu sha mao*, for it. But other members in Yiwu Municipal Government said they would support the decision too, so all of us took the responsibility for deciding to support the market".

When critics pointed out the negative impact of farmers' trade, like tax evasion and disrupting public order, Xie issued regulations, 'Strengthening the Management of Small Commodity Market,' and announced the opening of a small commodity market in Hu Qing Men in September 1982. Local people needed to register and obtain a local government certificate to trade inside the market. By the end of 1982, Yiwu had 833 registered traders, including 800 farmers, 33 jobless, and youth. In 1986 there was a nationwide discussion about the merits of socialism and capitalism. People asked if the Yiwu model was attached to capitalism or socialism and pointed out Yiwu's problems, like low quality and fake goods. The debate shocked Yiwu, and trading volume was reduced due to doubt and uncertainty. But the local government lobbied the central government. In 2011, Yiwu was formally nominated an International Trade Comprehensive Trial Spot and given a unique Customs tax code to speed and simplify exporting. Traders could use just one code for all small commodities, and customers could trace products to their original producers in case of complaints.

Yiwu International Trade Center covers eight hundred acres. It is a terminus for the Eurasian Silk Road Railway.

Though Yiwu's Trial Spot took thirty years to mature, it pales beside the Trial Spot that birthed the Three Gorges Dam.

John L. Savage, chief design engineer for the US Bureau of Reclamation, surveyed the gorges in 1944 and proposed a 'Yangtze River Project'. His proposal gathered dust until, after devastating floods killed thirty-three thousand people in 1954, Mao revived it, but retired engineers, foreign consultants, and a million people in its path condemned the project. Undeterred, officials, most of whom were engineers, drafted legislation but Congress demanded a Trial Spot to test its viability.

Planners duly built the successful Gezhouba Dam in 1992 but only sixty-two percent of congresspeople, daunted by the Three Gorges' cost, scale, environmental impact, and social disruption, voted for it. Though the vote was the lowest ever recorded and the media assailed the government for 'ramming the dam down people's throats,' Beijing relocated thirteen cities, one-hundred forty towns, one-thousand six-hundred villages, and 1.3 million people and built a reservoir so vast that it slows the rotation of the Earth. Planners had the last laugh: the project recoups its entire construction cost every four years[124].

After floods and droughts in the nineties, the government distributed $100 billion for two programs: the Sloping Lands Trial Spot for returning hillside farms to forest, and the Natural Forests Trial Spot for nature reserves. A complementary project, the Fast-Growing and High-Yielding Timber Construction Trial Spot, funded by the private timber industry, covers eighteen high-rainfall coastal provinces. Its thirty-two million acres of fast-growing, high-yielding timber provide one-third of the nation's commercial timber consumption–almost enough to balance the demand-supply gap.

Agro-ecology is a Trial Spot hotbed. In 2005 farmers used four times more nitrogen than the global average, so Trial Spots[125] tested hundreds of farms across the country to develop sustainable, localized practices. A thousand scientists, sixty-five thousand bureaucrats and technicians, and one-hundred forty-thousand agricultural industry staff used data to tailor local solutions. They conducted fourteen-thousand workshops and distributed high-quality seeds and fertilizers to attendees. Northeast rice farmers cut fertilizer use twenty percent by planting seedlings closer together and applying more nitrogen late in the season. By 2019, twenty-million farmers had increased their yields eleven percent, lowered nitrogen use by fifteen percent, and fattened their wallets by twelve billion dollars.

Wildlife has its own Trial Spots. In 2010 the Academy of Sciences approved a National Park Trial Spot for Siberian Tigers and Amur Leopards and a southern Trial Spot for Giant Pandas. Females Pandas are fertile for one day each year and, as their ranges fragmented, their encounters with potential mates had fallen, along with natural births. By 2017,

124 Construction cost $20 billion. The dam generates 100 billion KWh annually at US $0.084/KwH. Three Gorges Tours Earn $3 Billion annually. Flood mitigation and irrigation enhancements save as much again.

125 Millions of Chinese farmers reap benefits of huge crop experiment. *Nature*. March 7, 2018

populations of target wildlife in the Trial Spots had doubled and should redouble by 2030. Workers are busily consolidating thirty isolated parks, forty-three scenic protection zones, thirteen forest parks, four geographic parks, and two natural heritage sites and demolishing dozens of dams to create Giant Panda National Park, an uninterrupted nature reserve bigger than the State of Massachusetts. Soon eight thousand animal and plant species will once again range freely over ten thousand square miles.

In 2012, after President Xi began promoting officials who improved local inequality, and Inequality Trial Spots proliferated. Regional capital Chengdu imposed a progressive tax on luxury real estate to finance[126] low-income housing and, by 2019, three-hundred thousand handicapped, elderly, unemployed, and large, low-income families had new homes, and local restauranteur[127] who advertised free meals for the needy confessed that only two had accepted her invitation. Her experience is reflected nationwide:

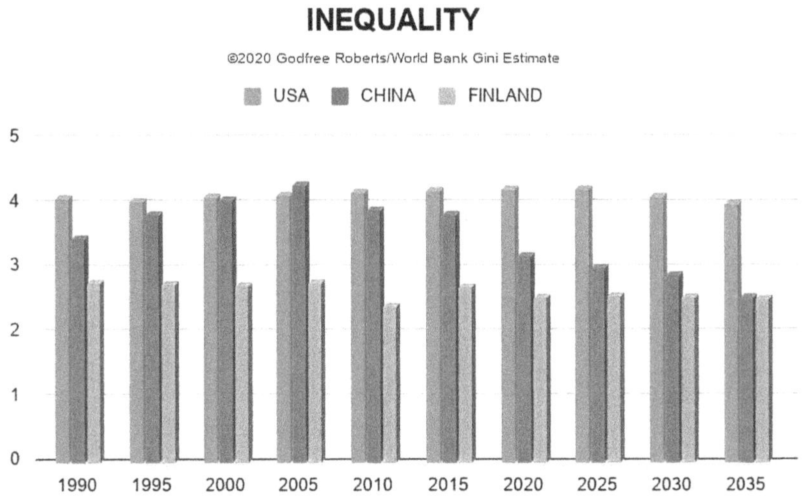

In 2018, the Health Commission asked provinces to bring childhood obesity under control by 2030. Provincial health ministers turned

126 Understanding Slums: Chengdu, China, by Tian Jun. UN Case Studies, Global Report 2003
127 Chinese woman offers oodles of free noodles to the needy, but no one seems to want them. SCMP. Kinling Lo, July 20, 2018

to County Health Directors, and Childhood Obesity Awareness Trial Spots mushroomed across the country: in a remote southwestern city, the author saw a billboard warning, somewhat dubiously, that obesity reduces children's[128] life expectancy. In 2025, the best solutions will be implemented nationwide, and, by 2030, obese children will again be rare.

Critics who label China's Congress[129] a 'rubber stamp' miss the point: congresspeople vote based on data. They visit mature Trial Spots, survey[130] local opinion, audit statistics and cashflows, calculate budgetary impacts and scalability and debate political viability at the national level. Though few trials even reach the provincial level–where they can affect one-hundred million people–all contribute to the trove of data that shapes legislation.

They reached their goals for the Twelfth Plan, literally by trial and error, yet economic growth averaged 7.8 percent, services became the largest sector of the economy and consumption became the major growth driver. Energy intensity[1] fell eighteen percent and emissions dropped twelve percent, the urban-rural income gap narrowed, rudimentary health insurance became universal, three hundred million folk gained access to safe drinking water and one hundred million were lifted from poverty.

Trial Spots, and the data they generate, are one of China's most remarkable political strengths. They allow legislation to be rolled out confidently and rapidly and, largely thanks to them, most Chinese say the country is run for their benefit[131] rather than for particular groups.

---

128 There is a correlation between obesity and lowered IQ, but causation is unclear.

129 To recap: the three-thousand delegates to the National People's Congress are elected via a multi-tiered, hierarchical representative voting. The NPC meets twice annually and elects the President and State Council and passes all legislation.

130 The Chinese Labor Dynamics Survey, the Chinese Family Panel Survey, the Chinese General Social Survey, and Chinese Income Inequality Surveys. They scrutinize hundreds of polls by overseas scholars and institutions like Harvard University, Gallup, Edelman, World Values, and Asian Barometer.

131 World Values Surveys Wave 6

Harvard's Tony Saich[132], who conducts his own surveys, says ninety percent are happy with their government–and getting steadily more optimistic.

132 *Understanding CCP Resilience: Surveying Chinese Public Opinion Through Time*, co-authored by Edward Cunningham, Tony Saich, and Jesse Turiel, presents findings from the longest-running independent effort to track Chinese citizen satisfaction of government performance. For the first time, this new study provides a crucial long-term view of how Chinese citizens view their government at the national and regional, and local levels in China.

CHAPTER 8

Poverty, Work & Wages

The economy is in such a state that men don't have enough money to care for elderly parents and support their wives and children. Even in good years, their lives are bitter while, in bad years, they struggle to avoid starvation and death. Under those circumstances, how can you expect them to be civil–or even lawful? Mencius[133].

***

Assuming that market economies are necessary and good, critics insist that China's is not a market economy and should become one. But market economies are a recent invention whose track record is mixed at best, and the Chinese are understandably wary of them.

Around 1850, for the first time in history, Western capitalists created a market economy by privatizing credit, land, and labor, and subordinating human society to the market and to wealthy individuals who dominated it. A century later, in 1950, Chinese communists created a collective economy by subordinating credit, land, and labor to society's service and placed their trust in the government to regulate it.

Today, almost all Chinese own their homes[134] and urban poverty has

133 Mencius, Confucius' principle disciple, was born a century after the Master's death, in 372 BC, and died in 289 BC.

134 How People In China Afford Their Outrageously Expensive Homes, by Wade Shepard. Forbes, March 30, 2016

disappeared[135], but rural poverty, exacerbated by distance, remained a problem until, in 1993, Shanghai's Minimum Livelihood Guarantee Trial Spot became the national social safety net, *dībǎo*, that pays the difference between people's actual income and the '*dībǎo* line,' set based on local living costs. Though the qualifying process is daunting, the *dībǎo* gives recipients discretionary use of the money and opens the window to benefits like inexpensive medical insurance. Two years later, a surprised Voice of America reported[136], "China enacted a labor law granting all workers the right to a wage, rest periods, no excessive overtime and the right to carry out group negotiations".

In 2000, the United Nations set six Millennium Development Goals: eliminate extreme poverty, hunger, disease, inadequate shelter, exclusion, and gender bias in education by 2015. Ever since, on Poverty Relief Day, China's President and Prime Minister, trailed by TV crews, have visited remote villages and shown affluent urbanites the ugly face of rural poverty, typified by an ethnic Miao[137] family who owned a little adobe house, farmed their tiny plot, sold blood[138], and did odd jobs to get by.

With three children (minorities are exempt from family planning), they could not afford furniture, so folded their clothes on the floor and entertained themselves with a black-and-white TV. They received a monthly living allowance of two hundred dollars from the local government. The husband's occasional day jobs earned ten to twenty dollars, and blood-selling brought in another hundred dollars. His wife said this bought sixty pounds of rice, two packs of salt, a kilo of peppers, and a bag of washing powder, electricity, and transportation. Their village headman explained, "Our village population is 1,770 and more than two hundred people live on blood-selling. Our land is arid, seven hundred

---

135 China has almost wiped out urban poverty. Now it must tackle inequality. Elizabeth Stuart. The Guardian. Aug 2015

136 Labor Strikes Surge in China. By Shannon Van Sant. April 9, 2015. VOA News

137 Blood selling tells bitter story of poverty in China. Xinhua). 2010-09-22

138 A common practice world wide. The majority of Cleveland's donors generate more than a third of their income from "donating" blood. BEARING MANY BURDENS: Source Plasma Donations in the US . Case Western. By Olsen, Margolius, et al., Case Western University. August 1, 2018

villagers' homes have no arable land at all and, without a road, they walk three miles for drinking water".

Rural pensions, introduced in 2009, lowered poverty in the countryside to fourteen percent and five years later workers' compensation, maternity benefits, unemployment insurance, skills training[139] and equal access to urban employment cut it to seven percent.

Next, tens of thousands of anti-poverty teams moved into poor villages and showed villagers how to grow mushrooms, plant pear trees, raise mohair goats, or host eco-tourists: anything that would earn a cash income. By 2018, pinned to the door of every poor household was a laminated sheet listing its occupants, the causes of their poverty, their remediation program, a completion date, and the name, photograph, and phone number of the responsible official.

Corporations pitched in. Foxconn, Apple's assembler, moved two-hundred thousand jobs inland, Hewlett-Packard moved huge factories to Xinjiang, and Beijing moved entire universities.

But it was infrastructure–roads, railways, Internet, and drones–that tipped the scales. By 2019, high-speed, low-cost internet service bringing e-commerce, distance education, remote healthcare, and public services transformed lives in one-hundred twenty-three thousand poor villages[140]. Isolated settlements averaged four daily drone pickups and demand for drone piloting classes exploded. Within five years, off-farm employment like crop-spraying, land surveying, and product delivery accounted for the majority of rural income.

Next, Congress allocated $120 billion from vehicle sales tax revenues to build one-hundred fifty-thousand miles of new rural roads, one of which reached Mashuping[141], an isolated cliff village on the Yellow River and one of the poorest in Shaanxi Province, where villagers cultivated apples and Sichuan pepper trees. They sold their produce cheaply to the few dealers who came by motorbike until a new, five-hundred mile,

139 China: Skills Training for Rural Migrants Makes a Big Difference. World Bank. August 7, 2015

140 Over 90% of China's Poorer Villages to Enjoy Broadband Internet Access by 2019. China Banking News, June 8, 2018

141 China's iconic revolutionary base Yan'an bids farewell to poverty. Xinhua. 2019-05-07

riverbank highway brought a high-speed internet connection and 'targeted anti-poverty teams'. Now, said a grower, "Our apples sell out when they're still hanging on the trees". By 2019, per capita income was twice the national poverty level.

Villages like Liangjiahe, where Xi Jinping grew up, exploit unique niches. Though cabbage fields still line the single road, its canny inhabitants cultivate tourists, charging thousands of visitors eight dollars each to hear tales of Xi's Four Hardships: flea bites, bad food, hard labor, and assimilating into the peasantry. They give three hundred overnight guests a taste of his boyhood in cave inns decorated with vintage Mao posters and kerosene lanterns, furnished with hard brick beds warmed by earth stoves. "All authentic, of course. We want to protect the Liangjiahe brand image," a young guide brightly explained.

Dedicated software apps help rural laborers connect with employment opportunities, veterans and disabled folk find piecework, and young people returning home start businesses. In a Zhejiang Trial Spot, five hundred villages have organized clusters around market towns and employ 200,000 locals to promote local products and skills in e-commerce niches. By 2019, rural online stores employed thirty-million people and created an e-commerce market bigger than Europe's.

Beijing judges anti-poverty programs successful once ninety percent of villagers swear, in writing, that they are no longer poor. Roaming audit teams conduct follow-up studies and send their findings to anti-poverty officers with videos of every interview. As with most social programs, Beijing plans to recoup its investment in poverty alleviation by 2040, through e-sales taxes.

In 2016 the government shifted ten percent of the equity in the most valuable SOEs[142] into the social security fund and President Xi set a final goal, "If we lift ten million rural people out of poverty each year until 2020, the social security system will provide adequate financial support for our twenty-million disabled people". In 2018 he set a new goal, reducing inequality to world-leading levels by 2035–no easy matter, as

142 One-quarter of the world's most profitable corporations–mostly banks and insurance companies–are State-Owned Enterprises, SOEs.

former President Hu Jintao[143] explained, "Taking from each according his ability and giving to each according to his needs requires democratic rule of law, fairness and justice, honesty and fraternity, abundant energy, stability, orderliness, harmony between people and their environment, and sustainable development".

***

Employers now pay thirteen percent of wages into a tax-exempt fund for employees' housing deposits and a further[144] thirty percent into retirement, medical, unemployment, maternity, and occupational injury funds, and employees match those contributions one hundred percent. Workers with fewer than ten years of cumulative work experience are entitled to three months' sick leave[145] on sixty percent to one-hundred percent of salary, depending on seniority.

Beijing expects[146] employers to treat their workers well. "Entrepreneurs–especially state-owned entrepreneurs–should play a leading role in serving society as conscious models of political, economic, and social responsibility, and so serve the Party, the country, and the people". In 2018, a labor lawyer warned Guangzhou executives that their labor costs were about to rise dramatically. Stricter collection of social security payments, a ten percent rise in the minimum wage, and a growing number of workers filing labor disputes would force changes, "I think all of you will agree that one-third of small and medium-sized private entrepreneurs will shut down if they have to pay their social welfare contributions in full". In 2019, provincial Trial Spots began monitoring employer compliance.

143 'Holding the great banner of Socialism with Chinese characteristics and struggling to achieve the new victory of the construction of a prosperous society.' People's Daily, October 25, 2007. Hu Jintao preceded Xi as China's president from 2002-2012.

144 Mandatory Social Welfare Benefits for Chinese Employees: An overview of social welfare obligations and costs for employers of Chinese staff. By Adam Livermore. China Briefing, 2/21.2012.

145 Annual Leave and Sick Leave Entitlements in China: A Guide for Overseas Employers. Shield GEO. 2019

146 "State Council Opinions on Promoting Excellent Entrepreneurship and Giving Full Play to the Role of Entrepreneurs". NDRC October 2017.

The Wall Street Journal reported[147] that the socially oriented economy has doubled everyone's salary every decade for the past forty years. "In 2012 alone, the average wage rose by 14 percent. Western corporations such as Crystal Group, which produces clothes for Abercrombie & Fitch and Gap, have pulled out because of rising labor costs". Yet The New York Times found complaints of labor shortages are widespread[148], "Waves of migrant workers from the countryside filled China's factories for the last three decades and helped make the nation the world's largest manufacturer. Many companies now find themselves struggling to hire enough workers and, for the scarce workers they do find, pay has more than quintupled in the last decade".

The Labor Contract Law's 'termination for cause' clause forces employers to publish detailed regulations, keep careful records and negotiate with unions, because management can only terminate employees–with severance pay–if they remain incompetent after training or reassignment.

Strikes are rare, explains union leader An Jianhua[149], "China has a huge population, so striking doesn't help much. There are plenty of laborers ready replace workers". Instead, the All-China Federation of Trade Unions, ACTFU, resolves labor disputes through consultation, arbitration, and legislation. The ACFTU, whose three hundred million union members outnumber the rest of the world's combined, has persuaded the government to ratify four of eight United Nations Labor Conventions, two of its four governance conventions, twenty-two Technical Conventions[150]. If all else fails, the threat of legal action usually brings employers into line: unions rarely lose in front of communist judges.

Base wages, which rise with seniority, come with annual bonuses plus a thirteenth monthly payment at New Year. Workers covet overtime because labor laws stipulate that, after forty-four hours of work, they receive one-hundred-fifty percent of base salary, two hundred percent on

147 Rising Wages Pose Dilemma for China. WSJ. Tom Orlik. May 17, 2013

148 Cheaper Robots, Fewer Workers. The New York Times. April 24, 2015

149 China's labor movement keeping pace with globalization. People's World, June 18, 2018, by John Bachtell and Carol Ramos Widom

150 The US has sanctioned two, one, and seven, respectively.

Saturday afternoon and Sunday, and three hundred percent on national holidays. Employers can hire on contract only twice (two six-month agreements, for example), after which hires automatically become permanent. Tenure, based on cumulative experience with all previous employers, allows job-switchers keep their seniority and accumulated vacation time: five days annually for the first nine years, ten for the next nine years, and fifteen days thereafter. Factory workers are generally young, happy, and carefree, gossiping, flirting, listening to music, and–except in large corporations–wearing what they please.

Accelerating inland growth has triggered labor shortages in coastal cities, forcing employers to automate, raise productivity, and move up the value chain–just as Beijing intended. In 2019, Mentech, a telecom manufacturer in coastal Dongguan, offered regular wages plus $1,100 guaranteed monthly overtime, air-conditioned dorms, free Wi-Fi, and birthday presents. Monthly manufacturing wages average[151] $1800 in 2019 and overtime, bonuses, company housing, and free meals allow workers to send money home. Indeed, adjusted for productivity, regulations, and benefits, Chinese employees now cost[152] employers more than their American cousins and a friend of the author, who hires workers in both countries, explained why:

> At our US facility, our only requirement for assemblers is a high school degree, US citizenship, passing a drug and criminal background check, and a simple assembly test: looking at an assembly engineering drawing and then putting the components together. While the vast majority of American applicants were unable to complete the assembly test, in China, they completed it in half the time, and 100% of applicants passed. Hiring for an assembler position in the US would require thirty interviews a day and produce twenty-nine rejections, not to mention all the HR hassles of assemblers walking off shift, excessive lateness, stealing from work, slow work speed, and poor attitudes. The position

151 *Wages in Manufacturing in China*. Trading Economics–adjusted for purchasing power parity.
152 Oxford Economics, quoted in 'Made in China' labor is not actually that cheap. Sophia Yan CNN. March 17, 2016

> starts at $12 an hour in flyover country, which is pretty reasonable compared to other jobs that only require a GED and no prior work experience. It offers medical, dental, and annual raises with plenty of opportunities to move up in the company and earn an average Production Assembler salary, $33,029, if they stay beyond five years. Similar positions in China pay the same wages as other positions there with only a high school degree and no work experience. Yet the applicant quality is much higher, and this also applies to the white-collar support professionals: schedulers, quality inspectors, equipment testers and calibrators, engineers, supply chain managers, account managers, sales. Their labor quality is simply higher. At the end of the day, high-end and middling manufacturing is not moving to either the US or Mexico because average workers in flyover country cannot meet the demands of twenty-first-century manufacturing.

Barely two percent of citizens pay taxes, and most like it that way: Congressional consultations on income taxes attracted 130,000 submissions advocating the *status quo*. Yet despite low taxes, a powerful union, strong labor laws, sympathetic courts, and rising wages, China is no workers' paradise. Only three quarters of workers report having union representation, paid annual leave, and paid days off. In 2019, ten years after they were promised a union, Walmart's employees were still struggling to establish one. Foxconn, Apple's Taiwan-owned assembler, allowed employees to unionize only after media exposed its practice of forcing employees to stand for illegal, twelve-hour shifts and local officials moved in to lend muscle to workers' efforts.

Until recently, millions of migrant workers contributing to urban retirement funds could only collect full pensions in their home provinces. Local governments had no money for them when they returned at the end of their working lives. When, despite pleas from cash-starved inland provinces, rich coastal provinces clung to multi-billion surpluses, Beijing endowed a trillion-dollar National Pension Insurance Program and persuaded provinces to join. The People's Daily[153] drummed up support by appealing to national pride, "In developed countries like America–where the Gini[154] index sometimes reaches 0.4–income disparities are eased through gradually increasing taxation on the wealthy and improving welfare systems to help the poor. China should learn from America's experience". In 2014, civil servants and academics joined the national scheme. In 2019, Beijing issued a billion electronic cards and now everyone uses them to access social security benefits, personal and medical records, government subsidies and reimbursements, and pay bills.

CHINA TAX & BENEFIT DEDUCTIONS 2020

Taxable Income RMB	Taxable Income $PPP	Tax Rate
0-1500	$0-390	3%
1501-4500	$390-1,168	10%
4501-9000	$1,168- 2,337	20%
9001-35,000	$2,337-9,088	25%
35,000-55,000	$9,088-14,282	30%
55,001-80,000	$14,282-20,773	35%
80,000+	$21,000+	40%
Mandatory Benefit Deductions	**From Employee**	**From Employer**
Retirement Insurance	8%	20%
Medical Insurance	2%	9.50%
Maternity Insurance	0	1%
Workplace Insurance	0	0.2-1.9%
Public Housing Fund	7%	7%
Unemployment Insurance	0.50%	0.50%
TOTAL	**17.50%**	**38.2% - 39.9%**

153 New Gini figures show instability risks, need for reform By Du Liya. Global Times, September 17, 2012

154 Gini measures income inequality. A lower number indicates greater equality.

***

By 2020, the quality of life in Tier One cities like Beijing, Shanghai, and Shenzhen rivaled the world's best. Education is virtually free, low-income scholarships abound, and graduates carry no student loans. Most employers supplement the inexpensive state health coverage and give mid-level managers modest, non-taxable expense accounts and occasional use of a company car. Software engineers out-earn their foreign colleagues, and Shenzhen's salaries for teachers with a bachelor's degree rival San Francisco's $68,000, while post-grads begin at $73,000. All teachers receive priority housing, long-term subsidized rentals, and one-hundred sixty-five paid vacation days.

Says economist Weiwei Zhang[155], "Shanghai's life expectancy is already higher than New York's, its level of education is the highest in the world, and its overall scientific and technological power suggests a healthy economic future. The average wealth, even the living standard, of many Shanghai residents is higher than the Swiss, while urban housing is better than Japan's or Hong Kong's". Shanghai's high-speed trains, subways, airports, harbors, commercial facilities, and public safety outperform New York's and, says the New York Times' Thomas Friedman[156], "Just compare arriving at La Guardia's dumpy terminal in New York City and driving through the crumbling infrastructure into Manhattan with arriving at Shanghai's sleek airport and taking the 220-mile-per-hour magnetic levitation train to get to town in a blink. Then ask yourself: Who's living in the third world country?"

In 2019 Credit Suisse[157] reported, "This year, China recorded more members of the global top 10 percent (100 million) than the United States (99 million), and created 182 new billionaires[158]–compared to America's fifty-nine–taking its total to 799". Every week two more people become billionaires, and a hundred become millionaires. Yet

155 Weiwei Zhang. *The China Wave*

156 Thomas Friedman, "Biblical Seven Years", The New York Times, August 27, 2008.

157 Credit Suisse Global Wealth Report 2019.

158 2020 Hurun Global Rich List.

many of the super-rich, like Jack Ma of Alibaba, Lei Jun of Xiaomi, and Ren Zhenfei of Huawei, are 'Maoist entrepreneurs,' says a Harvard study[159], "All but one of fifteen CEOs we interviewed told us they often turned to Mao's teachings for management ideas". Liu Qiangdong[160], founder of e-commerce giant JD.com, suggested that robots would make Communism possible in one generation if the government simply nationalized all companies and redistributed wealth.

***

Happily, wealth redistribution is becoming a national priority and economists[161] discovered that statisticians had exaggerated inequality statistics. Though their quality is identical, land, housing, and food are much cheaper inland, and incomes in rural areas purchase fifty percent more than in coastal regions. Adjusted for temporary migration, inequality shrinks even further.

Until 2019, economists counted people by where their *hukou* was registered rather than where they actually lived, so the movement of three hundred million migrant workers distorted statistics severely. In reality, the coastal provinces have millions more migrant residents than their registered populations, and the inland provinces have millions less. A worker moving from the interior to the coast lifts inequality indicators because she contributes to aggregate income at her coastal destination but still counts as living in her rural home. When analysts corrected[162] the error, they found that regional inequality has declined by 1.1 percent annually since 1978. Thus in 2002, the combined earnings of fourteen Guizhou workers[163] equaled one Shanghainese, but by 2019, the

159 Mao's Pervasive Influence on Chinese CEOs. By Shaomin LiKuang S. Yeh. HBR December 2007

160 Tycoons spark discussion on the realization of Communism. By Shan Jie. Global Times: 2017/8/21

161 Spatial Price Differences and Inequality in the People's Republic of China: Housing Market Evidence, "Chao Li & John Gibson, 2014". Asian Development Review, MIT Press, vol. 31(1), pages 92-120, March.

162 Regional Inequality in China, allowing for Spatial Cost-of-Living Differences: Evidence from a Hedonic Analysis of Apartment Prices. Chao Li, John Gibson. IDEAS.

163 China's Got a $46,000 Wealth Gap Problem. Bloomberg News. May 21, 2018

number had dropped to five. Nor is the structural gap as painful as it sounds. Inlanders and their friends get richer every year, and, to them, Shanghai's glitzy lifestyle is no more relevant than Manhattan's to people in Little Rock, AR.

From a global perspective, Shanghainese were five times richer than people in inland Gansu in 2018, but Gansu folk were better off than Armenians or Ukrainians. Residents of wealthy Beijing, Shenzen, Tianjin, and Jiangsu not only earned more than the average American but their median savings, $130,000, were higher, too.

The Great Leveling, scheduled to start in 2021, has widespread cultural support, since everyone knows by heart Confucius' admonition, "The ruler of a state need not worry that his people are poor but that wealth is inequitably distributed for, if wealth is equitably distributed, there is no poverty".

CUMULATIVE INCOME GROWTH 1978-2015

©2020 Godfree Roberts/NBER/Global Inequality Dynamics

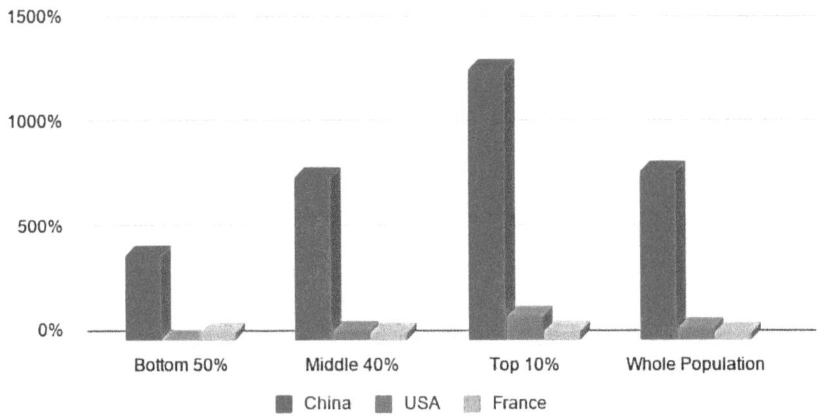

CHAPTER 9

Earth is My Mother

Only those who are authentic, true, and real can fully realize their own nature. If they can fully realize their own nature, they can fully realize human nature. If they can fully realize human nature, they can fully realize the nature of things. If they can fully realize the nature of things, they can take part in Heaven and Earth's transforming and nourishing process. If they can take part in Heaven and Earth's transforming and nourishing process, they can form a trinity with Heaven and Earth. Confucius, *Doctrine of the Mean.*

Ga'er Monastery in the Sanjangyuan Region, Tibet. Photo by Kyle Obermann.

Though more numerous today than ever, the Chinese still thrive on land they have tilled for five thousand years and that still hosts ten percent of the world's plant species and fourteen percent of its wild animals.

Thanks to the ancient observation that man and Mother Nature are mutually dependent, and man must care for his Mother, the world's first ecological legislation, banning tree-felling in Spring and fishing in July, was passed in 2000 BC. In 700 BC, the noted Taoist Guan Zhong advocated state monopoly of natural resources, "A king who does not protect the environment does not deserve to be called king". In 400 BC, the Law of Fields forbade the blocking of river courses and burning off vegetation in winter. In 200 BC Yang Fu advocated protecting an exhaustive list of endangered species. Four centuries later, Taoists chose twenty-four mountain sites as the first nature reserves in history and set detailed rules to protect the animals, plants, water, and mineral resources. They taught local people survival skills so that they could live without hunting or large scale agriculture. Their practice of boiling water (for sanitation) and steeping leaves in it (for enjoyment) gave birth to tea.

In 1030 AD Confucian Zhang Zhai[164] confessed, "Heaven is my father and Earth is my mother and even such a small creature as I finds an intimate place in their midst. Therefore that which extends throughout the universe I regard as my body and that which directs the universe I consider as my nature. All people are my brothers and sisters and all things are my companions". By 1200 AD, China counted one hundred and fifty nature reserves that have served as the settings for legends of animal deities and immortals. All still exist and still harbor rare and endangered animals and plants. Historian Jonathan Schlesinger says the First Qing Emperor practiced environmentalism five hundred years ago:

164 Zhang, who had studied Daoism, said all things are composed of a primordial substance, *qi*, that includes matter and the forces that govern interactions between matter, yin, and yang. In its dispersed, rarefied State, *qi* is invisible and insubstantial, but it becomes solid or liquid when it condenses and takes on new properties. All material things are composed of condensed *qi*: rocks, trees, even people. There is nothing that is not *qi*. Thus, in a real sense, everything has the same essence.

> I think of Changbaishan. It's a volcano on the border between North Korea and China, and the Manchus considered the lake inside the crater to be holy territory because it was the birthplace of the Manchus. The court had special rules on collecting ginseng or trapping sable and other fur-bearing animals on the mountain. When British explorers first climbed the mountain in the late 1800s, they referred to it as untouched and unspoiled nature. In fact, it was very much touched. People had poached on the land, but the court had been using its resources to protect that territory. The People's Republic of China has now converted the space into a nature reserve[165].

In 1909, concerned about America's deteriorating soil health Franklin King[166], chief of the USDA's Division of Soil Management, found Chinese farmers growing crops in the same soil year after year with no loss of fertility and called their technique 'permanent agriculture.' Today, we call it 'permaculture'.

In 1950, proclaiming that everyone has a democratic right to land since no one created it, Mao eliminated private land ownership. Thanks to public awareness of Western environmental catastrophes, China avoided toxic disasters like our Superfund sites–created on private land and repaired at public expense–and benefited from our fight for clean air. In 1952 air pollution killed twelve thousand Londoners on one weekend and hospitalized one hundred thousand–and London's NOx levels still exceed Beijing's. The Chinese devoured Rachel Carson's book, *Silent Spring*, and her depiction of the deadly impact of chemical runoff on American wildlife. They knew that Cleveland's Cuyahoga River once caught fire and watched newsreels of Tokyo traffic police wearing oxygen tanks in 1970. Their sailors found Japanese seas oily black many miles from shore, and their response typifies their cultural willingness to study and learn from others. Though developing countries rarely focus on the

---

165 The 400,000-acre Changbaishan Biosphere Reserve is located in the northeast of China on the border with the People's Democratic Republic of Korea.

166 Chinese Peasants Taught the USDA to Farm Organically in 1909. By Lina Zeldovich JSTOR Daily. May 21, 2019

quality of economic growth, forewarned by our experience, they never forgot their environment.

***

From seventy-four percent in 2006, coal now accounts for fifty-eight percent of energy consumption and, though air quality in some cities once approached Western peaks, it is falling twice as fast. Sulfur dioxide and NOx emissions, along with water pollutants like ammonia and nitrogen, peaked ten years ago and are falling steadily. China's share of global carbon dioxide emissions doubled from fourteen percent in 2001 to twenty-eight percent in 2011 but has not increased since, and the country is on track to reach its 2030 Paris Climate Agreement goals before the West and will complete its postindustrial cleanup three times faster.

Between 1980-2015, though the economy grew sixtyfold, energy consumption grew fivefold[167]–an eighty percent decline in energy intensity. Carbon intensity has fallen by fifty percent since 2005, and renewable power consumption is rising twenty-five percent annually and should reach twenty percent of total consumption by 2025. When London's Environmental Investigation Agency reported that dozens of Chinese companies were still using toxic CFC-11 to make foam, the government phased out the production of 280,000 tonnes of ozone-depleting substances and set quotas on the manufacture, import, and use of polluting chemicals like carbon tetrachloride. In 2015 the Pearl River Delta Industrial Trial Spot became the first region to reach America's EPA air quality standard, and, by 2017, ninety percent of China's cities had reached their targets. The World Health Organization says that, between 2013-2016, the sixty biggest Chinese cities lowered their particulate emissions by thirty percent and wealthy Beijing did even better[168]. Between 2014-2017, the city cut sulfur dioxide by seventy percent and

167 Energy intensity level of primary energy (MJ/$2011 PPP GDP) fell from 21.2 in 1990 to 6.7 in 2015 (World Bank)

168 A Review of 20 Years' Air Pollution Control in Beijing. United Nations Environment Programme, 2019
ISBN: 978-92-807-3743-1

particulate pollution by thirty-six percent, using ultra-Low Emissions (ULE) coal-fired power stations and natural gas plants that reduce[169] pollutant emissions of sulfur dioxide, nitrogen oxide, and particulate matter by sixty-five percent annually. They removed sulfur from road fuels, scrapped polluting vehicles, and reduced solid fuel home heating. In 2016 the mayor promised to reduce particulate density by one-third and delivering fifty-six percent good air quality days by 2020–and made it on schedule. Internal combustion engines will be gone from Beijing by 2025, and, by 2030, renewables will provide ninety percent of its energy.

The entire ecosystem has improved[170] since the government launched its 'ecological civilization,' reforms. The Loess Plateau, 250,000 square miles of yellow soil, had lost so much tree cover by 1902 that it was called 'China's Sorrow' for its flooding, drought, and famine cycles. Sparse vegetation, loose soil, and intense, heavy rains made it the most eroded area on Earth, and its billions of tons of yellow sediment gave the Yellow River its name. In 1978 volunteers began planting a hundred billion trees to form the Great Green Wall[171], a three-thousand-mile windbreak to stop the encroaching Gobi Desert. By 2018 they had reduced[172] dust storm frequency and shrunk rocky desert by fifteen hundred square miles, cut local poverty twenty percent, lowered sediment runoff by ninety percent[173], lifted forest cover from nineteen to twenty-five percent, and welcomed the return of long-forgotten birds and animals.

Since 2015 the Environment Ministry has created ten pilot national parks[174] with two-thirds the area of America's venerable park system. The four zones of these 'protected areas with Chinese characteristics with

---

169 Clearing the air in China. Valerie J. Karplus. Nature Energy 2019

170 Sugden, A. M. China's National Ecosystem Assessment. 2016. *Science*. Ecosystem services are the direct and indirect contributions of ecosystems to human well-being.

171 NASA reports, "China alone accounts for 25% of the global net increase in leaf area with only 6.6% of global vegetated area. The greening in China is from forests (42%) and croplands (32%)." Chi Chen et al., Nature Sustainability vol. 2, pp. 122–129 (2019)

172 China reduces total rocky desert area by 1.93m hectares By WANG KEJU | chinadaily.com.cn December 13, 2018

173 Revegetation in China's Loess Plateau is approaching sustainable water resource limits. Nature. https://www.nature.com/articles/nclimate3092

174 China's Attempt To Create The World's Largest National Park System. Conservation China. by Kyle Obermann. supChina.com. May 22, 2020

national parks as the main body' range from stringent (all human activity outlawed) to lenient, designed to spur ecological tourism and public visits. Each has 2025 goals, ranging from concentrating flagship species, to increasing forest cover, to reducing the number of mines. Sanjiangyuan National Park, at the headwaters of the Yellow, the Yangtze, and the Mekong rivers on the Tibetan Plateau, is stabilizing the population of nomadic herders and providing skills training so they can live and work in townships. The program has eliminated local poverty inside the park's boundaries.

In a 2017 TV address, President Xi referenced the environment eighty-nine times, "We want our modernization characterized by harmonious co-existence between man and nature–because any harm we inflict on nature will eventually return to haunt us. Since limpid waters and lush mountain forests are invaluable we must seek a simple, moderate, green, low-carbon lifestyle in eco-friendly communities". He consolidated seven agencies into a Ministry of Ecological Environment, made it responsible for the entire natural domain, and promised not to export pollution through investment or foreign policy. The new Ministry placed a fishing ban on the whole Yellow River basin, its tributaries, and lakes, and applied[175] new environmental standards, levied pollution penalties, and initiated an immense emissions trading scheme[176] that taxes pollution at its source and recycles the tax revenues into sustainable projects.

> China has embarked on what promises to be the world's largest carbon dioxide (CO2) emissions trading system (ETS). When fully implemented, this nationwide system will more than double the amount of CO2 emissions covered worldwide by some form of emissions pricing. China will rely on a tradable performance standard (TPS) as its emissions pricing instrument for reducing emissions. This mechanism differs fundamentally from the emissions pricing instruments used in other countries, such as cap and trade and a carbon tax. Our numerical model yields

175 How China cut its air pollution. BY JP. The Economist. January 25, 2018

176 China's Unconventional Nationwide CO2 Emissions Trading System. By Goulder, Xianling Long, Jieyi Lu, Richard D. Morgenstern. NBER Working Paper 26537

> results consistent with the analytical model's predictions, supplementing the theoretical model's qualitative results with a unique quantitative assessment closely geared to China's power sector. The key findings of the numerical model are as follows. China's forthcoming nationwide CO2 emissions trading system has the potential to make a very substantial contribution to the world's efforts to confront global climate change. The system will take a tradable performance standard and focus on the power sector in its first phase.

Iron ore from Australia, for example, will be taxed on the carbon used to extract, ship, smelt, and refine the ore, and to deliver the finished steel to consumers. Says Australia's Peter Castellas[177], "Our energy-intensive exports sit directly in the supply chain of the world's largest carbon market. Their regulations on supply chain emissions mean that Australians–and all of China's trading partners–will have to clean up our emissions since they regulate and tax emissions generated outside the direct control of Chinese businesses". Mining giant Rio Tinto struck a deal with Baowu Steel to reduce steelmaking's carbon emissions and curb end-users' emissions. Like smelting and cement, energy-intensive industries lost preferential electricity rates while eco-friendly businesses, like sewage treatment, electric vehicle charging, and water desalination, gained them. Wealthy Guangdong Province's successful Trial Spot canceled all sewage charges and began levying environmental taxes on air pollutants and water contaminants and was quickly replicated across the country. Four hundred thousand companies have started paying taxes on their noise, air, water, and solid waste pollutants since the Environmental Protection Tax Act in 2018.

By 2019 the Supreme People's Court had ruled on half a million environmental civil cases, eleven-thousand environmental damage

177 China's emissions trading scheme puts Australian companies on notice. The Guardian. Bianca Nogrady. October 3, 2017.

compensation trials, fourteen hundred public interest ecological litigation[178] suits and NGOs filed hundreds of high profile cases[179]. "A young environmental activist sued police for detaining her earlier this month after she spoke out about what she claims is illegal mining and water pollution. The district court accepted her case on Friday". Friends of Nature, an NGO, won a landmark action against three soil polluters. They were jailed and paid a multimillion-dollar remediation penalty. Three Xi'an officials were jailed for tampering with air quality monitoring equipment and seven were sentenced for falsifying environmental reports. Violators– and those who fail to report them–now incur daily penalties that accumulate as long as the violations continue. A friend of the author[180] describes the environmental enforcement process:

> China is the world's manufacturer, not just the USA's. The USA accounts for 11% of Chinese exports by value. So it should be no surprise that the concentration of factories would spew into the atmosphere, as they did in Blackstone valley in Massachusetts, in the Love Canal in New York and Petrolia in Pennsylvania.
>
> China had started to place restrictions on pollution, requirements on companies, and had regional meetings as early as 2003. But, also, not too much was getting done. Suddenly, in 2013, Xi Jinping started a "clamp down," and I had a front-row seat. What he did was send out two teams of "specialists" working in tandem. The first was the "Pollution Police". They weren't really "police" as we would consider them to be. But instead, they were government compliance inspectors. They would go to a factory and check the factory's status on all number of pollution, social, environmental, and other issues. They would talk with the factory owners about making changes, and then they would come up with a timetable to implement those changes. Usually, it required

178 Why the Supreme People's Court is harnessing the NGO "genie". January 26, 2015. Supreme People's Court Monitor

179 Environmental Whistleblower Sues Police for Unlawful Detention. Sixth Tone. Qian Zhecheng. March 31, 2018

180 Robert Vannrox, Executive Director / CEO, Smoking Lion Contract Manufacture & Engineering.

immediate implementation of specific practices. If they needed large capital expenditures, they agreed to a more extended schedule. The regulators would work with local banking and financial interests to ensure that capital would be obtained.

The second group was the "corruption police". This group was a paramilitary organization. It had armored vehicles, trained police forces, SWAT teams, and detectives. They also (like the USA IRS) had their very own court system and enforcement techniques. Of course, as you can expect, when they first hit the ground, they were ignored. Some minor "slaps on the wrists" and some fines. Nada action. Then all Hell broke out around 2015. They started making one on one raids to selected non-compliance factories. Not only did they shut the entire factory down, but they arrested the owners, their top management, and the supervisory staff and carted them off to re-education prison which, in China, is not a pleasant experience—and the word got around.

In 2016, they organized into teams and utilized Blitzkrieg tactics. They would descend on a manufacturing region and park themselves there for two weeks. They would observe, interview, and set in place corrective actions. They intended to work with factories. If the factories could not meet the requirements, they would shut them down. During this time, I saw many of my coating factories going "underground". They only operated in the middle of the night. Factories conducting PPT coatings or metal finishing started to clean up their acts to meet the demand, as it increased for them, as the lesser factories shut down. In general, they had around two years to meet the clean air standards or risk shut down.

Of course, these capital expenditures cost money to buy and implement. So, many factories back in 2017 started to increase their prices–often by 20%. I can name several factories that did this, and I remember one in Zhongshan that was frustrated that they had to do this, but their German and English clients would not go along with this increase–while at the same time

> praising them for their "green policies". This battle continues to this day. The European manufacturing interests (our clients) want green-polices, but refuse to pay for it. Sigh. It's my life, don't you know.
>
> All in all, pollution in China is much reduced. I live in Zhuhai, and it's almost always blues skies and fresh air. When I lived in Dongguang, it was always white skies and burning eyes. It's a big difference—a significant change. China is doing things. Things are happening. And this is what I have observed as someone in the industry. It's a real shame that NONE of this is being reported in the West.

Planners have made environmental protection profitable by simultaneously prioritizing clean technologies *and* economic growth. The result is that China dominates research in all renewable technologies and is the biggest market for–and exporter of–them. Stanford's Professor of Environmental Science, Gretchen Daily, says, "China has gone further than any other country–as strange as that sounds given all the devastation that we read about on the environment front there. In the face of deepening environmental crisis, China has eagerly incorporated science into its environmental program and funded far-reaching efforts that could serve as models for other countries. It has become very ambitious and innovative in its new conservation science and policies and has implemented them on a breathtaking scale".

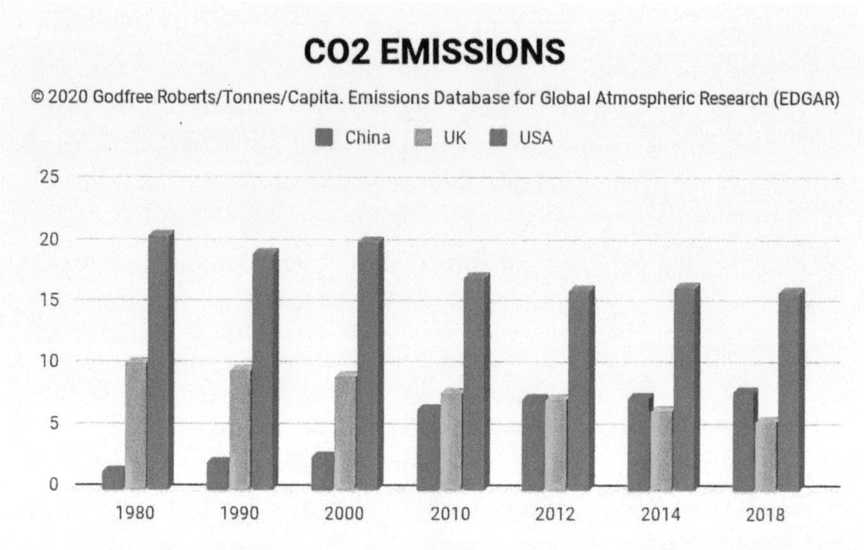
CO2 EMISSIONS
© 2020 Godfree Roberts/Tonnes/Capita. Emissions Database for Global Atmospheric Research (EDGAR)
China
UK
USA
25
20
15
10
5
0
1980
1990
2000
2010
2012
2014
2018

CHAPTER 10

Health Care

In fasting, he always alters his diet and alters again if absent from his usual seat at home. If the rice had turned sour, or the fish or meat had spoiled, he did not eat it. He did not eat food of bad color or bad odor. Nor food that was undercooked. He did not eat except at the proper times. If food had not been correctly cut, he did not eat it... Though there might be much meat, he did not allow the amount of meat to exceed the amount of rice. Confucius, *Analects*

***

The public health system, like education, is financed out of general tax revenues as an essential service to provide the best treatment for the largest number of people for one-eighth of US costs ($8,233). Yet urban Chinese outlive the average American, and Chinese children will live longer, healthier lives than their American cousins.

Country folk are less fortunate. The Barefoot Doctor system collapsed after the Cultural Revolution and Beijing did not introduce rural health insurance[181] until 2005, "Providing wide coverage but low benefits, in keeping with our level of economic development". The program added two hundred million migrant workers the following year, and,

181 Individuals pay thirty percent of health care expenses. Government funding (thirty percent), public and private insurance (forty percent), covers the rest.

in 2009, the Ministry launched Healthy China 2020[182], "An accessible, affordable, efficient national health system designed to prevent chronic disease, promote healthier lifestyles, and raise awareness of obesity, physical inactivity, and poor dietary choices".

While reforming and streamlining hospital management in hundreds of cities, the Ministry constructed thousands of rural primary care clinics to provide treatment close to home. To cover those unable to afford its modest premiums, Beijing tripled the medical budget to $1 trillion, harmonized its three national insurance schemes[183], and merged them into a single system accessible through electronic Social Security cards. Health Minister Li Bin[184] went further, "It's crucial to the poverty relief campaign that everyone receives free treatment by 2020. No one can be left behind," and, two years later, he announced *Healthy China 2030.*

The program calls on everyone to participate responsibly in their own health care, rather than being passive consumers, and to make health a strategic priority for the nation by innovating, using evidence-based prevention, cure, and control, and treating rural people fairly and justly. The goals are ambitious: measurably improve everyone's health every year; lift life expectancy above America's by controlling health-impairment factors; substantially improve and expand the health industry, and establish inclusive health-improving regulatory systems. Provinces have boosted health education in schools, propagandized healthy lifestyles and exercise, enhanced healthcare access, improved healthcare providers' service quality, increased health care for women and the elderly and disabled, and reformed local health insurance, pharmaceutical, and medical benefit systems.

---

182 He reinforced and expanded the program in 2016, with Healthy China 2030, to incorporate Sustainable Development Goals (SDGs) and propel Healthy China reform into the SDGs era. One goal: eliminate childhood obesity.

183 Chen spent five years as a barefoot doctor, then obtained his master's degree from Shanghai Jiao Tong University, his Ph.D. from the Paris Diderot University, where he completed his medical residency and postdoctoral research. He is former President of the Shanghai Institute of Hematology and Director-general of the China Human Genome Center in Shanghai.

184 Development of China's Public Health as an Essential Element of Human Rights. Xinhua. Sep 29, 2017. Maternal mortality fell from 88.9 per 100,000 persons in 1990 to 19.9 in 2016; infant mortality declined from 34.7 in 1981 to 7.5 in 2016. Chinese infant and maternal mortality rates are lower than those in Texas.

***

For-profit hospitals, private insurance, denied claims, refused treatments, and patients dying in parking lots are rare in China thanks to affordable procedures like $3.75 for 3-D, 360-degree dental X-rays. ECGs cost $3.50 and full-body MRIs cost $47.00, while hospital stays cost five percent of US prices. In Shanghai, the world leader in cataract eye surgery, the procedure costs $1,500 for both eyes.

Physicians' time is the most expensive component of health care and Health Minister Li became a telemedicine enthusiast after seeing a hybrid system invented by Ping An Insurance[185], the country's largest private insurer. Ping An Good Doctor, a one-stop healthcare management service, covers online medical treatment, triage, referral, hospitalization, and followup. Its online clinic combines the database of an 'AI Doctor' and the experience of seventy-thousand MDs working eight-hour shifts in Ping An's offices to provide prompt medical assessments. Ping An's AI analysis of X-rays and scans keeps diagnostic error rates under eight percent and three thousand hospitals use it too. Annual premiums of $285-$1,400 cover unlimited online consultations, guaranteed medical appointments, health checks, accompanied hospital visit service for seniors, and discounts on prescriptions, delivered to patients' homes in sixty minutes.

Still, one-third of Chinese are dissatisfied with public health insurance, people in poor regions complain that they must wait months for reimbursement, and only fourteen percent say they have enough saved to cover unexpected health emergencies. Since they cannot afford catastrophic health insurance, $600 annually for $70,000 coverage, two-hundred million of them formed a mutual health club online to share critical illness costs. Because the semi-automated platform takes only eight percent of revenues for administrative fees–compared to thirty-eight percent for private plans–they receive one-time payouts of $28,000 for an annual premium of $28.

185 Ping An Insurance, the world's largest insurer, had $200 billion in revenues in 2019.

But the importance of personal health care pales compared to public health, as the Health Ministry learned in 2002 when a SARS Coronavirus outbreak killed hundreds. When research showed that early detection could have saved those lives, the Health Ministry funded a nationwide network of seventy-thousand Coronavirus detection nodes.

On December 27, 2019, Dr. Zhang Jixian, an ICU specialist at Hubei Central Hospital, notified his local Health Commission of an unfamiliar pneumonia. When three more cases showed up, the Commission sent samples to Beijing and announced the discovery on local television. A week later, Beijing classified the new virus as highly pathogenic and, a week later, uploaded the virus' genetic sequence to an international database.

The Health Ministry could have treated the novel virus as another element in a bad flu season, as most countries do but chose to follow WHO guidelines and placed a *cordon sanitaire*[186] around fifty-million people in the travel hub of Wuhan. Beijing[187] orchestrated a rapid, scaled, differentiated, whole-of-society approach, tailored it to fit every province, municipality, locality, or village, depending on the severity of their outbreak. Officials repurposed the machinery and infrastructure of national, provincial, and local governments toward disease prevention through collective action and cooperation and underpinned their science-based approach with AI, Big Data, 5G communications, and advanced logistics. The Ministry's supercomputers monitored individual cases and updated interventions, resource allocation, and tactics in real-time and provided all virus-related medical services free of charge.

Helped by enthusiastic compliance and neighborhood committees which coordinated local tasks, health officials overrode market forces in favor of the common good and city officials coordinated the delivery of goods, supplies, and services. Administrators made on-the-fly policy adjustments while citizens communicated, worked from home,

---

186 *A cordon sanitaire* is a "sanitary belt" around a quarantine zone from which those inside are not allowed to leave. Wuhan allowed people to come and go under stringent conditions. A *quarantine* ('forty days') requires isolation.

187 Yellow-caking an epidemic: The Chinese "fight for mankind" against Coronavirus, by KJ Noh. March 05, 2020. MROnline

held meetings, consulted doctors, and ordered and received goods by drones and robots. Schoolchildren received new face masks daily, and school health staff became outreach officers. Contact surfaces in grocery stores were sterilized every two hours by gloved and masked staff, even banknotes were sterilized, and Post-Its on elevator buttons prevented contamination of shared surfaces.

The Wuhan region was cordoned for sixty days, movement was restricted, and public gatherings and interactions were restricted or banned. Only those who had been diagnosed with the virus were quarantined. At the same time, each city or apartment complex was 'siloed' by designating a neighborhood park where residents were free to move, restricting contagion to small, isolable units. Leaving and entering neighborhoods was limited to three times a week, and infrared scanners checked every movement and limited the number of people interacting. Across Hubei Province, planes and trains stopped, and schools, malls, and supermarkets closed, but the nation's most important chipmaker, Yangtze Memory Technologies, stayed open around the clock. Special trains brought engineers with priority permits and medical certificates to relieve engineers to keep the plant running.

At apartment complex checkpoints, shopping malls, and office buildings, it became routine to scan QR codes through WeChat or Alipay. Building security staff checked occupants' temperatures and scanned a QR code that led them to an online page that requested an ID number and contact phone number. The terminal issued a color-based personal health code and asked users to answer questions including their whereabouts during the previous two weeks, whether they had symptoms of illness or infection, and whether they had traveled to virus-hit areas or contacted infected people. Low-risk people returned to work, and those with green QR codes traveled relatively freely within the city. In contrast, those with yellow codes stayed home and reported their temperature daily to neighborhood committees while those with red codes–confirmed coronavirus cases–were quarantined.

Eighty percent of people were back at work in three months, but

CCDC Director Dr. George Gao[188], was furious that Wuhan officials had obstructed the notification process. "It is a great pity that the direct reporting system to monitor infectious disease that we set up after the SARS outbreak didn't play its due role during this epidemic. Under the rules, whenever there are more than three unknown pneumonia cases, they should be submitted to the system. The system's network covers 70,000 reporting points across the country, and, with a simple mouse click, doctors can report simultaneously to the CCDC's national and local offices. The idea of the direct reporting system reduces administrative intervention and saves time in the face of an epidemic. But, unbelievably, our efforts turned out to be in vain because hierarchical review and administrative intervention were back in place. How could such actions, which violate the Law on the Prevention and Control of Infectious Diseases, happen in government and law enforcement departments? Why didn't local experts fulfill their duty according to the infectious disease reporting rules? And why did the National Health Commission and its experts fail to collect important information in a timely way? Whether we can find true and adequate answers to these questions will be important to the success of our future work".

188 Dr. Gao is a virologist and immunologist who has contributed to the study of inter-species pathogen transmission.

CHAPTER 11

A San Francisco Every Month

The strength of the nation derives from the integrity of the home. – Confucius. *Analects.*

***

In 2018, San Franciscans—unable to afford one bedroom apartments for $3,600 monthly—slept in their cars. Across the Pacific, in Beijing, a quarter-million migrant workers slept in condemned buildings and, when fires, police, or demolition crews drove them out, TV cameras recorded their misery and Beijingers complained and the city fathers built one-hundred-thousand low-rent apartments and solved the problem. The locals barely noticed. China has built San Francisco's entire housing stock–homes for a million people–every month since 1950.

***

For three thousand years, landlords maintained their grip until, as we saw earlier, Mao placed all land in public trust, divided[189] it equitably, and launched a series of experiments that continue to this day. In 1960, he combined individual plots into communal farms for the Great Leap Forward then, in 1978, Deng redivided them into plots. The plots proved inefficient but attempts to recombine them failed until 2012 when a

189 In *Fanshen*, William Hinton tells how this was accomplished in a single village.

Trial Spot in Sihong County created land *management* rights that farmers could rent or pledge–but not sell–so long as the property remained agricultural. A local man, Sun Zeshun[190] leased his plot to an agribusiness corporation, became a roofing contractor, and used his new income to build a house and buy an SUV. "Life is much better now. I have more freedom, and my income is less affected by weather". Beijing promoted Sihong's solution nationwide, and farmers began unlocking twenty-two-trillion dollars of previously inaccessible rural wealth.

Urban experiments are equally ingenious. In 1953, to maintain food production and prevent urban slum formation, city governments issued residency permits, *hukou,* to rural people only if they attended university, joined the Army, or worked in state-owned enterprises then, as the need for urban workers rose, cities built hundreds of millions of apartments for the biggest baby boom in history. Though individual floor space was only forty square feet, rent was nominal, but planners complained that housing was capital-intensive and nonproductive. Tenants stoutly resisted reforms until 1981, when a Housing Privatization Trial Spot let them purchase their homes cheaply, unleashing a real estate boom that has never stopped. By 1988, tenants had purchased two-thirds of all urban housing–worth one-third of national GDP–and filled urban coffers. The economy soared and housing became a pillar of the national welfare system.

When markets overheated, cities released more land for development, and, when demand waned, they converted rural *hukou* into urban permits, keeping supply in line with local wages. When oversized apartments threatened to squeeze out low-income buyers, a Trial Spot taxed floorspace progressively, halved McMansions' value, and forced speculators to release hundreds of thousands of units onto the market.

Two-million poor villagers were stranded in regions prone to natural disasters, desertification, or erosion until the government spent thirty-billion dollars building new cities for them. Families paid only five-hundred-dollars for their homes and, since urbanization adds two percent annually to average wage growth, planners expect to recoup the

190 China's Reforms allowing villagers to rent out land have boosted incomes. Bloomberg 09-26-2017

balance over thirty years. Meanwhile, ecologists are spending five billion dollars restoring and reforesting the land they vacated.

Many country dwellers remain interested in urban life. Age, parents, family ties, and rural life hold them in place, and more are returning as local prosperity rises. When the economy in remote Guizhou Province began growing at ten percent, returnees doubled to 1.2 million annually. A young woman[191] in a provincial capital, said, "I plan to save more money and then move back home and start my own business, maybe a clothing shop in the next couple of years. When I was little, there was a big gap between here and my hometown, but not anymore. Now life is good back there".

Local price bubbles sparked unrest because, though eighty percent of buyers paid cash, the other twenty percent–rural folk moving to cities, students, migrant workers, and cash-strapped young couples–found city prices out of reach. A 2007 Trial Spot let first-time buyers pay half the deposit on new homes while the government covered the other half and guaranteed to buy or sell its interest on demand. Then an Affordable Housing Trial Spot packaged land, permits, utilities, and loan guarantees for apartments and fixed rents at fifteen percent of local wages and developers pre-sold entire projects to retirement funds eager for steady, long-term cash flows. Says the UN's Alain Bertaud[192], "Urbanization didn't happen because the government wanted the country to urbanize. They kept the *hukou* to slow it down, but the economy asked for it, and people voted with their feet. The government has to cope with urbanization rather than it being a deliberate policy decision. In a way, they are paying the price of this rapid urbanization now".

Despite the lure of city life, rural folk are reluctant to leave ancestral villages until their new towns have utilities, public transport, schools, shops, and jobs, and their hesitation led to tales of 'ghost cities,' says Wade[193], "I've been chasing reports of deserted towns and have yet to find

---

191 China's Factory Workers Head Home. By Dexter Roberts. Bloomberg. July 13, 2016

192 Endless cities: will China's new urbanization simply mean more sprawl? Helen Roxburgh. The Guardian. Bertaud, formerly the World Bank's urbanization advisor, now advises Beijing.

193 Ghost Cities of China: The Story of Cities without People in the World's Most Populated Country. by Wade Shepard. (Asian Arguments). May 15, 2015

one. Over and over, I would read articles in the international press claiming that China is building towns that are never inhabited–only to find something very different upon arrival. Ordos, the most famous 'ghost city,' took ten years to populate but now has a thriving downtown and rising home prices. Xiangluowan, Lanzhou, Zhengzhou, Zhujiang, and Zhengdong, former 'ghost cities,' currently host the biggest urban migration in history. Newer cities–backwaters a decade ago–are complete and awaiting occupants while others, like Xinyang New District, are finishing construction".

Rather than individual homes, the Chinese prefer entire communities of apartment complexes with their own management, parks, recreational areas, and parking. With no additional taxes or regulations, homebuyers receive membership in a community with clinics, schools, fire and police stations. The absence of property taxes and negligible carrying costs create local bubbles and Beijing regularly warns, "Houses are built to be lived in, not traded. If you lose money speculating on residential real estate because of policy changes, you have only yourself to blame".

In 2020, household debt reached fifty percent of GDP and housing accounted for sixty percent of personal assets, twice the US level. Individual living space was 450 square feet (half the US average), but its quality exceeds Japan's. Owners spend one-third to one-half of their incomes on mortgage payments and home loans comprise sixty percent of household wealth[194]. Eighteen percent of homeowners have mortgages[195] and the default rate is one-third US levels.

A young Kunming accountant told the author that he needed a thirty-percent deposit when he bought his first home, of which $30,000 came from his savings and $60,000 came from his father, sister, and friends. Banks demanded a sixty percent cash deposit for second homes. Still, he was frustrated when he tried to buy another condo, "Over the last few days I must have gone to a dozen banks, and none of them will let me mortgage my property for a loan to buy a $300,000 apartment that is coming on the market in my block. The bank managers all told me that the government imposed tough restrictions on loans since last

194 In the US, the figure is eighty percent.

195 63% of US homeowners have mortgages

year. If I want to borrow the money, I will have to pay shadow bankers thousands in extra interest. Also, I cannot buy normal houses in my market because I already own one, so I cannot buy or sell my current one inside three years according to their policy. Even when I bought my current apartment last year, I could not buy in locations the city zoned for college graduates who want to settle here. So our local real estate bubble isn't going to burst anytime soon as far as I can see".

Kunming (pop. seven million) is a remote, second-tier city and, compared to coastal Shenzen (twelve million), its transformation is sedate. Says Alain Bertaud, "When I first saw the original plan for Shenzhen, a fishing village across the bay from Hong Kong that became one of China's richest cities, I told them, 'You're too ambitious'. But I underestimated China's enormous ability to get these things done".

An airline stewardess of the author's acquaintance owns a fifteen-year-old[196], one-thousand square foot, $300,000 apartment in Shenzen. Since her annual salary is more than twice the minimum deposit, loan approval was simple, and her employer's Housing Provident Fund matched her deposit. She said her fiancé's flat inside Shanghai's Inner Ring Road cost one million dollars, while a similar flat in her inland hometown would cost one-hundred thousand. Shenzen's twenty-five percent homeownership is China's lowest because the price-to-income ratio is 46:1 (San Francisco's is 8:1). In 2020, Shenzen announced thirteen public housing projects[197] priced at $270 per square foot, half the local market price, and promised two million new units by 2035, of which half will be affordable homes and public rentals.

Urban development and poverty alleviation go hand in hand, nowhere more than in Shaanxi Province, the Xi family's ancestral home.

> Central Western Xi'an, home of the Terra Cotta Warriors, earns eight percent of its GDP from cultural tourism, double the national average. New records for annual tourists, now exceeding 3 million, have been set and broken each year. In 2009, Zhao Leji,

196 Chinese housing has a designed life of thirty years

197 Public housing is on the rise in Shenzhen. By Huang Wanyi, Xu Jiangshan, Tr by Nadeem. Asia Times November 04, 2019

Shaanxi's Party secretary and a rising star, received the central government's endorsement to turn greater Xi'an into an "international metropolis". The designation elevated the municipality's growth targets and clinched massive state commitments to achieve them. Additional bus routes were mapped, and excavation began on a sprawling subway network. The Xi'an-Xianyang International Airport added a new terminal and a second runway in 2012, and the Xi'an North Railway Station serves 82 million passengers annually, making it one of Asia's largest rail terminals. The most recent project, iHarbour, in the Xixian New District, epitomizes the city's quest to be global and metropolitan. It features industrial development zones and special hubs for aviation, trade, technology, and culture.

More than 2,000 years ago, the city was the starting point of the Silk Road. Now plans for One Belt, One Road–President Xi's signature initiative to redraw trade lines through Central Asia and Europe–are building the Xixian New District into a central hub for expected vast flows of commerce. Locals aren't shy about their sense of destiny. "This is a once-in-a-million-years opportunity for Xi'an and Shaanxi to reemerge as the focal point for a national initiative," Qiang Xiao'an, director of Xi'an's development and reform commission, told state media[198].

To keep population density[199] low, Tier One cities are capping their populations and non-residents moving to Shanghai must buy with cash and pay city taxes and social insurance for five years before applying for a local *houkou*. Tier Two cities are deleveraging, and Tier Three and Tier Four cities are optimizing their population density, infrastructure, and efficiency by blurring the urban-rural divide. Soon only Tibet will have *hukou*–to stop its burgeoning population moving to the country and overgrazing fragile ecosystems.

Shanghai capped its population at twenty-five million but needs

---

198 Xi'an readies for crucial role in 'One Belt, One Road' initiative. By Catherine Wong Tsoi-lai. Global Times. 2015-4-21

199 London's population density is twice Beijing's.

to attract investment to pay off its social insurance deficits, so it assesses would-be immigrants' educational background, employment, professional titles, and tax payments. Candidates scoring above one-hundred-twenty points receive privileges like access to world-class, centrally-located schools. Low scorers wait for spaces in lower-quality schools on the city outskirts, and those without permits have no access to city schooling at all.

Chongqing[200] (pop. fifteen-million), is clustering with Chengdu (nine-million) to create one of two hundred planned eco-cities, says Chongqing's mayor, "We became part of the high-speed rail network in 2017. Today we're seeing China's old pattern of provincial production based on self-contained industries being replaced by a more rational division of labor and production across the nation in a unified, efficient domestic market. Our objective is to be the economic center and major growth pole of Western China by 2020 and for our large urban and rural areas to balance our urban-rural development. Today, fifty-one percent of us live in urban areas and forty-nine percent in rural areas. Once our urban population reaches seventy-percent we will have three urban layers: one large metropolis, thirty medium cities, and a hundred small cities. We're creating a livable, green, drivable, safe, healthy Chongqing".

Urban growth has boosted competition for skilled workers. The island province of Hainan (pop. nine million), bent on developing medical tourism, advertises, "Talented people coming to Hainan won't have to worry about housing". Medical professionals receive eighty percent equity in their homes after five years and clear title after eight. Researchers get subsidized rents and home finance, cash incentives, prioritized service at banks and hospitals, discounts on subways, and free entry to museums and events. Nanjing, plagued by labor shortages, lowered home deposits to five percent and was rushed by cash-strapped couples.

***

The Sante Fe Institute[201] found that cities generate ninety percent of the

200 The China Wave: Rise of a Civilizational State by Weiwei Zhang

201 The Fate of our Cities, by Geoffrey West. Seed Magazine.com December 15, 2017

world's economic growth. Wages, wealth, the number of patents, and the number of educational and research institutions all increase by approximately fifteen percent as an urban population doubles–a phenomenon called "superlinear scaling". The bigger the city, the more goods, resources, and ideas the average citizen owns, produces, and consumes. Based on this data, China is creating nineteen supercities that will generate ninety-percent of the country's GDP.

Each of the five biggest megalopolises–the Pearl River Delta, Yangtze River Delta, Beijing-Tianjin-Hebei, Yangtze Mid-River, and Chengdu-Chongqing–will house 110 million people, three times more than Tokyo.

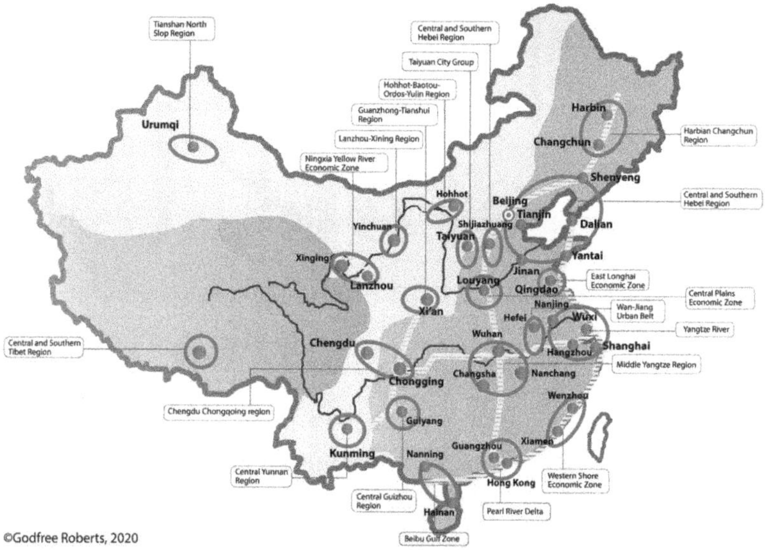

©Godfree Roberts, 2020

China State Railways is investing thirteen billion dollars in the Yangtze Basin alone. The first phase, already under construction, strengthens intercity links horizontally–via the Northern Land Bridge Corridor and the Yangtze River Corridor–and vertically, via the Coastal Corridor and the Harbin-Beijing-Guangzhou Railway Corridor. The Yangtze Corridor's airports, railways, highways, and waterways will anchor the land 'belt' of the Belt and Road Initiative, while the Coastal Corridor will anchor its maritime 'road'.

New free trade zones will help bigger cities attract innovation-based investments and focus on the *Made in China 2025* industrial strategy. Clustering will reallocate resources from bigger cities to smaller ones, helping them move up the value chain and away from polluting industries. In a 2018 Trial Spot, Beijing shared its world-class education, healthcare, employment, social welfare, and housing with seven million poor residents in its rural hinterland. Public response was so positive that the city added the rural poverty belt in adjacent Hebei Province. Now Hebei is building Xiong'an New District on a greenfield site sixty miles south of Beijing.

Bigger than Greater London, Xiong'an New District will connect the world's most prosperous city to its impoverished hinterland and re-house industries incompatible with Beijing's needs. Two-thirds of Xiong'an's forty square miles will be wetlands and forest, and its eco-city model features low-energy construction materials, light mass transportation, and green urban pockets. To optimize space, much of its transportation, water, and electricity infrastructure is underground. Seven hundred miles of new commuter lines connect its urban centers, universities, factories, hospitals, offices, institutions, and government departments, which keeps all commutes under sixty minutes. Downtown Beijing is only thirty minutes away and four high-speed lines connect the three new airports–Beijing Daxing, Tianjin, and Shijiazhuang–with the national high-speed rail network.

To raise energy efficiency and reduce time, manpower, and management overhead, planners designed Xiong'an around 5G, the Internet of Things, artificial intelligence, big data cloud computing, smart sensors, smart lighting, and integrated facial recognition. Locals predict it will have no traffic lights (nor traffic jams) because computers and remote-controlled, self-driving vehicles will manage traffic automatically.

China's urban-rural ratio and per capita GDP have now reached Japan's 1970 level, when that country's economic takeoff began. On present trends it will not reach fifty percent until 2049. By then, hundreds of millions more people will be living in new cities, like Xiong'an, that repay their capital cost by boosting their productivity–just as the Industrial Revolution increased England's productivity in the nineteenth century and made it the world's dominant power.

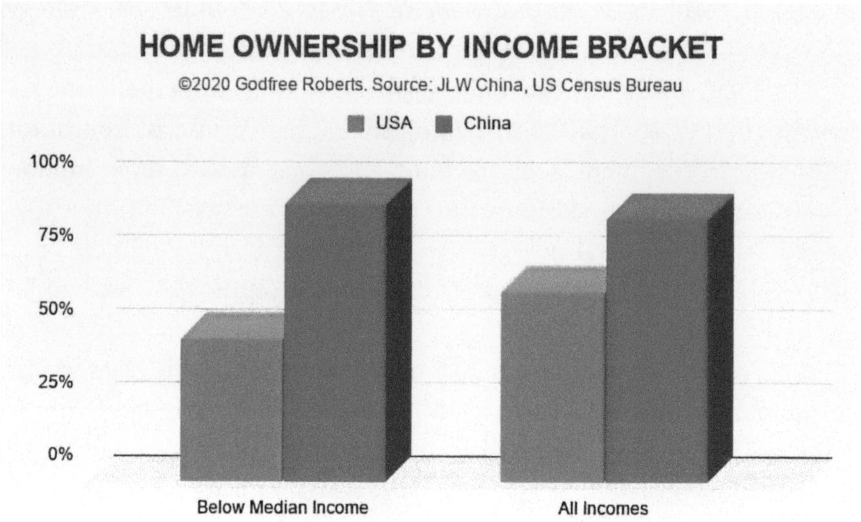
HOME OWNERSHIP BY INCOME BRACKET
©2020 Godfree Roberts. Source: JLW China, US Census Bureau
USA
China
100%
75%
50%
25%
0%
Below Median Income
All Incomes

CHAPTER 12

Charismatic Mega-projects

Enrich the people. Confucius

***

In 272 BC Li Bing, governor of Shu, watched the Min River burst its banks each spring, when meltwater overflowed a heavily-silted stretch but, because it carried grain to frontier troops, he could not dam it. Instead, Governor Li spent eight years heating, cooling, and cracking the river's rock bed to create a channel, sixty-feet wide, through Mount Yulei. The new watercourse discharged half of the river's flow onto a dry plain, transforming it overnight into a wealthy rice bowl whose capital, Chengdu, is home to fourteen million people today. Every year, millions visit Erwang temple to burn incense in grateful memory of the God[202] of Waters, Li Bing.

Li's Dujiangyan Water Diversion is celebrated today not only for its ingenuity but because it recovered its capital cost in seven days–and has done so for two thousand years–making it a model for mega-projects and Governor Li a model for officials seeking immortality. Since then every dynasty, including the present one, has immortalized itself with gigantic engineering projects the most famous of which–in a country plagued by floods–involve water management.

202 Chinese gods are democratically elected and are often historical figures like Li Bing.

Dujiangyan Irrigation System and Erwang temple,
honoring Governor Li Bing, 272 BC

A thousand years after Li's death, an official, Qiao Weiyue, invented the pound lock to lift grain barges across the Shandong mountains, which led to the completion of the eleven-hundred-mile Grand Canal[203], the world's oldest, longest manmade waterway. The canal allowed cargo to be shipped inland, avoided Macao's pirates, cut national freight costs in half, and repaid its capital investment every year thereafter.

The current (Mao?) dynasty has already completed more charismatic mega-projects than all previous dynasties combined, the biggest of which was born when Mao observed, "There's plenty of water in the South but not much in the North. If at all possible, borrowing some water would be helpful".

Four-fifths of China's water is in the South, while eight northern provinces–including the four biggest farming provinces that also produce half the country's GDP and electricity–are water-stressed. Finding

203 The Beijing–Hangzhou Canal, Jīng-Háng Dà Yùnhé,

ninety-six percent of the Yangtze River flowing into the Pacific, engineers proposed transferring enough water north each year to fill a dam one-hundred miles long, ten miles wide, and a mile deep: the capacity of Lake Michigan.

Work on the South-North Water Transfer Project began in 2002 and, by 2014[204], the East and West arms were carrying seven percent of China's total consumption, twenty-five billion cubic meters of water, every year. The Eastern arm passes *under* the Yellow River and the seven-hundred-mile Western arm, which runs through shelter forests and delivers seventy percent of Beijing's water, has halted local groundwater depletion. The middle route transfers ten Olympic swimming pools of water every minute to the thirsty North, where economic activities once constrained by dearth of water now run normally. Though its $48 billion cost is twice the initial budget, it boosts national GDP by three-tenths of one percent[205] each year and repays its bonds through increased tax revenues.

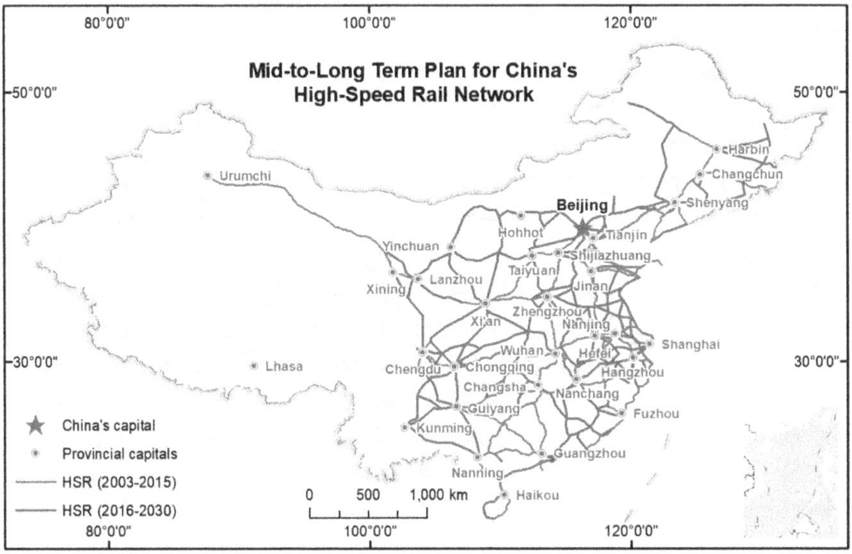

Beijing invests in moving people, too. In 2004, the government paid

204 The controversial Western Route should be ready by 2050.

205 The South-North Water Transfer Project: a Cost-Benefit Analysis. Margaret Louise Mallonée, University of Pittsburgh, 2016

$11.4 billion to license foreign high-speed rail, technology, upgraded its engineering, and began constructing the world's biggest, fastest, safest railway network. Today, four north-south and four east-west lines stretching 20,000 miles carry two billion passengers annually at 350 mph to eighty percent of the country's major cities. The next stage, the 24,000-mile Eight Plus Eight network, will connect to stations in every one of the country's hub cities whence 100 mph magnetic levitation trains, with no moving parts, will silently waft passengers to local towns.

Generating sufficient power to move oceans of water and billions of people requires both thrift and ingenuity. Since conventional coal plants waste sixty percent of their energy, engineers raised their efficiency by twenty percent, saving sufficient fuel to recoup their cost in fifteen years while reducing their pollutants by thirty percent. By 2021 every plant will have been upgraded to this standard, removing billions of tons of NOx, SO2, CO2, and particulates from our atmosphere every year. But replacing dirty coal-fired plants with less dirty coal-fired plants is clearly a stopgap. Given China's commitment to carbon neutrality by 2060, clean power generation is the new priority. Planners are now focusing on the world's fifteen-hundred gigantic coal-fired plants, each generating one thousand megawatts which, together, are responsible for thirty percent of the world's carbon dioxide emissions.

Engineers plan to replace their furnaces with stacks of self-heating, uranium-cored graphite spheres, 'pebbles,' cooled by circulating helium gas that conducts their heat to the boilers. Overheated stacks melt a plug that allows the pebbles to roll into a cooling area. The first plant will come online in 2022, and, if all goes well, a factory will begin to mass-producing them in 2024. Shipped in modules and reassembled, they will replace the mega-plants' coal-fired furnaces. The big plants will continue operating with their existing staff, buildings, transmission lines, water supplies, roads, railroad tracks–but without their emissions. Meanwhile, the country operates forty-five conventional nuclear plants, is building twelve, and plans to mass produce another forty-two at a unit cost of $11.5 billion, one-third of the international price.

China's Academy of Sciences and Oak Ridge National Laboratory are collaborating on an even cooler nuclear project, fueled by safe, cheap, abundant, thorium. Thorium, with its high energy efficiency and low radioactivity, allows compact power plants to be installed close to consumers, says nuclear scientist Kirk Sorensen, "Thorium is so energy-dense that 6,600 tonnes of it could replace the combined 5 billion tonnes of coal, 31 billion barrels of oil, 3 trillion cubic meters of natural gas and 65,000 tonnes of uranium that the world consumes annually". The schedule calls for a pilot plant to be operational in 2025.

Engineers have also reduced the cost of solar panels ninety-five percent. Since renewable energy tends to be plentiful in remote locations like seas and deserts, they have developed ultra-high voltage transmission lines capable of carrying the output of twelve power plants for two thousand miles with little transmission loss. The national UHV grid carries 150 gigawatts, four times Britain's maximum electricity output. Chinese researchers also lead the world in wind, ocean, and solar power, smart grids and intelligent buildings.

Another network challenge, online security, led engineers to develop the Beijing–Shanghai Quantum Secure Communication Backbone, whose three thousand miles of dedicated fiber optic cable connect the nation's banks, finance companies, and security services. Its designers also operate the first quantum communication satellite, QUESS (it transferred an image between locations without sending physical particles) and have demonstrated quantum imaging of low-contrast tissues like cancers. The program's godfather, physicist Pan Jianwei, says that a quantum computer could compute one trillion trillion, 10^{24}, simultaneous equations in one-hundredth of a second–an operation that would occupy today's supercomputers for a century. He plans to build a demonstration unit in 2021 and, by 2030, another with a million times the throughput of all the computers on earth. Pan says that the quantum age will have sufficient computing power to crack the mysteries of fusion and solve all of Earth's clean energy challenges.

In space, scientists face a different set of challenges. Expensive satellites are abandoned after fifteen years because they run out of fuel after regularly repositioning themselves. Now engineers have begun refueling them in orbit, and accurately repositioning them with millisecond pulsars, stars that pulse with the precision of atomic clocks. China's Beidou satellite GPS system uses the world's new timing standard, the Cold Atomic Clock in Space, to provide global navigation with ten-centimeter accuracy–and Beidou chips are built into every vehicle made in China, even bicycles.

Nor are the life sciences neglected. Francis Collins, Director of the US National Institutes of Health, says China took the lead in genomics years ago. "If you ask me where is the largest investment in genomics in the world, it's not in the United States. It is in Shenzhen, China, at BGI". BGI plans to extend the useful human lifespan by five years, increase global food production by ten percent, decode half the world's genetic diseases, and cut congenital disabilities by fifty percent. Its geneticists are working to identify thousands of unique genetic clusters from high-IQ donors and hope to allow parents to choose their smartest embryos. Says the project's leader, "People in the West think this is controversial, but not in China". Another startup, iCarbonX, collects DNA from millions of patients, teaches its computers to understand their diseases, and provides more reliable medical advice than most MDs–a diagnostic boon to developing countries.

None of this progress is surprising. When we adjust for purchasing power parity, China outspends the US fourfold on research and development, as this survey of scientific research papers confirms:

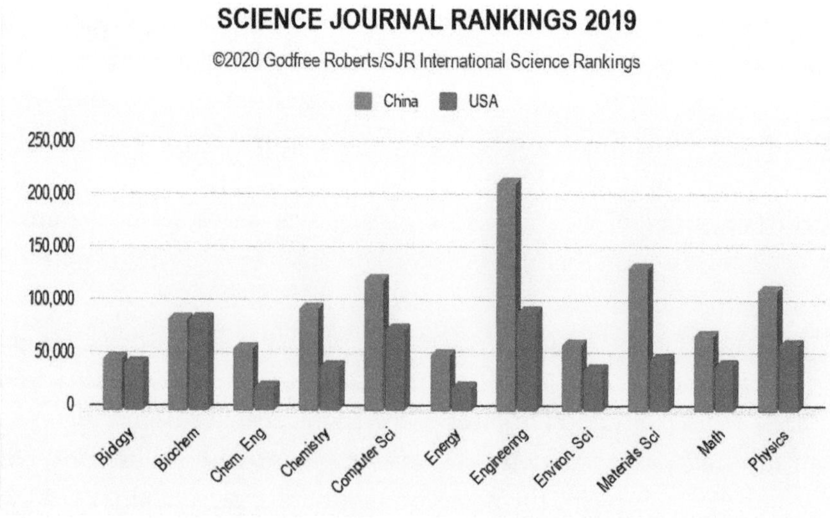

PART IV

DEMOCRACY AT THE BOTTOM

CHAPTER 13

Dimensions of Democracy

Without constant means, most people will not have constant hearts and, lacking constant hearts, will go astray, fall into excess, and become desperate. Since punishing people after they have broken the Law is just setting a trap for them, the government must take responsibility for their material and moral well-being. The people's interests must always come first; the rulers' interests come last. Mencius[206].

***

While there is an obvious tension between the ideals of democracy and the realities of power, it is fair to say that governments that consistently produce the outcomes their citizens desire are democratic, while those that consistently fail to produce the outcomes their citizens desire results are not[207]. By that definition, China is clearly democratic and the United States is clearly not.

***

In our Roman tradition, wealthy oligarchs sponsor eloquent candidates

206 Mencius, Confucius' principle disciple, was born a century after the Master's death.

207 Those that talk democracy and hold elections but fail to produce democratic outcomes are called formal democracies, a term coined by Sheldon S. Wolin, in 'Democracy Incorporated: Managed Democracy and the Specter of Inverted Totalitarianism'. Princeton University Press, 2017.

(usually lawyers, even in Ancient Rome) and stage colorful elections at which citizens impotently vent their frustrations, then the newly-elected politicians delay progress indefinitely by staging endless quarrels. Britain pioneered this model, the United States adapted it, and most Western nations emulate it today–to the great dissatisfaction of their citizens.

But our political model is not the only one–or the most successful. Three non-Roman democracies–Switzerland, Singapore, and China–consistently produce better outcomes. The Swiss hold four annual national voting sessions in which everyone participates, Singapore maintains a captive opposition, and China has used the Carter Center to create a Confucian democracy.

Since the Swiss and Singaporean models are probably suited only to small states, we will compare America's and China's by examining their constitutional, participative, elective, consultive, legislative, operational, substantive, and financial elements.

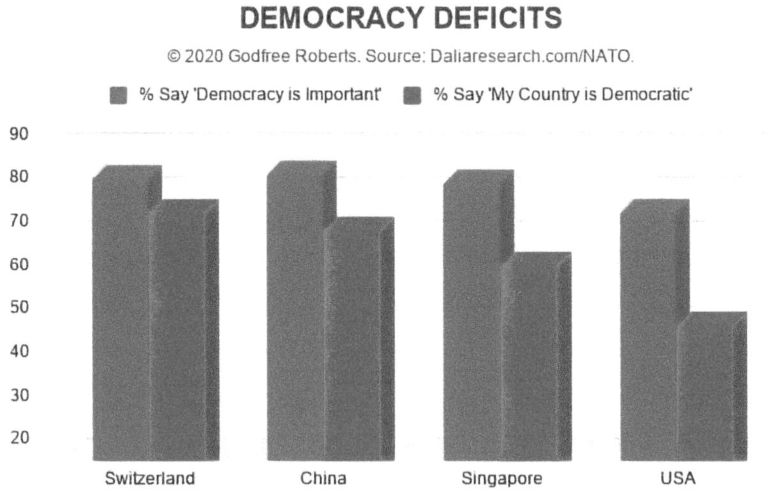

In the Confucian tradition, geniuses have led the nation by moral example but, beyond beneficial infrastructure, produced few benefits for the rural majority until Mao updated it. In 1945, when a Reuters[208] correspondent asked him what kind of nation he envisioned, Mao replied, "A free and democratic China in which all government levels, including the central government, are created by general and equal secret balloting and are responsible to the people who elected them. It will implement Dr. Sun Yat-sen's three principles of democracy, Lincoln's principle of 'of the people, by the people, for the people,' and Roosevelt's Atlantic Charter[209]. It will assure the independence and unity of the nation and cooperate with all democratic powers". Five years later, in 1950, he subjected Confucian officialdom to democratic oversight and created what he called *'socialism with Chinese characteristics'*.

How democratic is it?

While the US Constitution makes no mention of democracy (the Founding Fathers[210] loathed it), China's employs it thirty-eight times. A typical passage: "The State organs of the People's Republic of China apply the principle of democratic centralism. The National People's Congress and the local people's congresses at various levels are constituted through democratic elections. They are responsible to the people and subject to their supervision. All administrative, judicial, and procuratorial organs of the State are created by the peoples' congresses to which they are responsible and by which they are supervised".

Mao introduced universal suffrage in 1951 (ten years before the US

208 Written answer to Mr. Campbell, the Reuters correspondent in Chongqing. *Xinhua Ribao*, September 27, 1945. From *Collected Writings of Mao Zedong*, Takeuchi Minoru, Tokyo: Hokubosha, 1970-1972.

209 The Charter focused on territorial rights, self-determination, economic issues, disarmament, and ethical goals including freedom of the seas and a determination to work for a world free of want and fear.

210 "The Federalist Papers are very clear. The founding fathers and one of the people who was inventing the Constitution start to get apoplectic at the mention of Athens, the mention of Pericles, the mention of democracy. They go on and on about mobs, and we don't want this, and we don't want that. We're an oligarchy of the well-to-do. We were at the very beginning, when the Constitution was made, and we're even more so now". Gore Vidal: *History of the National Security State.*

[211]), and Quaker William Sewell[212], a professor at Jen Dah Christian University in Szechuan, voted in the first election in Chinese history.

> As a labor union member, I was entitled to vote. The election of a government in China is indirect. We at Jen Dah were to vote for our local People's Congress. Then the Local Congresses would, from among their own members, elect the Duliang Congress. From these members and the congresses of the great cities and many counties would be elected the Szechwan People's Provincial Congress. Finally, the National People's Congress emerged, every member of which had in the first place been elected to a local body. The National Congress made the laws, elected the Chairman, and appointed the Premier and the State Council members. In our chemistry group, we discussed the sort of men and women who might best represent us; then we put forward half a dozen names.
>
> Each group in our Jen Dah section did the same. All the names were then written on a board so that everyone might see who had been suggested. The names which several groups had listed in common were put on a shortlist. They amounted to over a dozen, any groups being still at liberty to put forward any name that they considered should not have been omitted. Those whose names were on the shortlist had then to be persuaded to allow their names to remain. This took some time, as a genuine sense of inability to cope made many reluctant to undertake such responsible work. Each person was discussed at length by the group. Those who were unknown were invited to visit the various groups so that they might be questioned. At length, a still shorter list of candidates was obtained, which was cut down eventually, after further discussion, to the number desired.
>
> When the day of the election came, the flags were flying, and the bands with their cymbals and drums with their constant rhythm made it all pleasantly noisy. Voting slips were handed out

211 The Voting Rights Act of 1965 initiated universal suffrage in the US .

212 *I Stayed in China*, William Sewell

> at one end of the booth, and students, all sworn to secrecy, were available to help if you couldn't read. Then alone, or accompanied by your helper, you sat at the table and cast your votes. The list contained names which had by now become very familiar, but there was a space at the bottom for additional names to be added should you so desire. A ring was to be put around those you wished to be elected, and the paper dropped into the box. In England, I had voted for a man I didn't know, with whom I had never spoken, who asked for my vote by a circular letter, and who had lost to his rival by over 14,000 votes. I had felt that my vote was entirely worthless. In China, in this one election, I had at least had the happy illusion that my voice was of real significance.

Thirty years later, powerful family clans dominated local elections and villagers regularly petitioned for 'a capable Party Secretary to straighten things out,' so, Beijing invited The Carter Center to supervise the process. By 2010, voter turnout had outstripped America's and the Prime Minister urged them on, "The experience of many villages has proven that farmers can successfully elect village committees. If people can manage a village well, they can manage a township and a county. We must encourage people to experiment boldly and test democracy in practice". Five years later, President Xi asked the Carter Center to reevaluate the country's electoral laws and to educate candidates about ethical campaigning, adding, "Democracy is not only defined by people's right to vote in elections but also by their right to participate in political affairs on a daily basis. Democracy is not decorative, it's for solving people's problems".

China's democratic process begins with millions of candidates–who need not be Party members–standing for election in six-hundred-thousand villages. New village secretaries start with a trial year (they are dismissed if they fail to meet their assigned goals) then prepare for three years of implementation, hoping that their policies will win national acclaim. They elect peers to represent them at the district level, where further voting elects county representatives. They repeat the process until three thousand national congresspeople convene in Beijing. The Party cannot completely control this process since candidates need strong support from peers below them, with the result that one-third of national congresspeople are not Party members. Non-Communist parties and minorities are overrepresented[213] and the China Democratic League[214], the Kuomintang[215], and the Jiusan Society[216] (for PhDs only) have produced outstanding Ministers.

A supermajority of the three-thousand Congressional representatives must approve all senior appointments and legislation–and regularly refuse to do so. In 2016, the Agriculture Ministry promised to provide genetically modified maize and soybeans to eager farmers and launched a two-year PR campaign extolling their benefits, then sent enabling legislation to Congress in 2018. But mandatory congressional surveys[217] found half the country opposed to GM (eleven percent thought it 'a bioterrorism weapon'), and only ten percent supported it, and legislation was shelved. These days, researchers, experts, media, academics, stakeholders, and obstreperous citizens set the agenda. The episode was in keeping Mao's reminder to colleagues, "If we don't investigate public opinion, we have no right to voice our own opinion. Public opinion is our guideline for action". High government approval ratings suggest that officials and Congress still heed Mao's advice.

The democratic process is not merely superficial. Engineers, economists, statisticians, and sociologists who develop policies do so

---

213 Ethnic minorities account for 21 percent of the Standing Committee of the NPC; 9.6 percent of vice-chairpersons of the National Committee of the CPPCC, one of the leading members of the State Council, two ministers, and heads of government of 155 ethnic autonomous regions, prefectures, and counties.

214 The China Democratic League is for teachers from elementary school to universities. Since Confucius is China's archetypal teacher and society holds teachers in high regard, this is a high-status, highly influential Party.

215 KMT (*Guomindang*), often translated as the Nationalist Party of China) is a major political party in the Republic of China on Taiwan, based in Taipei and is currently the opposition political party in the Legislative Yuan.

216 The Jiusan Society is for Ph.D. scientists, mostly physicists, and engineers, whose position is 'everything should be run by science'. It pushes climate initiatives, environmental protection, a larger R&D budget, and better health policies.

217 Public perception of genetically-modified (GM) food: A Nationwide Chinese Consumer Study. Kai Cui & Sharon P. Shoemaker. Science of Food volume 2, Article number: 10 (2018)

democratically. Cabinet members vote unanimously to send legislation to Congress and Congress, as we saw, requires a two-thirds majority to pass it. Such data-driven democracy keeps policy support as high as Switzerland's, above Singapore's, and far above America's, where[218] 'the preferences of the average American appear to have a near-zero, statistically non-significant, impact upon public policy'.

Operationally, no Chinese leader has powers like American Presidents. As William Henry Seward[219] said, "We elect a king for four years and give him absolute power within certain limits which, after all, he can interpret for himself". American Presidents take the country to war, hire and fire all senior officials, ban fifty-thousand citizens from flying, order kidnappings, torture, imprisonment, and assassinations–all without consulting Congress, while Chinese Presidents cannot even choose their prime ministers or cabinet members, hire or fire officials, or elect, assign, or suspend congresspeople.

Though discussion of economic democracy has always been taboo in Western democracy, it is central to the Chinese–which explains why they have doubled their incomes every decade for forty years. Meanwhile, says Stanford's Raj Chetty[220], "Absolute income mobility in the US has fallen across the entire income distribution, with the largest declines for families in the middle class".

Harvard's Tony Saich[221] found ninety-six percent of Chinese satisfied with their government and Edelman[222] found that ninety percent of them trust it. World Values Surveys found that eighty-three percent of

---

218 Using data drawn from over 1,800 different policy initiatives from 1981 to 2002, Martin Gilens and Benjamin Page concluded that wealthy, well-connected individuals on the political scene now steer the direction of the country, regardless of or even against the will of the majority of voters. "The central point that emerges from our research is that economic elites and organized groups representing business interests have substantial independent impacts on US government policy. Mass-based interest groups and average citizens have little or no independent influence". Democracy in America? U. Chicago Press. 2018.

219 Seward was Abraham Lincoln's Secretary of State.

220 The Fading American Dream: Trends in Absolute Income Mobility Since 1940. By Raj Chetty, David Grusky, Maximilian Hell, Nathaniel Hendren, Robert Manduca, Jimmy Narang. NBER Working Paper No. 22910. Issued in December 2016, Revised in March 2017.

221 Governance and Politics of China (4th Edition) by Tony Saich. MacMillan, 2015

222 Spring 2020 Edelman Trust Barometer, May 2020.

them (compared to thirty-eight percent of Americans) say their country is run for everyone's benefit rather than that of privileged groups.

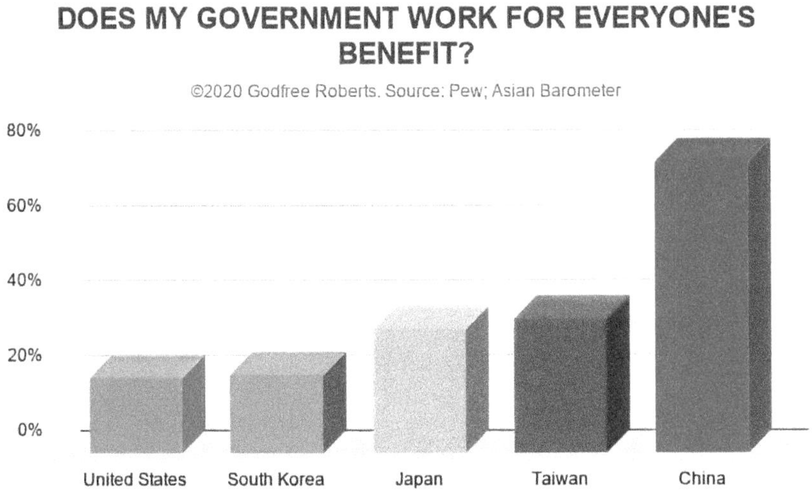

Nor is democracy a barrier to getting things done in China, says the New York Times' Tom Friedman, "If we could just be China for one day, we could actually authorize the right decisions".

CHAPTER 14

Corruption: The Worst kind of Treason

A student asked Confucius about the essence of good government. He replied, "The requisites of government are that there be a sufficiency of food, enough military equipment, and the confidence of the people in their ruler".

The disciple asked, "If it were necessary to dispense with one of these, which of the three should we do without?"

Confucius answered, "The military equipment".

The disciple persisted, "If it were necessary to dispense with one of the remaining two, which one should we forego?"

Confucius replied, "Part with the food. Death has always been the lot of men but if the people have no faith in their rulers, then the state cannot survive". Analects.

***

No nation has suffered more from corrupt government nor benefited more from honest government than China, and none is so culturally sensitive to it:

> Had I thoroughly eradicated corrupt officials in addition to those already imprisoned, I would have been dealing with two

> thousand men from just two prefectures, men with no useful occupation who used my prestige to oppress people. No-one outside government knew how wicked they were, so everyone said my punishments were harsh, for they saw only the severity of the law and didn't know that these villains had used the government's good name to engage in evil practices. In the morning, I punished a few and, by evening, others had committed the same crimes. I punished those in the evening, and the next morning there were more violations! Although the corpses of the first had not been removed, others were already lined up to follow in their path, day and night! The harsher the punishment, the more violations. I didn't know what to do, but I couldn't rest. If I was lenient, the law became ineffectual, order deteriorated, people thought me weak, and criminals engaged in still more evil practices. If I punished them, others regarded me as a tyrant. How could I enjoy peace of mind in those circumstances? Really, my situation was dreadful. The Hongwu Emperor, 1328-1398 AD.

Corruption has been subverting governments since governments were invented. Roman politicians were scandalously corrupt. Their legacy of impunity, bribery, influence peddling, patronage, nepotism and cronyism, electoral fraud, embezzlement, kickbacks, unholy alliances, and organized crime still afflicts governments in the West. Corruption has plagued China's government for millennia, too, but the Confucian tradition gave rise to heroes unknown in the West: corruption fighters.

On May 5, 278 BC, after the King of Chu ignored his warnings about official corruption, State Minister Qu Yuan[223] protested by drowning himself in the Miluo River and, ever since that fateful May day, Dragon Boats have renewed their search for his body.

223 Qu Yuan, 340-278 BC, was a Chu Kingdom official and government minister who wrote some of the most outstanding poetry in Chinese history.

Table 1. The Punishment Scale for Salaried Persons* Who are Convicted of Corruption

Punishment	Bribes for Unlawful Favors (*wangfa*)	Bribes for Lawful Favors (*bu wangfa*)^ Value of the Spoils	Influence Peddling (*zuozang*)^
Light Bamboo (*chi*)			
20 blows			under 1 tael
30 blows			1–10 taels
40 blows			20 taels
50 blows			30 taels
Heavy Bamboo (*zhang*)			
60 blows		under 1 tael	40 taels
70 blows	under 1 tael	1–10 taels	50 taels
80 blows	1–5 taels	20 taels	60 taels
90 blows	10 taels	30 taels	70 taels
100 blows	15 taels	40 taels	80 taels
Penal Servitude (*tu*)			
1 yr and 60 blows	20 taels	50 taels	100 taels
1 1/2 yrs and 70 blows	25 taels	60 taels	200 taels
2 yrs and 80 blows	30 taels	70 taels	300 taels
2 1/2 yrs and 90 blows	35 taels	80 taels	400 taels
3 yrs and 100 blows	40 taels	90 taels	500 taels
Exile (*liu*)			
2000 li and 100 blows	45 taels	100 taels	N/A
2500 li and 100 blows	50 taels	110 taels	
3000 li and 100 blows	55 taels	120 taels	
Capital Punishment (*si*)			
Strangulation after the Assizes (*jiao jianhou*)	over 80 taels	over 120 taels	N/A

Corruption in Eighteenth-Century China. Nancy E. Park. The Journal of Asian Studies, vol. 56, no. 4, 1997.

China has been able to keep corruption at bay because the culture expects officials to exemplify the Four Confucian Principles–decency, justice, honesty, and honor–and promotes those who demonstrate the Eight Virtues: loyalty, filial piety, benevolence, love, integrity, righteousness, harmony, and peace.

They also take more precautions than our Roman governments. From the earliest days, officials transferred to provinces were forbidden to bring their parents–lest their needs conflict with the Emperor's–and were rotated every three years. After each rotation their successors were encouraged to report discrepancies for fear of being blamed for them. In the capital, palace officials were regularly moved between departments and the incorrigibly corrupt were strangled and their families were sold into slavery. Though punishments are less draconian today, little else has changed.

In 1950, six months after taking power, Mao launched his first anti-corruption campaign, observing, "Today, you can still buy a branch secretary for a few packs of cigarettes, not to mention marrying a daughter to him". His slogan, "The masses have sharp eyes," encouraged people to report wrongdoing, and corruption fell dramatically. His insistence on merely shaming corrupt officials worked surprisingly well, says Sydney Rittenberg[224], "Nobody locked their doors. The banks–there was a local bank branch on many, many corners–the door was wide open, the currency was stacked up on the table in plain sight of the door, there were no guards and they never had a bank robbery, ever".

But contemporary China's greatest advantage is its freedom from corruption at the policy-making level, where the Roman model has historically been weakest.

The PRC recruited and promoted honest men and, anticipating low-level corruption, designed incentives so that bribers and dishonest officials still expedited Beijing's plan, says Yukon Huang[225], "The system countered the growth-inhibiting aspects of corruption by setting investment and production targets that gave local officials incentives to promote expansion. It fostered a unity of purpose so that, even when corruption flourished, the collaborators still made growth the guiding principle of their actions. This was reinforced by competition between localities to meet targets and support productivity-enhancing economic reforms. The competitive element helped curb waste and ensured a modicum of efficiency despite the high degree of state intervention in commercial activities".

Yet, despite their precautions, things occasionally got out of hand.

Acting on a smuggling tipoff in 1999, Beijing secretly sent

224 An old friend of the Party assesses China's new leaders. Rob Schmitz. Marketplace. November 19, 2012

225 Yukon Huang was the World Bank's Director for China. The Diplomat

investigators to Xiamen Port but someone tipped off the crooks, who set fire to the detectives' hotel, killing them as they slept. The following day, on national television, Premier Zhu Rongji declared war and ordered a hundred coffins, "Ninety-nine for the crooks and one for me". Detectives converged from across the country and were staggered to find that four million tons of imported diesel fuel had bypassed customs in just two years. They tracked hundreds of suspects, locked them in a hotel with armed guards on each floor, and spent three years unraveling a case so complex that the customs files alone would be higher than a ten-story building. The gang had bribed the Vice-Minister of Public Security, Li Jizhou, through his wife and daughter. Li and thirteen accomplices were sentenced to death, his wife to thirty months in prison, and three hundred officials were tried for aiding or abetting the criminals. The ringleader, farmer-turned-smuggler Lai Changxing, fled to Canada, was extradited, and jailed for life in 2009.

The decades of booming growth solved many social problems, then nepotism–to which China is uniquely vulnerable–precipitated a scandal that presaged a new episode in the struggle with corruption.

In 1985 Bo Xilai, son of a Revolutionary Immortal and Xi Jinping's schoolmate, ignored his father's pleas to stay out of politics, "You know nothing of the sufferings of ordinary people and just want to capitalize on my name". Bo cultivated a charismatic image, was named one of *Time's* Most Influential People, became a provincial governor, and publicly campaigned for a cabinet position. But, as scholar Cheng Li[226] said at the time, "Nobody really trusts him. A lot of people are scared of him, including several princelings who are supposed to be his power base". Michael Wines[227] wrote, "Despite his prodigious charisma and deep intelligence, he possessed a studied indifference to the wrecked lives that littered his path to power...Mr. Bo's ruthlessness stood out". Bo even suborned Justice Minister Zhou Yongkang and persuaded him to wiretap President Hu's office.

Despite massive internal resistance, Vice Premier Wu Yi, the nation's

226 Profile: Bo Xilai. September 2013. BBC
227 In Rise and Fall of China's Bo Xilai, an Arc of Ruthlessness. By MICHAEL WINES. MAY 6, 2012. NYT

highest woman official, demanded an open investigation and a 2012 trial revealed that Bo owned expensive properties worldwide and that his wife had murdered a British agent. The couple was jailed for life.

Bo's prosecution marked the end of the go-go years and triggered the election of Xi Jinping, the most honest official of his generation, to the presidency.

In his first year in office, Xi's anti-corruption campaign sidelined ten thousand officials for concealing information and demoted or disciplined one-hundred thirty-thousand for making false declarations. Within four years, prosecutors had charged sixty-three senior officials and ministers with corruption and released confessions from fifty-seven thousand Party members who made restitution and accepted demotions. Yunnan's unrepentant Party Secretary, Bai Enpei, was sentenced to death[228]. By 2018, anti-corruption squads had investigated 1.3 million officials, filed a million court cases, issued one hundred thousand indictments, captured thousands of overseas fugitives, and jailed or executed one-hundred twenty high-ranking officials, including five national leaders, twelve generals, and a dozen CEOs.

These days, even deputy county officials sign sworn statements, in the knowledge that ten percent of them will be audited. They declare their marital status, overseas travel, criminal record, wages, other earnings, family properties, stocks, funds, insurance, and investments. They are detained immediately if they refuse to answer questions, or collude with or protect accomplices.

Graft inspections resemble professional athletes' doping tests. Anhui inspectors telephoned one official four times between 7:31-7:35 one evening, to ask about his poverty alleviation efforts. When he failed to pick up his phone they reported him for obstruction and moved to dismiss him. The poor man had been showering and, happily, the public came to his defense and he was exonerated.

Bureaucrats with leadership ambitions endure increasing scrutiny as they advance, says Zhao Bing Bing[229], "The selection criteria are: a

---

228 Following Mao's prescription, most death sentences are stayed for two years and, if the criminal displays adequate contrition, commuted to imprisonment.

229 Daniel Bell and Zhao Bing Bing, *The China Model.*

person must have 'both ability, and moral integrity and the latter should be prioritized[230].' Midlevel officials must report the assets of their parents, wives, children, children's spouses and cousins, children from previous marriages, children born out of wedlock and foster children, their income, savings, real estate, stock portfolios, insurance policies, unit trusts, bonds, assets in overseas accounts. Income shall include salary and various bonuses, allowances, subsidies, and payment you receive from lectures, writing, consultation, reviewing, painting and calligraphy". Says the scion of a prominent family:

> I am a Party Member in China, and all my family are Party members. What I think of Xi is that life is really changing after he came to power. A relative of mine works for the government as a vital governor in my city Chengdu (which is a big city like BeiJing or ShangHai), then all my family people are like in the hierarchy of privilege. We pay nothing when going out for dinner, the Party pays. We pay nothing for filling in oil, the Party pays. It seems like we don't need to pay for anything with our salaries, cause either the Party pays, or someone will pay for us (who wants to flatter us). I smoke the best, and I drink the best, sometimes I even drive without a license when drunk, because I fear no one.
>
> In past times, yes, we did have privilege everywhere. I felt so arrogant to be superior to others. That's also true. But the problem is, there is a tradeoff. We drank quite a lot of alcohol to show respect to others. We had to accept bribes even we know it's risky, cause we have to consider our Clan (like the interest of my boss). We had to do many things we don't want to do, that's the rule of living in Party, care about Clan's interest more than your own. That's how we united. We have to fear a lot of threats from ordinary people, colleagues, and bosses. We cannot keep our passports. The Party keeps it in case we flee.
>
> But life changed after Xi came to power. He did real things

230 A Tang Dynasty Chief Censor first used the phrase.

> on anti-corruption. No one dares to present gifts to governors, and the abuse of public funds is strictly monitored. The Party took back the public cars from my family, and even we have to pay for the parking fee now! But..my family and I are actually happy with this. We are thankful to President Xi. Cause he seems like dragging China to a healthier future. My relatives don't need to go out for dinner with other governors as social intercourse daily; they don't need to drink so much on the table. And they start to learn to pay for the bill by turns, cause the Party will no longer do this for them. They begin to learn how to take the bus or metro. That's good, actually. People start to think about what kind of lifestyle is called 'healthy,' they are more like a human now, no longer some conceited stupid with expanding power. That's how our life changed after Xi came.

The lives of senior officials are excruciatingly transparent. Their private activities are scrutinized and their children must adopt assumed names to avoid influence-seekers. Their meetings must have third-party observers because one-on-one appointments are taken as evidence of impropriety. A record of excessive or low-quality government debts is *prima facie* evidence of corruption and triggers an automatic investigation. Senior officials are audited annually after retirement and remain responsible for the consequences of all their decisions until they die–after which clawback provisions apply.

Beijing publishes a monthly anti-corruption scoresheet and citizens text tips and complaints to the Rules and Discipline Committee (founded in the Tang Dynasty) at #12388, post accusations, and evidentiary photographs on social media, and solicit witnesses. Following an accident in Shaanxi Province that killed thirty-six people, netizens scrutinizing a news photograph of a work safety official grinning as he assessed the twisted wreckage spotted his expensive timepiece. Their tipoff led to Yang Dacai, Brother Watch, being jailed for fourteen years for taking a million dollars in bribes. When a 2019 industrial explosion in Tianjin killed one-hundred sixty-five people, and the magistrate found that petty bribery had led to weak code enforcement, she sentenced the responsible official to death and jailed forty-nine of his colleagues.

Until 2018, anti-corruption work was divided between four agencies, then Xi united them in The National Supervision Commission, and created a fourth, independent, political arm of government that ranks with the Supreme Court and the Department of Justice. Congress appoints its senior staff and they can never work in another arm of government for the rest of their lives.

The most potent such agency on earth, the NSC's mission is to make corruption impossible. It exercises authority over all civil servants within and outside the Party, the government, the Peoples' Congresses, the local supervisory commissions, the people's courts and procuracy, the Peoples' Congresses, the eight democratic parties, federations of industry and commerce, and everyone who works in, or consults for, organizations managing public affairs. Its writ runs to managers of state-owned enterprises, state educational, scientific, research, cultural, health care, sports, and similar agencies, think tanks, village and urban residents committees, and 'all other personnel who perform public duties,' and oversees provincial, city, and county level anti-corruption agencies.

The Commission employs the peoples' sharp eyes enhanced by digital technology–including face recognition and AI–and its extensive powers to interrogate, search, wiretap, and detain suspects and freeze their assets. It is a political body, exempt from the procedural constraints on administrative organs like the police, and does not provide a right of further recourse through the courts (though the law requires staff to pay compensation for infringing suspects' lawful rights and permits them to appeal to higher-level organs and to challenge unlawful conduct like prolonged detention). If the Commission succeeds, grateful citizens will credit Confucius for designing honesty into government and Xi Jinping for creating the most potent corruption-fighting agency in their history.

Today, visitors still burn incense at the shrines of great corruption fighters, Dragon Boats still search for Minister Qu on May 5, and millions watch TV dramas about Justice Bao Zheng, the incorruptible Prefect of the Capital in 1000 AD. A popular TV series, 'In the Name of People,' depicts current-day intra-Party power struggles in the fictional city of Jingzhou, where a prosecutor and a few honest local officials help laid-off workers fight corrupt land deals, foil corrupt bureaucrats trying to sabotage arrest warrants, and stop fake police bulldozing honest citizens' homes. The show's writers say they have no shortage of material.

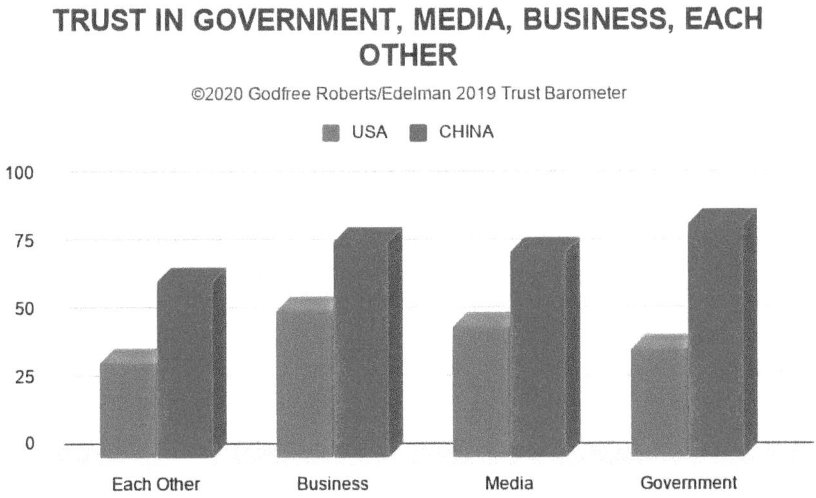

CHAPTER 15

Discussion is Suspended

If language is incorrect, then what is said does not match what was meant and, if what is said does not match what is intended, what is to be done cannot be accomplished, and disorder will prevail. Officials should therefore choose their words judiciously and only promise what they can achieve. Confucius, *Analects.*

***

Trustworthy media are a precondition for democracy and civil society as Thomas Jefferson said, "An informed citizenry is at the heart of any true democracy". If our picture of the world is distorted or incomplete, how can we participate in a democratic government? Not knowing about Good China, we wasted our taxes on wars because our famous 'free press,' let us down.

Our media today suffer from the same shortcomings as they did did thirty years ago, when Singapore's Yew[231] criticized them [*emphasis added*]:

> The Philippines' press enjoys all the freedoms of the US system but fails the people: a wildly partisan press helped Philippines' politicians flood the marketplace of ideas with junk and confuse and befuddle the people so that they could not see what their

231 A Third World Perspective on the Press. RH Lee Kwan Yew, Prime Minister of Singapore. C-SPAN, APRIL 14, 1988

> vital interests were in a developing country. Because vital issues like economic growth and equitable distribution were seldom discussed, they were never tackled, and the democratic system malfunctioned. Look at Taiwan and South Korea: their free press runs rampant, and corruption runs riot. The critic itself is corrupt, yet the theory is, if you have a free press, corruption disappears. Now I'm telling you, that's not true. Freedom of the press, freedom of news critics, must be subordinated to the overriding needs of the integrity of Singapore and to the primacy of purpose of an elected government.

Our 'free press' was born during the religious wars of 1644, when the Roman Catholic Church was the global censor. John Milton, England's great poet, praised Oliver Cromwell as the reincarnation of Moses–a claim Rome called heretical.

Milton's protest made him a *protestant* against Church censorship, "Give me the liberty to know, to utter, and to argue freely according to conscience, above all liberties," just when entrepreneurs were borrowing money to buy printing presses.

Their priority repaying the loans and religious screeds (both pro- and anti-Rome) were big sellers. Authors, paid by the word, churned out propaganda for political parties, and scandal sheets sold on every street corner. Publishers seeking the broadest audience promoted belief over evidence, scandal over accuracy, and war over peace.

The results were disastrous, said Bernhard von Bülow[232], "Most of the conflicts the world has seen in the past century have not been called forth by princely ambition or ministerial conspiracy, but by the passionate agitation of public opinion which, through press and parliament, has swept the executive along".

232 Bernhard von Bülow was Germany's Chancellor in 1909. *The Sleepwalkers: How Europe Went to War in 1914* by Christopher Clark.

***

Clearly, no nation that places such power in the hands of private publishers can survive long, which is why the US has always censored its media.

Eugene Debs, the US Socialist Party's candidate for the presidency in 1912, characterized America's entry into World War I as 'a dispute between capitalist ruling classes in which working people have no stake' (and modern historians agree). President Wilson charged him and thousands of his supporters with sedition, judges sentenced them to ten years in prison, and the Supreme Court upheld their judgments. Later, Edward Bernays[233] admitted, "The conscious and intelligent manipulation of the organized habits and opinions of the masses is an important element in democratic society. Those who manipulate its unseen mechanisms constitute an invisible government–which is the true ruling power of our country". Or, as Noam Chomsky put it, "Propaganda is to a democracy what the bludgeon is to a totalitarian state".

CIA Director William Casey's[234] advice to President Reagan exemplifies the truth of Chomsky's critique, "We'll know that our disinformation campaign has worked when everything the American public believes is false".

Casey relied on five information filters:[235] wealthy media owners and advertisers;[236] powerful news sources like the White House; endless, imaginary foreign threats; and public relations experts who create editorials, interviews, petitions, lawsuits, speeches, and legislation.

If individual's opinions escape that net, governments censor them, too. Since 9/11, the US Government has issued a million national

---

233 *Propaganda.* Edward Bernays, Freud's nephew, the father of America's public relations industry.

234 William Casey was President Ronald Reagan's CIA Director from 1981 to 1987 who traded arms to the Islamic Republic of Iran and diverted some of the income to aid the rebel Contras in Nicaragua, in violation of US law.

235 Manufacturing Consent: The Political Economy of the Mass Media. 2002. by Edward S. Herman and Noam Chomsky.

236 In a 1992 US study of one-hundred-fifty news editors, ninety percent said advertisers tried to interfere with newspaper content, and seventy percent tried to stop news stories altogether. Forty percent admitted that advertisers had influenced a story.

security letters that resemble Louis XIV's *lettres de cachet:* administrative subpoenas with gag orders enjoining recipients from ever divulging their existence. Formally, the President controls all information through Executive Orders 10995 and 12472 and executes without trial citizens and non-citizens who express unpopular ideas. For criticizing US foreign policy, President Obama executed without trial an American preacher, Anwar al-Awlaki, and, separately, his sixteen-year-old son and eight-year-old daughter.

News about China reaches us through the additional filter of linguistic and cultural differences. Instead of a *government*, China has a *regime* that does not *fire* officials but *purges* them. Its leaders don't *strengthen* laws, they *concentrate power*. Its media don't *report news*, they *spew propaganda*, and, instead of *challenges,* China faces *threats to its rule*. We have *deterrents* while they have *nuclear weapons* and, instead of *bribing* politicians as they do, we *lobby* ours.

Writing propaganda pays well in the West, too, says Carl Bernstein.[237] More than four hundred American journalists and all major US media outlets have carried out CIA assignments. Victor Marchetti[238] testified that the Agency spent a quarter billion dollars annually on NGOs like The Asia Foundation for "Anti-communist academicians to disseminate a negative vision of mainland China[239]". Udo Ulfkotte[240], Editor of the *Frankfurter Allgemeine Zeitung*, says no significant European journalist, including himself, is free of CIA influence.

Publishers add their own disinformation, says Ann Lee[241], "A reporter and friend of Michael Massing,[242] who worked at the Beijing office of

237 "The CIA and the Media: How America's Most Powerful News Media Worked Hand in Glove with the Central Intelligence Agency and Why the Church Committee Covered It Up". Carl Bernstein. Rolling Stone, 1977.

238 The CIA and the cult of intelligence – 1976. by V. Marchetti. (It is the first book the US Government ever went to Court to censor before its publication).

239 Some of those writings resurfaced in 2017 when China's Censor asked Cambridge University Press to retract three hundred journal articles about a non-existent massacre in Tiananmen Square. Claiming academic freedom, Cambridge refused, and the Censor yielded.

240 Gekaufte Journalisten (Bought Journalists), Udo Ulfkotte. Kopp Verlag. 2014. The English language edition, Journalists For Hire: How The CIA Buys The News, has been suppressed.

241 What the US Can Learn from China: An Open-Minded Guide to Treating Our Greatest Competitor as Our Greatest Teacher, by Ann Lee, 2012

242 Michael Massing was the former editor of *The Columbia Journalism Review*.

The Wall Street Journal told him that, by the time his stories went to press in Washington, his editors had taken advantage of the twelve-hour time difference and replaced all their Chinese interviews with statements from American talking heads who work at think tanks promoting anti-China perspectives".

While researching in Kashgar, Xinjiang Province, China, engineering Professor Patrik Meyer[243] saw, first-hand, how anti-China perspectives are manufactured:

> What CCTV billed as a 'Renovation Combining Tradition and Modernity,' The Washington Post headlined as, 'An Ancient Culture, Bulldozed Away,' The New York Times,' 'To Protect an Ancient City, China Moves to Raze It' and TIME, 'Tearing Down Old Kashgar: Another Blow to the Uyghurs.' As a tourist, these headlines resonate with me, too. I wish to keep the Kashgar Old Town untouched and be able to wander along its narrow, shaded alleys lined by adobe houses. However, if I were responsible for the living conditions and safety of its residents and the modernization of Kashgar writ large, I would see Beijing's transformation in a more positive light.
>
> Given the almost unprecedented access I was granted between 2010 and 2013 to conduct ethnopolitical research in Xinjiang–and my robust background in civil engineering–I consider myself well-positioned to provide a broader perspective on the issues raised by Western journalists when criticizing the KOT renewal project. A simple survey of Western media outlets shows that harsh criticism of Beijing's renewal of the KOT is built on four central arguments: demolition of Uyghur's historical heritage, destruction of Uyghur's social fabric, absence of Uyghurs' voices in the project, and the sufficient seismic performance of existing houses. Moreover, Western journalists often argue that the goal of Beijing's works in Kashgar is to weaken, or even erase, Uyghur identity, not to improve their living conditions.

243 Western Journalistic Confirmation Bias: Reporting on Kashgar's Old Town Renewal Project. By Patrik K. Meyer. The Diplomat, September 19, 2016

KOT's historical value is indisputable, but it is not as significant as assumed by Western critics. While some houses are centennial, with charismatic courtyards and beautifully decorated wooden frames, most of the houses are a poorly-built patchwork of old and new mud and masonry walls. Hence, while the old town as a whole has significant historical value, many of its houses are not historically valuable. Kashgar is one of the few Chinese cities where the old town is being partly preserved and remodeled following traditional standards. There is indeed some damage being caused to the Uyghurs' historical heritage. Still, it is far less significant than the Western critics claim, and it is intended to modernize Kashgar, not to "Demolish the Uyghur History," as argued by the Smithsonian.

The second dominant argument, the tearing apart of the Uyghur identity, is also happening, but again, not to the extent or for the purpose that it is being reported in the West. China's fast modernization results in numerous communities being reshaped and displaced, including the one in the KOT. However, when asked for their view about Beijing's renewal of the KOT, most of its dwellers welcome it. And for good reasons. Their houses are often very small, poorly ventilated, dusty and dark, have no toilets, and are impractical. It is those who *do not* live in the old town–Uyghurs, tourists, and Western journalists–who are most critical of the renewal project. Hence, I believe that the KOT project is causing Uyghur identity change, not its destruction, as argued by the West.

As for the third argument, that the Uyghurs have no say in the project, it is again only partially correct. Their voice is indeed absent from the upper levels of the project's decision-making process. However, most homeowners decide whether to stay or leave the KOT and how to proceed with the repair of their houses. They are offered three options to choose from, the first being to permanently move to a free, new apartment larger than their old house. Second, they can opt to let the Government tear down the old house and replace it with a new structure for free, which

> does not include finishing works such as flooring, windows, and decoration. When this work is being done, the families can rent an apartment subsidized by the Government at about $900 per year. If the house is deemed structurally sound, the homeowners are given a subsidy (about US $ 90/m2) to upgrade the house themselves.
>
> Additional subsidies are also offered for those willing to finish the façade using traditional Uyghur style. While there might be some irregularities within this system, most homeowners affected by the renewal of the KOT have the choice to stay or leave, which the Western critics seem to ignore. Finally, a fourth dominant argument against Beijing's KOT project is that the old town must be seismically safe because it has survived hundreds of years without being destroyed. Again, this is only partly true. Some houses were built properly over a hundred years ago. Still, the majority have been either poorly constructed or structurally modified in the last 30-50 years, making them prone to structural damage in case of a significant seismic event. Based on my expertise in adobe structures' seismic performance and my countless visits to the KOT, I can confirm that it is not feasible to retrofit most of its houses because of their deficient structural condition.

Though China's economy has grown faster, longer, and more consistently than any in history, our media remain relentlessly pessimistic. Reporting on China's Fourteenth Party Congress thirty year ago, in 1992, *The Economist* said the Party had 'stepped backwards' and called its socialist market economy 'an oxymoron.' At the next Congress[244] it reported, 'hollow promises, from privatization to unemployment goals, made and broken' and warned that 'raising people's expectations is a recipe for civil strife.' The Seventeenth Congress found the Party facing 'inevitable, looming crisis and unrest'. At the next Congress, *The Economist* found 'the entire country unstable at the grassroots, dejected at the middle strata

244 Out of the shadow of Deng–Print edition | Asia. September 18, 1997. BEIJING

and out of control at the top.' At the Nineteenth Congress, in 2017, China was at death's door. "Though Mr. Xi talked about a new era the next five years sound, from his speech, to be much like the past five–only more so … a risky assertion in a country where many are prospering but many feel left out," warning "not to expect Mr. Xi to change China, or the world, for the better".

Our media invariably celebrate the fictionalized memoirs of Chinese who criticize the PRC. They were fulsome in their praise for Jung Chang's *Mao: The Unknown Story*, though she is the daughter of a senior government official and was raised in a walled compound by a wet nurse with a nanny, maid, gardener, and chauffeur and educated in a special school for officials' children. After spending three weeks in the countryside during the Cultural Revolution (she found peasant students 'semi-literate' with 'little aptitude' for scholarship) she fled, exclaiming, "Mao intended me to live the rest of my life as a peasant," and was given a scholarship to study at a British university–a distant dream for millions. Yet literary reviewers–who doubtless shared her horror of being reduced, even briefly, to the status of an ordinary person–lauded her heroism.

***

Media censorship in China has changed little since 600 BC, when officials discussed the injunction[245] that, "Trying to stop the peoples' mouths is more difficult than stemming a river". A century later, when a disciple asked Confucius his first action if he were governor he replied, "I would make officials' words correspond to reality, *zhèngmíng*. Otherwise, undertakings cannot be completed". His disciple, Mencius, warned that without *zhèngmíng*, political plans and promises would never correspond to reality.

245 From The *Guoyu*, a collection of speeches attributed to rulers during the Warring States Period, 771–476 BC.

The world's first mass media were Chinese Buddhist sutras[246] printed on woodblock presses in 700 AD, and they were followed by millions of dictionaries, medical texts, and almanacs. A cheap, standard edition of the Confucian classics expanded access to the Imperial Examinations and the first extant book printed with moveable type, the *Manual of Agriculture*[247], was followed by manuals on dam building, surveying, irrigation, and fertilization. As John Stewart Mill[248] observed, "The Chinese are remarkable in the excellence of their apparatus for implanting, as far as possible, their best wisdom in every mind in the community".

Senior officials practiced propaganda, *xuānchuán*, 'transforming the people through honorable behavior and instruction,' and lectured on the Emperor's Sacred Maxims while exemplifying them in daily life. Edgar Snow[249] saw Communist *xuānchuán* in 1937.

> However badly the Communists have erred at times, however tragic have been their excesses, however exaggerated has been the emphasis here or the stress there, it has been their sincere and sharply felt propaganda aim to shake, to arouse the millions of rural Chinese to their responsibilities in society; to awaken them to a belief in human rights; to combat the timidity, passivity and static faiths of Taoism and Confucianism; to educate, to persuade and, I have no doubt, at times to beleaguer and coerce them to fight for 'the reign of the people,' a new vision in rural China; to fight for a life of justice, equality, freedom and human dignity as the Communists see it.

Mao[250] was emphatic, "Unless you have investigated a problem you

246 The world's oldest, dated, printed book, the Diamond Sūtra, is marked, "For free public distribution". The sutra aims to emancipate practitioners from the fundamental ignorance of not knowing how to experience reality as it is. It promises the liberation by giving without attachment to self, liberating beings without notions of self or other, living without attachment, and cultivating without attainment.

247 Wang Zhen's Manual of Agriculture, was published using Bi Sheng's invention, movable type in 1045 AD.

248 *On Liberty.* John Stewart Mill. 1863.

249 Snow, Edgar. *Red Star Over China*, Victor Gollancz 1937. p.120

250 Oppose Book Worship. May 1930

will be deprived of the right to speak on it. Is that too harsh? Not at all! When you have not probed a problem and know nothing of its essentials, nor investigated the relevant facts and their history, whatever you say about it will unavoidably be nonsense, and talking nonsense solves no problems, as everyone knows. So why is it unjust to deprive you of the right to speak? How can a Communist keep his eyes shut and talk nonsense? It won't do! It won't do! You must investigate! You must not talk nonsense!"

The Chinese, though they speak freely in private, understand that they have no special right to opine publicly on any subject, "Only those who do should speak. Those who speak must do".

For thousands of years their Chief Censors, who are responsible for accurate public information, have been distinguished scholars. The present incumbent, Wang Huning[251], is China's leading public intellectual. President Jiang persuaded him to join his staff by quoting passages from his celebrated books[252] from memory. President Hu promoted him to the Politburo, and President Xi brought him onto the six-man Steering Committee. Wang's authority is Constitutional: "Once a policy has been widely discussed, voted on, and legislated, discussion is suspended and everyone unites to implement it". Thus, as Ren Xianliang[253] explains,

> The relationship of the Government and the Party to the media is different from that in western countries. In the West, these relationships are often adversarial debates with the media, with many pointed questions. This is not true in China because the political system is quite different. The core value of the Chinese Communist Party is 'to serve the people with all your heart,' and it embodies the fundamental values of Marxism. The people are

---

251 Chairman of the Central Guidance Commission on Building a Spiritual Civilization

252 His Master's thesis, *From Bodin to Maritain: On Sovereignty Theories Developed by the Western Bourgeoisie*, won wide acclaim, and his Ph.D. thesis, *Comparative Political Analysis*, is considered a classic.

253 The Art of Guiding Public Opinion—How Leading Cadres Handle the Media. By Ren Xianliang, Vice Chairman of the China Journalists' Association. David Cowhig's Translation Blog.

> the masters of China, and officials are their servants[254]. This is often said, but many leaders don't know what it means and do not put it into practice. They don't take seriously the problem of creating an effective system for releasing news to satisfy as much as possible the people's right to know.
>
> People have a constitutional right to know, express themselves, participate in management and decisions about public life, and exercise oversight of the state. The media supports the right to know, warn society, exercise government oversight, participate in the market economy, and reconcile various interests. The media are the ears of the Party and Government and their microphone. A classic example of the news media in action was the Watergate affair. Watergate's lesson is that failure to understand the media can be fatal to a government or a ruler. Lies cannot substitute for the truth, and the truth cannot long be concealed.

The Constitution is explicit: "Citizens have the right to criticize and make suggestions regarding any State organ or official, to make complaints or charges against relevant State organs and expose any State organ or functionary for violation of law or dereliction of duty".

However, we must bear in mind that, for every Western advocate of mass shooting, racial pogroms, hate crimes, and war, there are four Chinese, four times crazier, doing the same. The Censor imposes mass media rules on them and anyone with more than five thousand social media followers. No infringing, fake accounts, libel, disclosing trade secrets, or invading privacy; no sending porn to attract users; no torture, violence, killing of people or animals; no selling lethal weapons, gambling, phishing, scamming, or spreading viruses; no organizing crime, counterfeiting, false advertising, empty promises or bullying; no lotteries, rumor-mongering, promoting superstitions; no content opposing the basic principles of the Constitution, national unity, sovereignty, or

254 *The People are supreme, the state is secondary, and the Ruler is least important. Only those who please the people can rule.* Mencius. Mengzi (372–289 BC), 孟軻, was born near modern Zoucheng, Shandong Province, just south of Qufu, Confucius's birthplace. An itinerant teacher and sage, he was the principal interpreter of Confucianism.

territorial integrity; no divulging State secrets or endangering national security.

His explanations of sensitive topics in 2019 are instructive[255]: The China-US trade war (irresponsible speech could derail them). US sanctions on Huawei (don't inflame anti-America sentiments). The arrest of Huawei's Mèng Wǎnzhōu (don't inflame anti-Canada sentiments). The first genetically-edited baby ([256]). The Changsheng vaccine scandal (self-reported, no harm done, don't sensationalize). Movie star Fàn Bīngbīng's tax scandal (her first offense, she was poorly advised, she made restitution, she apologized, so leave her alone).

In 2016, Wang's office reprimanded the nationalistic *Global Times* for publishing surveys about reunifying Taiwan by force, President Trump's election, and the release of a Tiananmen arsonist. "These surveys are serious violations of news discipline, sensitive issues likely to cause offense to foreign nations. They have created political fallout and publishers should learn from this and refrain from polls". The *Global Times* publisher grumbled, "The *Global Times* is pro-government but it's also market-based, not just State-controlled". But Wang's biggest headache is rumors.

A 2017 story about RYB Kindergartens torturing children went viral, and the censor intervened[257], "Please prevent malicious hyping of the RYB Kindergarten matter. Social media accounts that exaggerate the situation should be closed on sight or have content deleted". Investigators heard that a teacher had pricked children with a sewing needle and detained her, but they found that the accusations had been fabricated by parents who confessed and apologized. Wearily, the Censor concluded, "Public security organs will always thoroughly investigate and punish real illegal and criminal harms to minors in accordance with the law and also strictly handle intentional fabrication and dissemination of rumors. At the same time, we appeal to everyone to approach information on the

255 Censored on WeChat: A year of content removals on China's most powerful social media platform.
256 The babies were born into a village with 30% HIV infection
257 The police again report on the Red, Yellow, and Blue kindergarten. 2017/11/28 China Law Translate Legal News

Internet rationally and cautiously". But the Censor intervened too late: a class action lawsuit reduced RYB Kindergartens' valuation on the New York Stock Exchange by forty percent.

In 2018, censors yanked a viral essay[258] about the capital's migrant workers, *Beijing Has 20 Million People Pretending to Live Here.* "This essay polarizes relations between prosperous Beijingers and the immigrants who sweep our streets and may thus inflame bad feelings towards these vulnerable people". In 2019, netizens blamed Wang for not censoring enough when a female doctor committed suicide after being targeted by social media.

Today, twenty-five-thousand independent outlets publish romances, pornography, intellectual journals, political, financial, and tomes on Swiss democracy. Seven-thousand periodicals, three-thousand cable channels, a thousand radio stations, and seven-hundred T.V. stations struggle to distinguish themselves in a cutthroat market where niches are worth billions. Says Alice L. Miller[259],

> Virtually every topic of conceivable interest to Chinese politics and policy students now has specialist periodicals devoted to it. This diversity includes publications on previously sensitive issues like foreign affairs and military issues. Since the early 1980s, previously-restricted specialist publications dealing with various aspects of international affairs–journals such as American Studies and Taiwan Studies–and new publications such as Chinese Diplomacy became openly available. In military affairs, the Academy of Military Science's premier journal, Chinese Military Science, became available for home delivery to Western students of the PLA. In the 1990s, PRC media began routinely to carry opinion pieces by the growing community of foreign policy. National security specialists in China frequently offered competing–even clashing–perspectives on international

---

258 , "Beijing Has 20 Million People Pretending to Live Here" (Full Translation) by Zhang Wumao. What's on Weibo. July 26, 2017. By Manya Koetse

259 Alice L. Miller. Analyzing the Chinese Leadership in an Era of Sex, Money, and Power. China Leadership Monitor, Issue 57 (Fall 2018).

issues, raising fundamental questions among Western analysts about what political authority to attach to them in Beijing's policy process… The proliferation of websites hosted by news agencies such as Xinhua has given immediate access to streams of information and commentary far surpassing anything easily accessible by traditional means.

Maria Repnikova[260] found journalism alive and well:

In the past decade, a popular depiction of Chinese media has been that of a fearful, loyal agent of the ruthless party-state, which exudes no tolerance towards its critics. Indoctrinated to channel official propaganda to the public, silenced by censorship, and threatened by coercion, Chinese journalists function in one of the world's most challenging places when it comes to media freedom…

What goes unnoticed beneath the stark imagery of collision between the mighty state and the fearless, isolated critics is the web of complex negotiations between some Chinese journalists and party officials. Specifically, whereas the majority of Chinese reporting still adheres to the propaganda model, in the past three decades, an exceptional practice of what I term 'critical journalism,' including investigative, in-depth, editorial, and human-interest coverage of contentious societal issues, has emerged in China amid the restrictive environment. What unites these journalists is their pursuit of social justice and their quest to push the envelope of permissible reporting.

They exposed stories such as the 2002 AIDS epidemic in Henan province, the 2003 Sun Zhigang case of a migrant worker illegally detained and beaten to death in Guangzhou, the scandalous school demolitions in the 2008 Sichuan earthquake, the 2008 milk-poisoning scandal, widespread environmental protests, and food safety crises among other contentious issues. In

260 *Media Politics in China: Improvising Power under Authoritarianism by Maria Repnikova, C.U.P., July 15, 2017.*

> most cases, their stories raised a wide public outcry, as manifested in active discussions online. In some cases, they also produced a moderate policy shift ... recently demonstrated in the courageous investigative reporting of Tianjin's major chemical explosion.

Investigative journalism is flourishing. Cui Yongyuan[261], whose talk show, *Tell It Like It Is*, garnered twenty-million Weibo followers, catalyzed a national debate in 2013. By vehemently opposing the Government's plan to introduce genetically modified food and making heated, personal attacks on G.M. food supporters, he helped defeat the legislation. Then he charged China's highest-paid actress, Fan Bingbing, with cheating on her taxes, triggering a tax audit that cost the entertainment industry two-billion dollars in taxes and fines. He publicly accused Shanghai police of taking huge bribes while investigating the case and of ignoring death threats to himself and his daughter. He publicly ridiculed them when they claimed they had been unable to reach him. In 2020, Beijing charged Shanghai's police chief, Gong Daoan, with corruption.

Cui then turned his sights on the Supreme Court and published an obscenity-laden Weibo post accusing the President of the Supreme Court of malfeasance and demanding to know why critical case files were missing. A leaked videotape showed a Supreme Court judge hinting that CCTV cameras had been sabotaged when the documents were stolen from his office. A leaked image of the case file's cover page showed a judge's directive to keep the case secret. After first denying them, the Court admitted Cui's allegations were valid and promised to investigate. The public uproar caused President Xi to intervene personally and he told the judiciary to 'investigate the scandal openly and scrape away the poison.' Cui said that he challenged the Court to uphold justice and to educate people about the law, "In China there today there are too many damn people afraid of getting into trouble and too few with the guts to speak the truth".

The Censor is remarkably tolerant of contrary points of view. For thirty years, Beijing funded a monthly journal, *China Through the Ages*,

261 Meet Sui Yongyuan, Chat Show Host: China's Unlikeliest Whistleblower. SCMP January 26, 2019

whose one-hundred-thousand subscribers enjoyed its attacks on 'the Party's self-serving narrative about the Cultural Revolution,' its advocacy of constitutional, multi-party democracy, and privatization of State assets. Only after the journal praised Zhao Ziyang, the Cabinet Minister who collaborated with the CIA during the Tiananmen demonstrations, did Beijing lose patience and cancel its subsidy. The editor went down fighting, "This magazine will stop publication due to policy changes reflecting the establishment's intolerance of reformers and liberals". Imagine the US Government funding *America Through the Ages* for thirty years while it advocated one-party rule, workers' ownership of the means of production, and the abolition of competitive, multi-party elections.

Deborah Fallows[262] found that eighty percent of citizens want the media controlled and almost all want the Government controlling it. University students say the censorship is too strict, adults think it strikes the right balance, and older folk criticize its laxness, but few find it repressive. One graduate student praised[263] it, "Our Internet is already in chaos and the Chinese Government is not the only one having paid commentators, for sure. Western governments and others also hire people to create and circulate opinions about democratizing China or colonizing China again. They probably want a Chinese version of the Arab Spring. I believe censorship is necessary to resist some of these influences".

In 2009, the Censor blocked Facebook and Google[264] for ignoring content guidelines, but interest in them was never high, as researchers found in 2018[265], when they gave two-thousand elite Beijing University students free software that bypassed the Great Firewall. The students

---

262 Most Chinese Say They Approve of Government Internet Control, by Deborah Fallows, Pew Internet & American Life Project. March 27, 2008.

263 A Confucian Look at Internet Censorship in China. Yubo Kou, Bryan Semaan, Bonnie Nardi. September 2017

264 The 2009 Urumqi religious rioters killed over 200 civilians and injured thousands through a coordinated Facebook campaign. When the Government asked Facebook to cooperate with the Police, Facebook refused. The Government has blocked it ever since. In 2010, Google announced that it would not conform to China's censorship laws. China blocked it, along with Twitter and YouTube, which took the same stance. Google simply withdrew from the market rather than follow the Censor's guidelines.

265 The Impact of Media Censorship: Evidence from a Field Experiment in China. Yuyu Chen, Guanghua School of Management, Peking University; David Y. Yang, Department of Economics, Stanford University. January 4, 2018

showed little interest in Western opinions and, even after repeated reminders, only half activated the software. Fifteen percent of those soon uninstalled it and the most active users browsed non-political content. Only when offered small cash prizes did they visit the New York Times or other suggested sites. When the trial finished, the few who renewed their subscriptions used it for Google searches or to access social media and entertainment.

Other investigators found that those who accessed international media using VPNs[266] were more critical of Western governments and media than those relying on domestic media alone–probably because Chinese media rarely criticize other countries. Says Professor Deborah Cai[267], "Chinese reporting on the US appears to be relatively balanced overall. Extremely negative tones toward the US are rare and appear mostly during periods of overt Sino-US confrontation, such as the [South China Sea] reconnaissance plane incident".

Harvard's Gary King[268] adds, "Contrary to much research and commentary, the purpose of the censorship program is not to suppress criticism of the State or the Communist Party. Despite widespread censorship of social critics we find that, when Chinese people write scathing criticisms of their Government and its leaders, the probability that their post will be censored does not increase. Instead, censored tweets were equally likely to be against the state, for the state, irrelevant, or factual reports about events. Negative, even vitriolic criticism of the state, its leaders and its policies are not more likely to be censored".

What's the bottom line?

Do China's government-censored media inform their citizenry better than our media?

---

266 Virtual Private Networks

267 Deborah A. Cai, *Perspectives Toward the United States in Selected Newspapers of the People's Republic of China.* University of Maryland Institute for Global Chinese Affairs and the Department of Communications, May 2002, pp. 6–7.

268 "Reverse-Engineering Chinese Censorship". Harvard Magazine, Gary King, September 12, 2013

Each year Reporters Without Borders[269], RSF, funded by Western media owners, asks publishers to grade their media markets' freedom by pluralism, independence, political environment, self-censorship, legislation, and transparency. The RSF survey ranks America's media freedom forty-first, Singapore's government-regulated media at #154 and China's dead last, at #176.

But when asked by the Edelman Corporation[270] what news sources they *trust*, readers voted overwhelmingly for government media. Australians trust the ABC, Canadians trust the CBC, Britons trust the BBC, Singaporeans trust SBC, and the Chinese trust CCTV. And the American Press Institute[271] found, "Just six percent of Americans say they have a lot of confidence in the media, putting the news industry about equal to Congress and well below the public's view of other institutions".

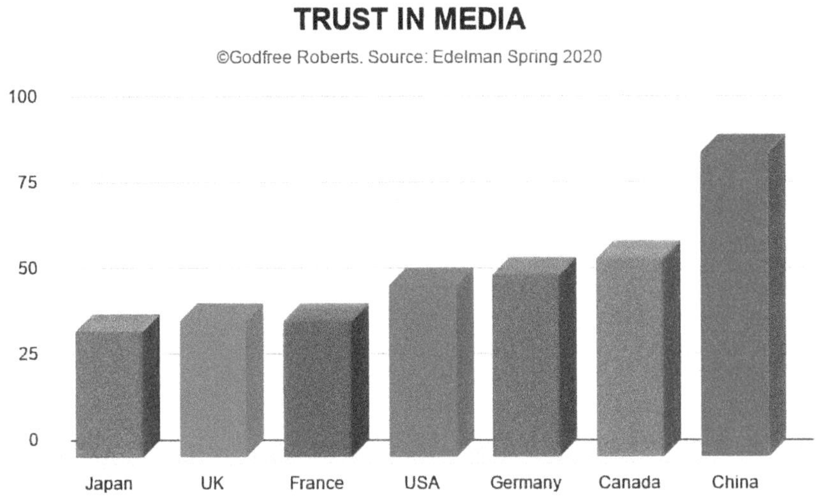

269 2018 World Press Freedom Index
270 2018 Edelman Trust Barometer, January 2018.
271 An alarmingly low number of Americans say they trust the media. Carole Feldman and Emily Swanson, Associated Press April 18, 2016.

CHAPTER 16

Law and Virtue

If people are ruled by uniform laws and penalized uniformly, they'll try to avoid punishment but never develop a sense of shame. If admirable leaders' fine example inspires them, they'll emulate them, internalize their ethics, and gradually become good themselves. Confucius

***

Western legislators, who once claimed Divine authority for their laws, now endorse 'the rule of law[272]' for its own sake. But this raises a question we have never satisfactorily answered: who keeps the lawgivers honest? *Quis custodiet custodes?*

Confucius' answer, on the other hand, has satisfied the Chinese for two millennia.

272 Gallup found one-fourth of us trust our criminal justice system. Says Jiang Shigong, in *Philosophy and History- Reading the China Dream*: "The rule of law and the rule of man are not completely opposed to one another but are complementary. A society governed by the rule of law cannot ignore the need to provide people with ideals, beliefs, and moral education. It cannot ignore the positive role played by moral values and a healthy social climate in governance, nor can it ignore the key historical function of leaders and great people, political parties and the masses".

In 340 BC, Lord Shang[273], Chancellor to Duke Xiao advocated the rule of law because, he said, people are too lazy and passionate to create peace and prosperity themselves, so a system of collective responsibility and surveillance must frighten them sufficiently to suppress crime. Lord Shang instituted a harsh code of penalties and rewards, "If small faults are pardoned, crimes will be numerous". Shang replaced clan-based law with a harsh, intrusive, law-and-order code that weakened families and communes. He prescribed horrific punishments for those who fled the battlefield while heavily taxing merchants, scholars, and 'parasites' and giving aristocratic titles to those with high grain yields and military successes. Though his code transformed the State of Qin into a victorious Sparta, it generated such profound resentment that, when the Duke of Qin died, Lord Shang fled. He tried to hide at an inn, but the innkeeper turned him away because Shang's code forbade inns to admit guests without identification. Following Shang's law, the innkeeper reported him to the authorities and, according to the punishment that his code prescribed, Shang was fastened to five chariots and torn apart and his family, to nine levels of kinship, was annihilated by *lingchi*, death by a thousand cuts. Popular reaction to Shang's regime of terror led to the overthrow of the Qin Dynasty, and 'the rule of law' retains its odium in China to this day.

Confucius, born when Lord Shang's gruesome fate was still fresh in popular memory, assumed that, once morality is established, the legal will naturally converge on it. He insisted that humans are born with four essential virtues–compassion, righteousness, propriety, and wisdom. Social influences and lack of education cause crime, but wrongdoers could learn to feel ashamed of improper actions if provided with good example, education, and moral suasion. Since good example was primary,

273 The Book of Lord Shang, Shāng jūn shū, dates from the 3rd century BC, and is regarded as a foundational work of Chinese Legalism and is named after the significant Qin reformer Shang Yang, who served as minister to Duke Xiao of Qin (r. 361 – 338 BC) from 359 BC until his death in 338 BC and is generally considered to be the father of that State's "legalism".[2] The book includes many ordinances, essays, courtly petitions, and discourses delivered at the Qin court. The book focuses on maintaining societal order through impartial laws that reward and punish citizens' actions. The first chapters advise promoting agriculture, suppressing secondary activities, encouraging martial virtues, and creating a state army for wars of conquest.

he said, society should revolve around superior men, *jūn zǐ*, who put righteousness and propriety before selfishness and pettiness, and only they should be admitted to Government for, "He who rules by virtue is like the North Star, which maintains its place and the multitude of stars pay homage".

If social roles–fathers, mothers, husbands, wives, subjects, and officials–are clearly defined and if rulers demonstrate filial piety, compassion, and virtue, and if citizens act according to ritual propriety, society will prosper. Therefore, rulers' primary responsibility is to sacrifice their own desires, perform expected rituals on society's behalf, and demonstrate compassion by providing livelihoods for all because "Only when the granary is full can we expect moral behavior".

Not every emperor was virtuous nor every official compassionate but, over the centuries, there were enough to transform society into Confucius's national family, says F.W. Mote[274], "More important than penal law and judicial procedures in maintaining order in the community were the methods of arbitration and compromise. That route to resolving disputes allowed the parties to retain their dignity, utilized social pressures as understood by all and gave problem-solving roles to senior figures acting as arbitrators that reinforced the community's recognition of its shared ethical norms. Some regions of China were known to be more litigious, more quarrelsome, less placid than others but, throughout their observations of ordinary Chinese life from the sixteenth century onward, early European travelers remarked on the mannerliness, good humor, and social graces of the common people".

***

When he launched his anti-corruption drive in 2012, President Xi promised[275] to govern by virtuous example, *hide zhiguo,* and to create a socialist spiritual civilization, *jingshen wenming.* Four years later, in langua-

274 Imperial China 900-1800. F.W. Mote. Harvard University Press. 2003.
275 Report, 18th Party Congress, November 8, 2012. Xi was quoting from Confucius' Analects.

ge that would have pleased Confucius, he reminded[276] a judicial study group that law and ethics are inextricably bound:

> Law is virtue expressed in words, and virtue is law borne in people's hearts. In the State's eyes, law and virtue have equal status in regulating social behavior, adjusting social relations, and maintaining social order. The rule of law must embody moral ideals that provide reliable institutional support for virtue. Laws and regulations should promote virtuous behavior while socialist core values–prosperity, democracy, civility, harmony, freedom, equality, justice, the rule of law, patriotism, dedication, integrity, and friendliness–should be woven into legislation, law enforcement, and the judicial process.

Even today, members of the National Family[277] still address older strangers as 'aunty,' 'uncle,' 'grandfather,' or 'grandmother,' every adult assumes responsibility for every child, and clans and families law settle ninety percent of disputes. Would-be criminals must struggle against family, friends, workmates, classmates, and neighbors who counsel, mediate, and compromise[278] to keep them on the path of virtue. Families use persuasion, education, and individually tailored solutions that they can enforce far more effectively than the police.

So effective is mediation that Congress now requires villages to maintain People's Mediation Committees[279], courthouses to maintain mediation offices, and lawyers to become certified mediators. In 2019,

276 Xi stresses integrating law, virtue in state governance. Xinhua. 2016-12-10

277 The Chinese term for the nation-state is 'nation-family,' and most Chinese take for granted that the nation-state is an extended family.

278 Failure to do so can bring consequences. In 2018, when Liu Zehnhua committed suicide after raping and murdering Li Mingzhu, the court ordered Liu's family to pay the Li family one-hundred-thousand-dollars for failing to socialize their son.

279 In addition to People's Mediation conducted by grassroots community mediators, China employs Judicial Mediation conducted by judges, Administrative Mediation led by government officials, Arbitral Mediation conducted by arbitral administrative bodies, and Industry Mediation conducted by specific industrial associations.

mediators handled six million disputes and reduced the national legal bill to one-tenth of America's[280].

Penal law still plays a minor role in everyday life and the judicial process–originally designed to protect the State from the people–remains a work in progress.

As in France, magistrates are regarded as neutral truth-seekers who interrogate suspects, examine evidence, hear testimony, render verdicts, and determine guilt and innocence pre-trial. A Shanghai Trial Spot provides defense lawyers for all criminal defendants but elsewhere, they are mandatory only for juveniles, the disabled, and those facing life imprisonment or death. If evidence for conviction is insufficient, magistrates suggest that the procurate either reduce the charges or investigate further. Since most casework involves paper depositions, the Western custom of cross-examining witnesses under oath before a judge is uncommon but, while American defendants lose their Fifth Amendment rights against self-incrimination if they testify, Chinese defendants may say whatever they wish in their defense or refuse to be cross-examined, without prejudice. If the investigating magistrate decides that the defendant is guilty, the case goes to a sentencing hearing and, even if a defendant confesses and wishes to end the matter, the magistrate must hold an open hearing and ask the defendant to confirm his confession publicly.

Though lawyers' reputations in Chinese society have always been poor, the profession was boosted in 2012 when Li Keqiang[281], an expert on English common law, became Premier, and the Supreme Court's internship program began attracting top students. Next, President Xi suggested establishing independent judicial committees with non-Party members to select judges based on merit and professional track record. By 2019, every province had an independent judicial committee to minimize local government interference, establish and oversee judges and prosecutors' work, and punish professional misconduct. Shanghai's

---

280 Average Person Spends $250 Per Year on Legal Services. Jay Reeves | April 14, 2015. Lawyers Mutual

281 At Peking University Law School in 1978, Li translated Lord Denning's "The Due Process of Law," becoming so proficient in the language that he broke protocol and spoke in fluent English at a Hong Kong University event in 2011.

committee expelled a High Court prosecutor, two sub-prosecutors, the Vice President of the Provincial Supreme Court, and a senior circuit court judge. National appeals courts now re-hear cases, overturn wrongful convictions, order restitution, and require lower courts to study their reversals.

The Supreme People's Court's website, with five billion visits, offers online courses on every element of the law, invites criticism of new regulations, and provides an artificial intelligence interface to its six-hundred-thousand recorded trials. Its website invites citizens to email the Chief Justice, whose answers begin cheerily, "Hello! We received your question, and after consideration, we respond as follows..." and end with, "Thank you for your support of the work of the Supreme People's Court!"

Since their ethical duty transcends their legal responsibility, the courts ultimately answer to the Party which, as the arbiter of national ethics, blocks unethical decisions[282]. Chief Justice Xiao Yang explained, "The power of the courts to adjudicate independently doesn't mean independence from the Party at all. On the contrary, it embodies a high degree of responsibility vis-à-vis the Party's [*dàtóng*[283]] program".

Citizens can video police, who must publish the status of all arrestees online. Police, prosecutors, and court officials are responsible for wrongful prosecutions until the day they die, but, though unarmed, police have powers of which their Western colleagues dream. Instead of removing miscreants from society, they can issue temporary restraining orders and mandate home confinement–which provides wrongdoers an opportunity to discuss solutions with their families. Convicted criminals, who can prosecute prison staff for breaching their rights, must receive humane levels of material comfort and dignity from arrest to release.

282 In 2010, the US Supreme Court ruled that corporations can spend unlimited money on elections because limiting corporations' "independent political spending" violates their First Amendment right to free speech.

283 A *dàtóng* society is the Chinese Dream, which Confucian scholar Kang Youwei rendered thus: "Now to have states, families, and selves is to allow each individual to maintain a sphere of selfishness. This infracts utterly the Universal Principle (gongli) and impedes progress... The only [true way] is sharing the world in common by all (*tienxia weigong*). This is the way of the Great Community, *dàtóng*, which prevailed in the Age of Universal Peace. *Commentary on Liyun*.

Sentences are typically short, prisoners must participate in career, legal, cultural, and moral counseling, and even murderers are expected to repent, reform, and rejoin society.

TV programs regularly explain new laws, while schools, offices, factories, mines, and army units discuss concepts like excluding illegally obtained evidence. After the success of a weekly TV show, *I am a Barrister*, the Legal Channel screened *The Lawyers Are Here*. Each episode introduces a legal issue, ranging from child custody to healthcare negligence, and experts offer opinions and advise real litigants on air.

Online Trial Spots are reducing legal costs, promoting equitable outcomes, and lightening the burden of enforcement. One app bundles free mediation, dispute settlement, and legal aid and connects plaintiffs to thousands of lawyers, notaries, and judicial appraisers. Another verifies plaintiffs' and defendants' IDs and combines face and speech recognition with electronic signatures, allowing them to go to trial without leaving home. Using voice-to-text, it submits their files, transcribes their testimonies, and stores their case records in case of appeal.

Beijing's Internet Court provides an artificial intelligence-based risk assessment as a public service and automatically generates legal documents, applies machine translation, and simplifies settlements through oral interaction with its knowledge base. In 2017 Hangzhou, home of Alibaba, launched the first cyber court exclusively for online e-commerce complaints, loan litigation, and copyright infringement. In its inaugural case, TikTok sued Baidu for ownership of user-generated video content.

With unarmed police, two percent of America's legal professionals, and one-fourth of its policing budget, the Chinese have the world's lowest imprisonment and re-offense rates. When Harvard's Tony Saich[284] surveyed them about their greatest worry, they ranked 'Maintenance of Social Order' highest, and when he asked which government service pleased them most, they again chose 'Maintenance of Social Order.'

284 How China's citizens view the quality of governance under Xi Jinping. Tony Saich. Journal of Chinese Governance. Vol 1, 2016

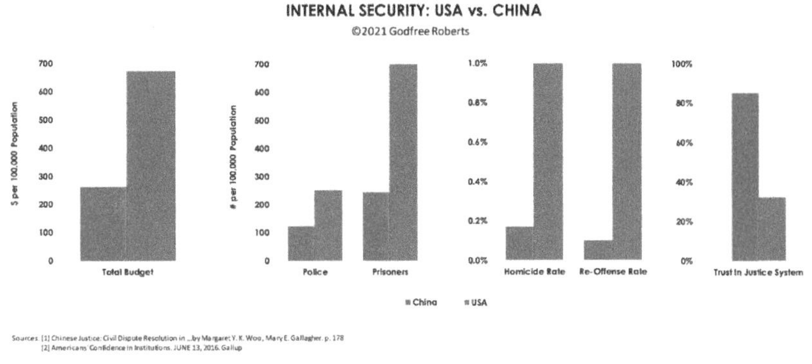

***

In 1982, as consumption began driving the economy, Beijing launched Consumer Rights Day. Vendors took to the streets, experts discussed product quality, and TV screens showed fake merchandise being shredded, crushed, and burned. Though consumers are more sophisticated nowadays, one element of the program remains popular: CEOs of cheating corporations are hauled before a billion gleeful viewers to beg forgiveness and promise to change their ways. Most CEOs are local, but Apple[285] persistently ignored China's two-year warranty law, Tim Cook apologized publicly and changed the policy. Volkswagen and Nikon's CEOs also took the Walk of Shame, groveled gratifyingly, and altered company policies.

Congress mandated[286] ethical manufacturing, truthful advertising, secure distribution, honest payment, and reliable delivery, but consumers remained reticent to transact business on the Internet, so legislators required retailers to accept returns unconditionally within seven days, pay doubled fines for false advertising, and refund three times the price of counterfeit goods. Nike, which had lobbied for the law, urged consumers to profit from it–and online counterfeits disappeared.

285 China Has a Way Better iPhone Warranty Than America to Go with Its Apology from Apple. The Atlantic. REBECCA GREENFIELD. APR 1, 2013

286 China Releases Draft Implementing Regulations for Consumer Rights Protection Law. By Ashwin Kaja and John Balzano. Global Policy Watch. August 26, 2016

In 2014, the State Council[287] issued its *Planning Outline for the Construction of a Social Credit System by 2020* and launched the most significant national attitude adjustment since the Cultural Revolution, "Declining trust has transformed us from a community of acquaintances into a society of strangers. Our integrity system is weak, and we suffer from unhealthy social phenomena like economic disputes, telecommunications fraud, mistrust, and indifference to human feelings. Integrity systems must begin with government honesty, promise-keeping, and respect for morality and customs. Next, we must make genuine efforts to strengthen the integrity of our entire society[288]".

Warning that officials and corporations would be the first Social Credit targets, the Academy of Social Sciences[289] encouraged Trial Spots to discourage corruption, cheating, debt-dodging, shoddy products, irresponsible medical treatment, commercial fraud, tax evasion, and product piracy. *The People's Daily* called for publicly accessible corporate credit dossiers to promote sincerity, *chengxin*, and trustworthiness, *yongxin,* and planners proposed a timeline: establish fundamental laws, regulations, and standards for social behavior; construct a social credit information system for the entire society; build credit supervision and management systems; then foster a social credit service market with mechanisms that encourage honesty and integrity.

Social Credit, SCS, is a data-sharing service[290], "Founded on laws, regulations and standards, based on a complete network covering the credit records of members of society and credit infrastructure, supported by the lawful application of credit information and services, it aims to establish a culture of sincerity, to keep trust, encourage traditional virtues, and employ incentives and constraints against breaking trust".

---

287 The 35-member State Council is chief administrative authority and national Brains Trust. Chaired by the Premier, it includes the heads of all the cabinet-level executive departments. It is one of three interlocking branches of state power, along with the Party and the PLA, and oversees the Provincial Governments.

288 'Legal Documents Related to the Social Credit System.' chinalawtranslate.com/

289 The Chinese Social Credit System Surveillance and Social Manipulation: A Solution to Moral Decay? Martin Maurtvedt KIN 4593. The UNIVERSITY OF OSLO. 2017

290 China's Social Credit System: An Evolving Practice of Control. By Rogier Creemers, University of Leiden

The first phase[291] focused on government and corporate transparency, and watchdogs discovered one-thousand government officials on the list[292] of violators. By 2019, one-hundred towns and cities had been listed as dishonest, their credit ratings downgraded, and their senior officials blocked from taking high-speed trains, visiting golf courses and expensive hotels, and purchasing real estate. Blacklisted companies' corporate officers are banned from heading other enterprises for three years and must submit to increased inspection frequency, and increased discretionary penalties and business-to-business and business-to-consumer platforms must alert users if they are listed. Professionals, like pharmacists, are simply de-registered. In its first full year of operation, SCS blacklisted seven thousand enterprises, denied air travel to ten-million deadbeats, and blocked four-million credit abusers from buying high-speed rail tickets.

In 2017, the Ministries of Finance, Customs, and Ecology cooperated to lower the wages of sin. They blocked crooked corporations from issuing bonds or receiving government subsidies, tax breaks, permits, and loans, purchasing real estate, owning land-use rights, exploiting natural resources, and issuing IPOs. They blocked crooked executives from company directorships, job promotions, asset ownership, establishing financial companies, receiving stock options, participating in government procurement, and working in high-trust sectors like food, pharmaceuticals, and chemicals. The system also blocked them from first-class travel, hotels, restaurants, resorts, nightclubs and golf courses, foreign holidays, sending offspring to private schools, and even buying homes and automobiles.

By 2020, sixty-one-thousand companies and government agencies had been penalized[293]. Counterfeiting and food and drug violations had fallen dramatically, and the EU Chamber of Commerce in Beijing warned members:

291 Social Credit Overview. Jeremy Daum. China Law Translate. 2018/10/31.
292 "Officials' dishonesty" cases? The court carries out special clean-up. People's Daily. December 21, 2017.
293 China Economic Daily. China Economic Net

> Under this far-reaching system, your company and executives will be subject to a series of rewards and punishments, with firms at risk of being blacklisted for non-compliance. The system has started monitoring the behavior of Chinese companies abroad–particularly those involved in the Belt and Road Initiative–in an attempt to safeguard the country's interests and reputation. Monitoring of European companies' behavior in other markets, including their cooperation and business relationships with Chinese companies–even if they are not present in China–is possible in the future.

Consumers, officials, and corporations now interact with SCS through innovative apps using data from the National Credit Information Sharing Platform to help the market weed out bad actors[294]. It crowdsources commercial supervision and acts as a neutral record keeper that consolidates government files into a central database and integrates and regulates data exchanges and information sharing across geographic regions and professional fields. It incentivizes trustworthy conduct and punishes untrustworthy behavior, increases reliance on credit evaluations in transactions, and employs these mechanisms, along with moral education, to foster a trusting social environment.

***

With the government and corporate program bearing fruit, planners turned to individuals. Professor Zhang Zheng[295] explained the program simply, "There are two kinds of people in this world: good people and bad people. Now imagine a world where the good ones are rewarded and the bad ones are punished, and untrustworthiness in one place leads to constraints everywhere".

When statistics revealed that a staggering seventy percent of individuals and organizations evaded enforcement or failed to perform court-ordered obligations, the Supreme Court ruled that their identities

---

294 *The apps of China's Social Credit System.* by Kendra Schaefer. Trivium. October 14, 2019
295 CREATING THE HONEST MAN. JULY 28, 2017. Kai Strittmatter. Schoolinfosystem.org

could be listed publicly for up to two years. The first targets were debt defaulters, *laolai,* so the People's Bank of China incorporated court records into credit reports, revised its penalties, and created The Deadbeat Checker, a public blacklist searchable by agency, department, institutional, and individual name.

Dengfeng's *laolai* Trial Spot used automatic recordings to warn callers, "The person you are calling is listed as dishonest by the Dengfeng People's Court. Please urge them to fulfill their obligations". Henan's court featured local *laolai* in video clips set to dramatic music and claimed its first victory when a deadbeat saw himself onscreen at a local movie theater and promptly paid his $78,000 judgment. By 2020, SCS had blocked *laolai* from fourteen million flights and high-speed train trips.

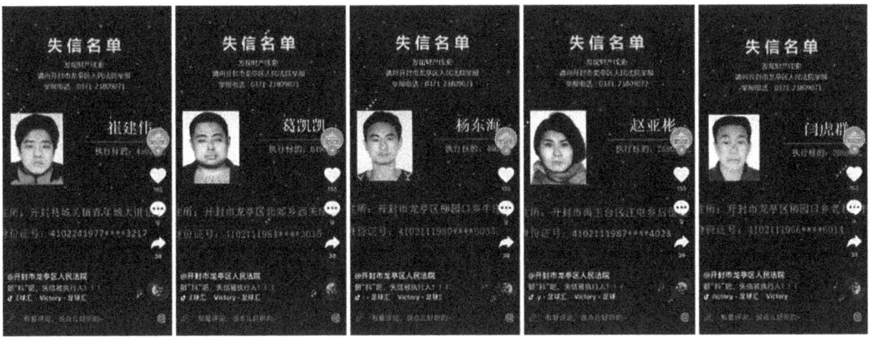

(Image: Douyin)

Individuals with good SCS scores receive cheaper loans, upgraded flights, no-deposit rentals, no-wait hospital visits, and desirable schools for their offspring. Japan and the Netherlands offer expedited visa processing for travelers with scores above 750, and landlords waive deposits if they're over 800. China Daily regularly talks up the benefits: "After graduation, Zhang Hao, 28, found a job at a Hangzhou securities company. On his mobile app, Alipay, he saw an apartment he liked. Alipay rates users' credit based on their consumption and investment habits and Zhang had a high score so was exempted from the $1,000 security deposit and the $200 broker's fee. The experience not only saved Zhang time and energy in renting an apartment, which is often complicated, but also gave him a positive impression of the city where he was about to build his career". One young man posted his high score and a video of himself collecting a Ford SUV from an unstaffed automobile vending machine for a three-day test drive, along with a discounted loan offer to buy it.

Jiangsu's Suining County[296] (pop. 3.3 million) launched a personal Trial Spot in 2007 that gave each citizen a thousand credits and deducted points for legal, administrative, and moral infringements. Drunk driving convictions cost fifty points; having a child without family planning permission lost thirty-five, and delinquent loans lost up to fifty. Miscreants could recover points after two to five years, depending on the infraction's gravity, and participants were categorized A-D based on their scores. A-class citizens received preferential access to employment opportunities while other applicants were scrutinized for government jobs and contracts, subsidized housing, social welfare, business licenses, and permits. The trial provided valuable data on the effects of naming, shaming, and rewarding citizens for compliance with local regulations but, when the county published the entire list of names and scores, critics compared them to the hated Good Citizen Cards issued by Japanese occupiers during the war.

Public nuisances, like unleashed dogs and uncouth passengers, are popular targets. A railway Trial Spot[297] penalizes fare dodgers, vandals, smokers, scalpers, and people who use false ID or invalid tickets. Some Trial Spots are[298] controversial. A private[299] university refused to enroll a Zhejiang businessman's son because his father had not repaid a $30,000 bank loan. The father promptly paid. Some netizens condemned this as collective punishment, while others argued that children should not enjoy privileges like private universities if they are purchased with unpaid debt.

To allay people's fears that Social Credit will become oppressive, government information on individuals will neither be considered in

296 China's Social Credit System: An Evolving Practice of Control. Rogier Creemers. The University of Leiden.

297 *Measures on the Administration of Railway Passenger Credit Records 2017 (Provisional)* China Law Translate, https://www.chinalawtranslate.com/subscribe/?lang=en

298 China Daily. 2018-7-14. 09:50:51

299 Public universities are forbidden to discriminate on any but criminal grounds.

evaluating their credit nor crafted into a unified score. Nor will SCS collect public or market credit information on individuals' religion, genetics, fingerprints, blood type, or medical history.

Provincial trials are developing a public appeals process for credit restoration if miscreants stop their negative behavior and work to undo its impact. Others are experimenting with credit objections, repair, appeals, and protection of civil rights, and the media are playing a critical role:

From: Gao Lu, editorial writer, Qianjiang Evening News[300],
Date: July 30, 2019
Re: Wulian No. 2 Middle School, Shandong Province.

Recently, a teacher's severe punishment by the school authorities and the local education department–for using corporal punishment to discipline two students for skipping class–has drawn public concern. According to official documents issued by the school and department, at the end of April this year, students Li and Wang (actual names withheld), from Class No. 3 of the Wulian No. 2 Middle School, skipped classes to go to the playground. Upon discovery, as punishment, their class teacher, Teacher Yang, beat them with textbooks.

As a result, the Wulian No. 2 Middle School suspended Teacher Yang for a month, issued a formal apology to the students and parents, and bore the students' medical and other expenses. These reparations all seem well and good, but the controversy lies in the additional sanctions for Teacher Yang proposed soon after. As issued by the Wulian County Education and Sports Bureau on July 2, the other sanctions proposed were:

1. Deducting Teacher Yang's performance-related pay from May 2019 to April 2020; 2. Directing the Wulian No. 2 Middle School not to renew Teacher Yang's employment contract; 3. Adding Teacher Yang to the Wulian County credit information evaluation system (credit system) blacklist from July 2019.

300 Original Mandarin: http://opinion.people.com.cn/n1/2019/0730/c1003-31262966.html

Among these additional sanctions, the last is most controversial. As is well known, a credit information evaluation system, narrowly defined, refers to the credit system of the People's Bank of China, and the appraisal of the borrower in the context of behavior such as the non-payment of bank loans, overdue credit card payments, overdrafts, and so on. However, in some places, the definition of "creditworthiness" has widened to include social behavior, thus a social credit system. In these places, jaywalking, spitting, and other uncivil behaviors are deemed detrimental and included in the credit system. This issue is not limited to just Wulian County. At least 20 other cities are developing credit systems to restrain personal conduct.

Although using corporal punishment to discipline students is almost certainly a failure to adhere to the teaching profession's ethical code, that relates somewhat to a teacher's trustworthiness. It is a different thing from staining their sincerity and honesty. Instead, it is already possible for the authorities to sanction teachers according to existing regulations. Those who exceed their authority can also be investigated under the law–there is no need to rely on the credit system.

The credit system is not the solution to every social problem. What kind of mess would it be if administrative and law enforcement offenses resulted in a loss to creditworthiness? The system would no longer be the traditional credit system we recognize. As implemented, a person's actual credit circumstances would be submerged within other systems. How useful would this be for the banks and financial institutions that only want to evaluate the person's ability to repay?

Why would they want to use the local credit system? If they used it, the banks and financial institutions would exceed their legal authority (by taking into account matters unrelated to the applicant's ability to repay). If they did not, the local authorities would have succeeded in creating a penalty system with no relation to financial behavior. Is that useful?

In some places, this is nothing more than a weapon used to

intimidate and reduce resistance to control. Peace of mind from credit evaluation gives way to paralysis by intimidation. The crux of the matter is this: the credit system can be misused to violate citizens' rights. In modern society, correctly evaluating credit is critical. For us, the public interest is at stake, and we must be cautious.

On July 28, the Wulian County People's Government announced that the Wulian County Bureau of Education and Sports had withdrawn the decision to seek additional sanctions for Teacher Yang. The Wulian County People's Government did not explain, but it is certainly worrying that one could be included or excluded from the credit system blacklist, just like that. We hope this incident spurs local authorities to approach creditworthiness more prudently and hope that more local governments recognize the problems inherent in building a credit system that preserves its citizens' legal rights.

Hundreds of Social Credit Trial Spots will parade their data in 2021, and, once public approval reaches ninety percent, legislators will integrate SCS into the social fabric and we will witness the most ambitious social experiment since the Cultural Revolution: digitally enhanced Confucian virtue.

Ask any Chinese about SCS and they will usually enthuse, "Just what we need! Perfect for us Chinese!"

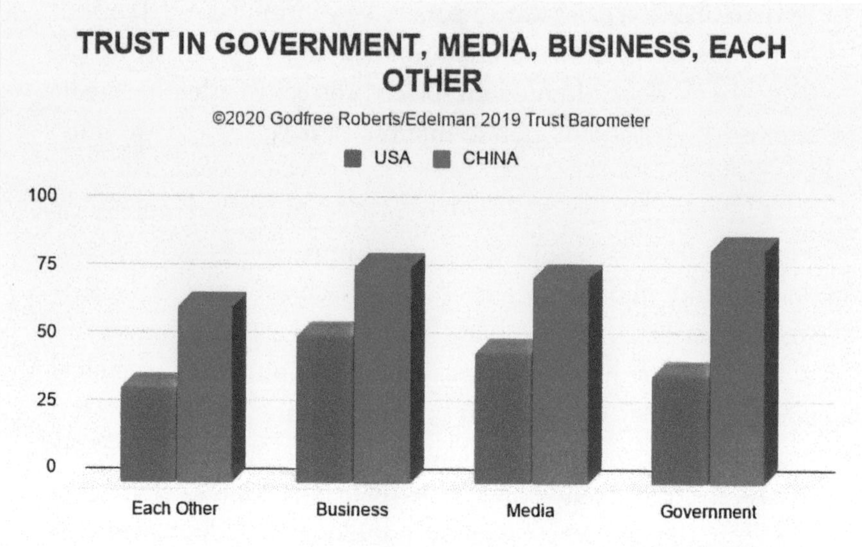
TRUST IN GOVERNMENT, MEDIA, BUSINESS, EACH OTHER
©2020 Godfree Roberts/Edelman 2019 Trust Barometer
USA
CHINA
100
75
50
25
0
Each Other
Business
Media
Government

CHAPTER 17

Lost Girls and Half the Sky

Of all people, girls and servants are the most difficult! If you are too familiar with them, they lose their humility. If you are reserved, they sulk. Confucius

***

Confucius was born into a selfishly hierarchical society in which women had always been subservient. Parents and brothers chose marriage partners who would control women's lives and own their property. Husbands took as many concubines as they could afford, and, when husbands died, sons assumed their responsibilities. A famous Confucian, Cheng Yi[301], urged widows–but not widowers–to starve themselves to death rather than remarry.

Yet Confucius neither denied women's agency nor their need for spiritual development, insisting that everyone, regardless of gender, could improve through education and self-cultivation. We associate his core teaching of *ren*, compassion, more with women than men as we do his notion of equality based on a social hierarchy of relationships, so it is no coincidence that some of the world's most liberated women appeared during a Confucian Golden Age:

> When a book was bought, he and I would always read it together, mending the text, repairing the manuscript, and writing the

301 Cheng Yi (1033–1107), a founder of the Neo-Confucian, *daoxue* movement of the Song period that crucially shaped our notions of Confucianism.

> captions. And when a painting or a bronze was delivered, we would together open it, play with it, study its merits, and criticize its defects. Every evening we studied together till our candle was burned up, and, after supper, we sat together in the Kuei-lai Hall and made our own tea. We wagered against each other that such and such a quotation was to be found on a particular page in a certain chapter of a specific book. We would give the exact line, page, chapter, and volume and then check them from the bookshelf. The winner was rewarded with the first cup of tea, but when one of us did win, the first cup was rarely drunk: we were so happy that our hands trembled with laughter, and the tea spilled all over the floor. We swore to grow old and die in that little world of ours. –Li Qingzhao, Poetess, Song Dynasty, 1000 AD.

Tales of Song women made a deep impression on young Mao who, at age twenty-six, published *The Death of Miss Chao*[302], about a local girl who committed suicide rather than marry a man she despised. "Miss Chao found herself in the following circumstances: One, Chinese society. Two, the Chao family of Nanyang Street in Changsha. Three, the Wu family of Kantzuyuan Street in Changsha, the family of the husband she did not want. These three factors constituted three iron nets, a kind of triangular cage and–once caught in these three nets–she sought life in every way possible, but in vain. There was no way for her to go on living. It happened because of the shameful system of arranged marriages, the darkness of our social system, the negation of the individual will and the absence of freedom to choose one's own mate".

Mao spent fifty years campaigning for women's rights, "A man in China is usually subjected to the domination of three systems of authority: political, family, and religious. Women, in addition to being dominated by these, are also dominated by the authority of their husbands. These four authorities–political, family, religious, and masculine–are the embodiment of the whole feudal-patriarchal ideology and the oppressive system it supports". He charged that Chinese women comprised

---

302 The Death of Miss Chao. Mao Zedong. 1919

the greatest mass of disinherited human beings the world had seen and, insisting that women volunteers be treated equally, attributed victory in the Great War of Liberation as much to them as anyone. He made colleagues promise that, if they won the war, they would 'grant freedom of marriage and equality between men and women' and, thanks to his efforts, Chinese women gained more democratic rights earlier than most.

His first official act as Head of State was signing the Marriage Law of the People's Republic of China, which he had drafted. A prequel to America's failed Equal Rights Amendment, it declares, "Women in the People's Republic of China enjoy equal rights with men in all spheres of life, in political, economic, cultural, social, and family life. The State protects the rights and interests of women, applies the principle of equal pay for equal work to men and women alike, and trains and selects cadres from among women".

To conservatives, Mao insisted, "Genuine equality between the sexes can only be realized through egalitarian transformation of our entire society. Men and women *must* receive equal pay for equal work". In 1955, he drove home his point by promoting Li Zhen[303], the sixth daughter of a peasant family, to the rank of Major General–the first female combat commander in history to reach that rank. He advocated gender balance in education and his successors have made steady progress.

In 2016, when the Education Ministry pledged to reach that goal by the 2021 centennial, they discovered thirty-million missing girls. Under Family Planning guidelines, second children were encouraged after birth spacing, though third children attracted a fine, and unregistered siblings were mostly girls. Thus was born the myth of the 'missing girls', which, like 'ghost towns,' captured imaginations but irritated political scientist John Kennedy[304], "Thirty-million girls–the population of California–are missing from the population, and they think they're just gone?" Kennedy

303 In 1929, Li Zhen (1908–1990) and her guerrilla unit, encircled by KMT forces, fought until night and, ammunition exhausted, retreated until their only escape was a cliff behind them. Li gave the order to avoid being taken alive and promptly jumped over the cliff. She landed on a tree and, after regaining consciousness, she and one other survivor buried their comrades. She survived the Long March, but starvation left her unable to nurse her baby, and it died.

304 *Delayed Registration and Identifying the "Missing Girls" in China.* The China Quarterly, Volume 228. December 2016, pp. 1018-1038

compared 2010 census figures with girls' enrollment and graduation rates in 2016 and reported:

> Most people are using a demographic explanation to say that abortion or infanticide is why girls don't show up in the census and that they don't exist, but we find there's a political explanation. The point of contention is the interaction between the central State's capacity to influence local officials and local officials' willingness to implement central policies–particularly unpopular ones. We find that millions of unreported female births 'appear' in older cohorts [school enrollment years], and this also reflects a cultural shift regarding the value of girls in China. The 'preference for sons' cultural argument suggests that parents see sons as necessary for elderly care and contributions to the family income while daughters are viewed as a burden.
>
> However, scholars suggest that, over the last few decades and especially since the introduction of economic reforms, daughters have contributed more to their natal families (i.e., increased their value). Still, 1990, 2000, and 2010 censuses show that unreported male births are overwhelmingly registered between the ages of one and ten years old, but that the vast majority of children registered after the age of ten are females. This implies an administrative bias towards sons whereby they are registered earlier than daughters, rather than a strict son preference (i.e., fewer daughters).

Kennedy interviewed a farmer who introduced his elder daughter and son by name but referred to his middle daughter as 'the non-existent one'. "He told us that his first daughter was registered but that when his second child, another daughter, was born they did not register her and instead waited to have another child. The third child was a boy and they registered him as the second child". To keep the peace, village officials, often clan relatives, turned a blind eye to children born outside family planning limits and left them unreported. Kennedy found that, though the government relaxed the rural one-child policy in the 1980s, village-level enforcement had already bypassed it, and the thirty-million girls were where they should be: in school.

Today, more girls graduate from university than boys and, normalized for job position and seniority, gender and wage gaps almost disappear. Modern women keep their surnames after marriage, take International Women's Day off, enjoy up to twelve-month maternity leave, and can retire younger. They also enjoy official favoritism in promotions and unofficial preference in transfers:

> My father was the deputy director of the labor department in my hometown ten years ago. I still remember my father got phone calls in the very early morning many times, maybe 3–5 AM, associated with overtime production issues and the illegal use of child labor (the factory owners think no one will inspect them overnight and in the very early morning). No alternative option and no excuse like "it's not office hours". He just had to go and do his work. Afterward, no compensation like a bonus and day off would be offered to him.
>
> Another example is my high school classmate. He is the officer of a rural village right now. Even though the village is not far from his own home, located in the more developed town, he must live in the village as required during weekdays and only stay home during the weekend. Being an officer means you have the power that the public cannot have, but at the same time, it forces you to sacrifice many personal benefits.
>
> I just read a news item months ago: two female officers refuse to be deployed into a poor village because they just do not want to give up the city's convenience and better life quality. CCP cannot fire them because the policy requires a certain percentage of female officers in the organization. CCP also cannot use Party principles to punish them too much because they are female. The only thing CCP can do is never promote them. But they don't care because their salary would not increase too much along with the promotion of your position, and they are satisfied with what they earn. But if they are male, the story would be thoroughly

> different. They would be punished based on the Party principles and even be kicked out of the Party, and their whole political career would be over. To sum up, there is no FREEDOM and HUMAN RIGHT for male officers in the CCP's organization if some people still want to find a perspective to criticize CCP's organizational principles.

Critics question the government's commitment to women in power because, though one-fourth of the National People's Congress delegates are female, there is only one woman in the twenty-five member Politburo, Health Minister Sun Chunlan, and none in the six-man Steering Committee.

Is this evidence of discrimination, or does it resemble Western women's participation in STEM research[305]?

Reaching the pinnacle of power in China is much harder than winning an Olympic gold medal. Today, as it has been for millennia, a Chinese political career is a single-minded, forty-year marathon that begins with decades of physical and mental hardship in poor, remote villages, frequent changes of location, relentless demands for performance, and increasing public scrutiny. If we blame anyone for the scarcity of women at the top, it should be their mothers and grandmothers, who fear that graduate studies and rural postings will dim daughters' marriage prospects–and sometimes to the ladies themselves:

> This July, Chinese state media[306] reported on punishments meted out to two civil servants in China's Yunnan Province. Their infraction? Neither corruption, nepotism, nor poor performance. Instead, they had both refused promotions, believing it better to suffer the consequences of disobeying their superiors' wishes than to give up the relative comforts of city life for a higher-ranking position in the countryside. Yunnan authorities defend the punishments handed down to two government employees who

305 Is it really just sexism? An alternative argument for why women leave STEM. By Karen Morenz. Medium. February 2, 2019

306 Government Employees Penalized for Rejecting Promotions. Sixth Tone, July 23, 2019

> passed on promotions. Discipline watchdogs in Suijiang County had reprimanded one of the employees, surnamed Zhong, with a demerit and recommended that another employee, surnamed Wan, be fired for "shirking responsibility".
>
> A county official told The Paper on Saturday that the two female party members must accept the decisions. A day earlier, the Central Commission for Discipline Inspection's official publication, the country's top disciplinary body, had accused the two women of "pursuing their own interests at the cost of the greater good". According to Friday's article, Zhong and Wan, who worked at separate government offices in Suijiang County, had been promoted to leadership roles last August because of their outstanding performance. While Zhong reportedly worried that the new position would mean less time with her family, Wan had cited health concerns when turning down the promotion. In the official write-up of the incident, the two women Party members were castigated for, in party parlance, "forgetting their original intention" and putting their "small families" at home ahead of their "big family," the collective good.

The story is quite different in education[307], where the family planning policy[308] accounted for half of women's additional education. While men born in 1950 had significantly more education than women born that year, men and women born in 1980 had about equal levels—nine years of schooling. This suggests[309] that Chinese women, anticipating having fewer children due to the policy, postponed having children while increasing their education.

Women now constitute fifty-three percent of university students and

---

307 What the US (and Rest of the World) Should Know About Higher Education in China. By Zhou Zhong, Lu Liu et al. Tsinghua University. May 28, 2019

308 Xuan Jiang. FAMILY PLANNING AND WOMEN'S EDUCATIONAL ATTAINMENT: EVIDENCE FROM THE ONE-CHILD POLICY, Contemporary Economic Policy (2020). DOI: 10.1111/coep.12462

309 Xuan Jiang, a postdoctoral researcher in economics at The Ohio State University, quoted in 'Having fewer children reduced the education gap in China: Study finds women got more schooling, delayed parenthood.' By Jeff Grabmeier, Ohio State News, February 12, 2020

forty-nine percent of academics. As in the US, one-third of full professors are women, and women graduates outnumber men in science and finance. Women professors, scientists, and entrepreneurs regularly lead glamorous projects. A woman designed the Navy's Houbei Class missile patrol boats, and the country's first native Nobel Laureate, Tu Youyou, is a woman whose discovery of artemisinin prevented millions of malaria deaths. Ms. Lu Yutong designed the world's fastest computer, Mme. Wang Shufang created Beidou, the world's most accurate GPS system, and Dr. Liang Jianying is lead designer for the new 500 mph maglev trains.

Half of all homebuyers are women. Eighty percent of venture capital companies have at least one female partner–which translates into real wealth. The 2020 Hurun Global Rich List found that ninety percent of the world's richest self-made women and eighty percent of the world's self-made female billionaires are Chinese. Zhou Qunfei, the most famous, was raised by her blind father in rural Hunan and dropped out of school at sixteen to make watch lenses for $1 a day. She invested her savings in a startup to make touch screens and went public in 2015. China's glass ceiling is higher, too. Sun Yafang chairs Huawei, the world's biggest telecom; Jean Liu is President of Didi Chuxing, the world's biggest ride-sharing company, Rachel Duan is CEO of GE China, and Dong Mingzhu is CEO of the world's largest appliance manufacturer, Gree.

Finally, as the 2021 gender equality deadline approaches, disadvantaged women are receiving more attention. Fan Yusu, a migrant worker and domestic helper in Beijing, raised two daughters in a ninety-square-foot room without running water. She attended a free writing course and, at aged forty-four, wrote *I Am Fan Yusu.*

> My life is like a book that's dreadful to read–fate has made its binding messy. I am from Xiangyang in Hubei and started to do private teaching at the local village school when I was twelve. If I hadn't left, I would have continued to teach and become a proper teacher, but I couldn't bear to stay in the countryside and view the sky from the bottom of the well, so I came to Beijing. I wanted to see the world. I was twenty then. Things were not

> easy after coming to Beijing, mainly because I was lazy, stupid, and unskillful with my hands and feet. What others did in half an hour took me three. My hands were too slow–slower than most people's. I worked as a waitress at a restaurant and would drop the tray and break the plates. I made just enough money to keep myself from starving. I wasted two years in Beijing; I was the type who couldn't see the flame of my dreams. Then I rushed into marrying a man from the northeast of China, and, within six years, we had two daughters. But their father's business was doing worse and worse, and he started drinking heavily every day.

After teaching her daughters to read from subtitles on TV, she bought a truckload of discarded books for a few dollars and today, she says proudly, her older daughter is a white-collar worker but, "Oh, the damned Education Ministry who made those policies to hurt the children of poor migrant workers!" Her cries personalized inequality, the urban-rural divide, and the seizure of farmland for development, and caught the nation's imagination. The People's Daily praised her "Matter of fact, thought-provoking prose. She is like an anthropologist who, by observing people from all walks of life in the city, offers readers a new perspective".

Thousands of years of sexism will not disappear by 2021, but stronger policy enforcement, dedicated family courts, vocal NGOs, and increasing social support are gradually turning women's dreams into reality–sometimes with unexpected results. The China Women's Association announced proudly that, in 2017, it received as many complaints from men about wives and girlfriends beating them as the reverse, and that forty percent of the women confessed to cheating on their partners. Zhou[310] Qiáng, president of the Supreme People's Court, revealed that women initiate seventy percent of divorces and this confession, by Sheng Yun,[311] explains a great deal:

---

310 Zhou made the revelation on November 6, 2019, in a speech (in Chinese) at Beijing's Tsinghua University.

311 Diary. Sheng Yun. London Review of Books.Vol. 40 No. 19 • October 11, 2018

I have never felt the need to call myself a feminist, no matter how often my late-developed gender awareness tells me I ought to be one. In my primary school in China in the mid-1980s, the most ferocious person in the class was a girl. She used to carry a tree branch to beat boys, and absolutely no one dared to offend her. Our desks were designed for two, usually a girl and a boy; the better student was supposed to help their neighbor. We drew a line (called the '38th parallel' after the line separating North and South Korea) down the middle of the desk, and neither side was allowed to cross the border. I had a compass with one needle leg as a weapon, ready to attack the boy when his elbow strayed into my territory. One day his mother found some blood on his sleeve when she was washing his clothes and asked him what had happened. He told her that he had had a minor nosebleed: it was too shameful to admit that he was being bullied by a girl (and male pride prevented him from retaliating). Poor boy. After the bloodshed, I stopped using the compass and adopted a softer tactic: pinching.

Somewhere, Miss Chou is smiling.

CHAPTER 18

Religion, Tibet & Xinjiang

Respect the gods and spirits, but keep them at a distance. Superior men don't go around talking about ghosts. Confucius

***

The civilization that Lao Tzu and Confucius founded is, simultaneously, the least religious and most tolerant on earth. The world's earliest, dated, printed book is a ninth-century AD translation of the Diamond Sutra, and its colophon reads, "For universal, free distribution". Though three-fourths of Chinese are non-religious, freedom of worship has been a tradition for millennia, and the Constitution guarantees it. The government supports seventy-four seminaries, one-thousand-seven-hundred Tibetan monasteries, three-thousand religious organizations, thirty-nine-thousand mosques, eighty-five-thousand sacred sites three-hundred-thousand full-time Catholic, Protestant, Buddhist, Traditional Chinese, Taoist, and Muslim clergy.

While our forebears demanded belief in Jesus and struggled to master Nature, theirs elevated reason over faith and saw Man, Nature, and the Cosmos as indivisibly psychophysical. While ours sought personal salvation in the afterlife, theirs pursued collective liberation in a *dàtóng* society. While our ancestors struggled against sin, theirs saw human error as temporary disharmony. While ours clung to beliefs, ideals, absolutes, and dogmas, theirs distinguished ideals from facts, and rejecting fixed positions. While our forefathers suppressed spirituality, theirs practiced harmony with the Tao, "A Thing, formless yet complete, That existed before heaven and earth. Without sound, without substance, It stands alone and unchanging. It is all-pervading and unfailing. We do not know Its name, but we call it *Tao*. Being one with Nature, the Sage lives in harmony with the *Tao*[312]".

Some Chinese rulers were so tolerant that they courted self-destruction.

When Dominique Parennin, a Jesuit missionary, requested permission to proselytize in 1724, the Yongzheng Emperor[313] explained that the Christian God posed a danger to the State because it invited foreign interference:

> You say that your law is not a false law, 非左道, and We believe you. If We thought it was false, what would have held Us back from razing your churches and expelling you from the empire? False laws are those which, on the pretext of teaching virtue, fan the spirit of revolt, as is the case with the White Lotus[314] Teaching.
>
> What would you say if We were to dispatch a group of monks and lamas to your country to preach their doctrines? How would they be received? Your Matteo Ricci came to China in 1572 when you Christians were few in number and did not have your people and churches in every province. It was only under my father's reign that you began to build churches everywhere and that your doctrines started spreading rapidly. We observed this, but we said nothing.
>
> You may have known how to deceive Our Father, but don't think you can deceive Us in the same way. You wish to make all Chinese Christians, as your law demands. We know this very well. But in that case, what would become of Us? Should We not soon become merely the subjects of your kings? The converts you have made already recognize nobody but you, and, in troubled times, they would listen to no other voice than yours. We know

312 Lao Tzu, Laozi 601-533 BC, is credited with authorship of the *Tao Te Ching*.

313 'Yongzheng's Conundrum. The Emperor on Christianity, Religions, and Heterodoxy', Menegon. An Emperor Confronts Christianity and the Heterodox, Part II: Eugenio Menegon.

314 White Lotus is the name of a revolutionary secret society founded in the 14th century.

> that we have nothing to fear at present, but when foreign ships start coming in their thousands and tens of thousands, perhaps then serious disorders will arise.

Sixty years later, foreign ships came in their tens of thousands and a Christian uprising killed thirty-million people. The dynasty never recovered.

***

Tang Dynasty religious regulations remain in effect today: civil law still trumps beliefs; public proselytizing is forbidden; believers may not give allegiance to foreign powers; religious explanations of the world may only be taught to adults; if followers incite treason, unrest, or violence, or practice tax-evasion or threaten public order, officials may raze their churches[315] (though not harm their congregants). The Chinese have always treated believers more leniently than Western governments[316].

Tang Dynasty principles were applied in Xinjiang[317] in 2009, when some Wahhabi Uyghurs massacred two hundred people. When a local court ignored testimony from forensic specialists (hired by the victims' relatives) that six men could not have killed so many, the censor blocked the families' public complaints. The defendants were ethnic minorities, he said, with a constitutional right to preferential treatment, and public discussion would only inflame ethnic tensions. The censor again intervened when the attacks resumed in 2014, ruling that publicity would rekindle dormant hatreds, and urging the government to provide more opportunities for illiterate, unemployed, rural Muslim youth.

The government relocated entire industries to Xinjiang and built

---

315 The famous Shaolin Monastery has been demolished a dozen times since 500 AD.

316 The US Government massacred 81 members of a Christian sect in Waco, Texas, in 1993.

317 Says US Ambassador Chas. H. Freeman, "The CIA programs in Tibet, which were very effective in destabilizing it, did not succeed in Xinjiang. There were similar efforts made with the Uyghurs during the Cold War that never really got off the ground. In both cases, you had religion waved as a banner in support of a desire for independence or autonomy which is, of course, anathema to any state". https://supchina.com/podcast/legendary-diplomat-chas-w-freeman-jr-on-u-s-china-strategy-and-history-part-3/

residential vocational schools across the province (which Western media called 'concentration camps'). Inspectors from twelve Muslim countries praised[318] them, graduates found good jobs, and the massacres stopped.

***

All the serfs and slaves take with them is their shadow. Their only legacy is their footprints. Tibetan saying.

Chou en Lai, the Panchen Lama, Mao, the current Dalai Lama. Beijing, 1952

Another border region, Tibet, was a different story.

When the Mongols arrived in 1271 AD, Buddhism, which had been established for a thousand years, had split into warring sects that united only to persecute members of the native Bon religion. In 1672, when the fifth Dalai Lama faced a rebellion from the Tsang province, he ordered a Mongolian army under his control to exact retribution:

> For the band of enemies who have despoiled the duties entrusted to them: Make the male lines like trees that have had their roots cut; Make the female lines like brooks that have dried in up

318 No cultural, religious repression of Uighur Muslims in Xinjiang: Pakistan diplomat. Times of India, January 24, 2019

> winter; make the children and grandchildren like eggs smashed against rocks, make the servants and followers like heaps of grass consumed by fire, make their dominion like a lamp whose oil has been exhausted. In short, annihilate any traces of them, even their names.

The British arrived in 1903, and were even more bloodthirsty. Lieutenant Arthur Hadow[319] wrote, "The machine gunners slaughtered the Tibetan soldiers; thirteen hundred died in the massacre. I got so sick of the slaughter that I ceased fire, though the general's order was to make as big a bag as possible. I hope I shall never again have to shoot down men walking away".

A journalist on the expedition, Perceval Landon[320], described the Thirteenth Dalai Lama's rule as 'an engine of oppression' and Captain W.F.T. O'Connor concurred, "The great landowners and the priests ... exercise each in their own dominion a despotic power from which there is no appeal, while the people are oppressed by the most monstrous growth of monasticism and priest-craft". Wrote Spencer Chapman[321], "Tibet's rulers invented degrading legends and stimulated a spirit of superstition among the common people. The Lamaist monk does not spend his time in ministering to the people or educating them. The beggar beside the road is nothing to the monk. Knowledge is the jealously guarded prerogative of the monasteries and is used to increase their influence and wealth".

After acknowledging China's suzerainty, the British departed in 1904 and the Buddhist sects resumed their wars until 1950, when the PRC arrived, ejected the warlords, Nazis, and spies who had fled there during World War Two, and negotiated the Agreement for the Peaceful Liberation of Tibet:

---

319 China Station: The British Military in the Middle Kingdom 1839-1997. Mark Felton

320 *The opening of Tibet, an account of Lhasa and the country and people of central Tibet, and the progress of the mission sent there by the English government in the year 1903-4.* (1905). Landon was one of the first Europeans to describe the holy city of Lhasa in detail.

321 Waddell, Landon, O'Connor, and Chapman are quoted in Gelder and Gelder, *The Timely Rain*, 123-125.

> The local government of Tibet will drive imperialist forces out of Tibet; China will not alter the existing political system, all government officials will maintain their positions, and the status, functions, and powers of the Dalai Lama will remain unchanged. Tibet will carry out reforms following the wishes of its people, through consultation with its leaders rather than by compulsion; the Tibetan people will exercise autonomy under their government, and Tibetan religious beliefs, customs and habits, monasteries, and their incomes will be respected; Tibet will remain a theocracy and retain its autonomy in most military and diplomatic matters; Tibetan troops will be trained and integrated into the PLA and Beijing will guarantee peace with bordering countries.

American diplomat Robert Ford[322] wrote, "There was no sacking of monasteries at this time. On the contrary, the Chinese took great care not to cause offense through ignorance. They soon had the monks thanking the gods for their deliverance. The Chinese had made it clear they had no quarrel with the Tibetan religion". The government allocated $500,000 to renovate the Buddhist temple in Beijing and granted additional funds to Tibetan Muslims for a pilgrimage to Mecca in 1957.

This intervention triggered a violent reaction amongst Tibet's wealthy elite, many of whom engaged in terrorism against peasants who 'collaborated' with the PLA. Mao[323] urged patience, "Although the establishment of the military and administrative committee and the reorganization of the Tibetan troops were stipulated in the Agreement you had fears, and so I instructed the comrades working in Tibet to slow down their implementation. The Agreement must be carried out but, because of your fears, it has to be postponed. If you are scared this year, it can wait until next year. If you still have fears next year, it can wait until the year after

322 The Making of Modern Tibet By A. Tom Grunfeld
323 Xinhua monthly, February 1952, p. 11.

that". With Mao's approval[324], a fifteen-year-old Chinese-born boy was installed as the fourteenth Dalai Lama[325].

Four years later, he and the Panchen Lama traveled to Beijing where he was greeted as a Head of State by Premier Zhou Enlai and Chief of General Staff Zhu De. Mao hosted dinners in his honor and the National People's Congress elected him Vice-Chairman of the Standing Committee[326]. In a speech to Congress, the Dalai Lama championed regional autonomy for all minorities, "Tibet's Agreement has enabled the Tibetan people to fully enjoy all rights of ethnic equality and embark on a bright road of freedom and happiness".

He was frank about conditions in his country[327] and enthusiastic about China, "Outside the monasteries, our system was feudal… The more I looked at Marxism, the more I liked it. Here was a system based on equality and justice for everyone which claimed to be a panacea for all the world's ills. From a theoretical standpoint, its only drawback was its insistence on a purely materialist view of human existence. This I could not agree with. I was also concerned at the methods used by the Chinese in pursuit of their ideals. I received a strong impression of rigidity. But I expressed a wish to become a Party member all the same. I felt sure, as I still do, that it would be possible to work out a synthesis of Buddhist and pure Marxist doctrines that really would be an effective way of conducting politics". In 1998, Professor Dongping Han[328] met the Dalai Lama when he visited Brandeis University:

> He agreed to meet Chinese scholars and China scholars in the Boston area behind closed doors. He said that in 1950, on his way to Beijing for talks with the Chinese central government,

324 All Dalai Lamas, including the first, required Chinese Government approval before they were installed.

325 Freedom in Exile: Autobiography of His Holiness the Dalai Lama of Tibet by Dalai Lama XIV Bstan-'Dzin-Rgya-Mtsho. Harpercollins 1990. (The title 'Dalai' means 'ocean' in Mongolian, and 'Lama' means 'Living Buddha' in Tibetan. In the 1950s, the US State Department titled him 'God-King of Tibet'.

326 The Panchen Lama was elected a member of the Standing Committee.

327 My Land and My People. By the Fourteenth Dalai Lama.

328 The Socialist Legacy Underlies the Rise of Today's China in the World–by Dongping Han. Aspects of India's Economy Nos. 59-60 (Oct 2014)

> he was filled with doubt about Tibet's future. But on his way back, he was filled with hope for Tibet and China's future because he saw with his own eyes how Chairman Mao and other Chinese leaders were working hard for the Chinese people. He also said that Chairman Mao treated him like a younger brother, and he was able to talk with Chairman Mao freely and candidly for three days with the help of an interpreter. No Chinese leader, he said, ever treated him like Chairman Mao did. It seemed that behind closed doors and in the absence of reporters, the Dalai Lama could be disarmingly candid and persuasive.

But, during his years in Beijing, the young man had forgotten the political realities in Tibet where the nobles had conspired with the leading abbots to murder the mildly reformist ninth, tenth, eleventh, and twelfth Dalai Lamas. Conservative Drepung monastery, the seat of fierce resistance to the Chinese, owned one-hundred-eighty-five manors and twenty-five-thousand serfs and employed sixteen-thousand herdsmen. Its lamas forced boys into monastic slavery, pilfered the country's wealth, and sold serfs along with the land. American journalist Anna Louise Strong[329] found handcuffs of all sizes at Drepung, including small ones for children, and instruments for cutting off noses and ears, gouging out eyes, breaking off hands, and hamstringing legs, hot brands, whips, and disemboweling implements.

By the time the Dalai Lama reached Lhasa, the reforms had stirred deep resentment among the elite. Public schools threatened their monopoly of education, training serfs as technicians upset the social hierarchy, and paying wages for road construction challenged the *ulag* tradition: in 1957 a lord beat his serf almost to death in Shann'an for failing to perform his unpaid *ulag* service. Like Virginian plantation owners a century earlier, the nobles saw emancipation as a threat and turned for help to Washington. Says US Ambassador Chas W. Freeman[330]

---

329 AL Strong (b.1885, d.1970) *Tibetan Interviews*, pp 91-96.

330 US Ambassador Chas. H. Freeman, Director for Chinese Affairs at the US Department of State from 1979-1981.

> I don't see why Tibet being part of China should be any more controversial than Wales being part of the United Kingdom. The periods when they were put into that position were about the same ... but the Central Intelligence Agency, with assistance from some of China's neighbors, put $30 million into the destabilization of Tibet and financed and trained the participants in the Khampa rebellion and ultimately sought to remove the Dalai Lama from Tibet–which they did. They escorted him out of Tibet to Dharamsala. The CIA programs were very effective in destabilizing Tibet, but did not succeed in Xinjiang".

The CIA persuaded Kashag[331] officials and Khampa[332] tribesmen to rebel, and the ensuing riot killed eighty-thousand people. It took the PLA twenty hours to hoist the Red Flag over the Potala Palace, and, when the smoke cleared, the nobles had fled to India, along with the Dalai Lama and the country's gold reserves. Their fear that the PLA would capture the Dalai Lama was unfounded, for Mao[333] had written the local PLA commander, "If the Dalai Lama and his entourage flee Lhasa, our troops should not try to stop them. Whether they are heading to southern Tibet or India, just let them go."

Mao said, "If the Dalai Lama is willing to return home and is able to get rid of the reactionaries, then we hope he will. But is it possible for him to change his own world outlook? If he wants to return, he can do so tomorrow... Indian newspaper stories say he plans to return but the two statements he made thoroughly oppose the Central Government and the big family of the motherland and advocate Tibetan independence. As a result, he has blocked his own way back. Even so, we must leave leeway for him by electing him Vice-Chairman of the Standing Committee

---

331 The Kashag was the governing council of Tibet during the rule of the Qing dynasty and post-Qing period until the 1959 rebellion.

332 The Khampa people of Tibet's Kham Province have a fearsome reputation as the most hostile and violent of Tibetans. "Tall and well-built men, fearless and open of countenance, they resemble Apache Indians, with plaited hair hanging from each side of well modeled heads." In 1950, the Chinese captured the town of Chamdo without firing a shot when they set off a huge fireworks display on the outskirts of the town, and the Khampa fled in terror.

333 Beijing's Power and China's Borders: Twenty Neighbors in Asia. By Bruce Elleman, Stephen Kotkin, Clive Schofield

of the National People's Congress and Chairman of the Preparatory Committee of the Founding of the Tibet Autonomous Region".

When the Dalai Lama declined to return, Beijing terminated the Tibetan government, separated Church and State, abolished slavery, serfdom, *ulag* labor, and debt peonage, and concluded, "The fundamental improvement of national relations, in the final analysis, depends on the complete emancipation of the working classes within each nationality: class struggle, aimed directly at the overthrow of the local elite". Hoisting the flag of class struggle, the CCP proclaimed itself the universal champion of the poor and set out to wean them from their allegiance to the elite by redistributing their wealth.

The government seized three-quarters of the rebels' property–five-hundred-thousand acres–and purchased one-hundred-fifty-thousand acres and a million head of livestock from serf-owners who had not rebelled. Local officials redistributed it to two-hundred-thousand households, closed ninety percent of the monasteries, and married off their inmates. Ex-slaves burned their bondage records on Serfs Emancipation Day and received cattle, farming tools, and title deeds to land they had tilled for centuries. Tibetans today remember the period as the English remember the Dissolution of the Monasteries: as the overthrow of religious tyrants who monopolized land and resisted social progress.

After centuries of persecution, the native Bon religion revived and ethnic minorities like the Loba, Monba, and Deng re-entered society. The government created jobs by piping clean water to the main population centers, building the first hospitals, and opening schools in every village. Modernization began humbly, says William Hinton[334], a Quaker professor in neighboring Henan Province:

> There was no doubt, as far as could be seen, that a better day had come for those who had been downtrodden in Tibet, the victims of the ruthless overlords and lamas who lived in security, supported and fed by the unending toil of the peasants, who were mostly serfs, denied even the minimum of education, medical,

334 I stayed in China, by William G Sewell – January 1, 1966

> and social care, which every one of us takes as his right. There were no sentimental feelings about holy monks, rather a horror of their unholy treatment of their less fortunate fellows. The latter came to Szechwan while, we believe, the former, the privileged class, found their way into India. Schools were being opened in Tibet, hospitals built, and roads made. Even from Duliang, there were teachers, nurses, and engineers going westward, over the snow-clad mountains that we could see from time to time. The Tibetans who found their way down from the mountains to Duliang were entering a new world. Special hostels were opened so that they might live as they were accustomed and enjoy their own food, doctors and nurses were set apart to look after them, their children were given clothes and taken to school. For these people from the high mountains, where everything had to be carried by man or beast, the wheel was largely unknown and indeed was useless before the new roads were made. One of the lighter and happier touches of welcome was the provision of bicycles on open spaces outside the city walls where they could be taught to ride. The crowds gathered daily to watch. Groans, 'Ah-ah!', would rise as they feared some burly Tibetan, supported on each side by slender Chinese, would fall from his machine, loud clapping when he stayed on.

The Party struggled to win over the peasants who, lacking a history of class confrontation[335], placed their hope of freedom in a Buddhist afterlife earned by enduring the misery of submission. At the same time, they had always viewed Chinese emperors as incarnations of the Bodhisattva, whom the Dalai Lama also incarnated, so they simply honored Emperor Mao, the mighty god who punished enemies and bestowed miraculous favors on the masses. The Marxist notion of predestination by class was entirely familiar, and they enjoyed the fact that, in this new theology, the elite suffered most.

The abolition of the *ulag* and taxes, miraculous airborne disaster

---

335 Reflections on Tibet. Wang Lixiong. New Left Review 14, Mar-Apr 2002

relief, mobile medical treatment, and the enrollment of peasant children in universities (which, to the peasants, resembled heavens) made Mao's extraordinary powers comparable to the Buddha's. Communist ideology resembled faith, communism's goal mirrored heaven, political studies echoed preaching, and Party discipline mirrored monastic asceticism. Bowing to Mao's picture in their home shrines and reciting his instructions while clasping his Little Red Book became their daily prayer ritual and, where once they carried Buddhist images and chanted Buddhist songs, they now carried Mao's picture and sang *The East is Red.* The content was irrelevant so long as the magic worked.

Their religious conversion became a two-edged sword during the Cultural Revolution, however when its goal of destroying the Four Olds–old customs, culture, habits, and ideas–wrought havoc. Zealous converts took Maoism to extremes, smashed the old world, declared their loyalty to the new, and embraced the Cultural Revolution with religious fervor. Tibet's culture, so closely intertwined with religion, bore the full brunt of their destructiveness but, says Wang Lixiong[336], "Only a limited number of Han Red Guards actually reached Tibet [then extraordinarily difficult to access] and, even if some did participate in destroying temples, their actions could only have been symbolic".

Temples and monasteries survived in the central cities where authorities could prevent the destruction and, in October 1966, Premier Zhou tried to persuade eleven Tibetan students to go slow in destroying the Four Olds, "Wiping out superstition is a long-term project," he told them, and suggested that temples and monasteries be converted to schools or storehouses. Tibetan activists, who did most of the damage, were mostly from poor social backgrounds, and many thought them rascals, thieves, and thugs. They reduced Gandan Monastery, a major center of the Yellow Hat sect outside Lhasa, to ruins. When they went to destroy the Juela Temple, the resident lama, Mimaciren, locked the gates, but Mimaciren's son, Lobu, opened them from inside.

336 Reflections on Tibet. Wang Lixiong. New Left Review 14, Mar-Apr 2002

In 2006, a young Tibetan woman, Woeser[337], tried to discover why Tibetans participated in the destruction of their own religion. Her first interviewee, an ordinary Tibetan woman in Lhasa, told her that Mao helped a lot of people, that the world cannot do without people like Mao, that Tibet used to be unfair when some were rich while some did not have enough to eat, and that Mao's revolution changed everything. Many interviewees held that there was not much ethnic conflict, and one Hui interviewee says the Han and the Tibetans were alike in making revolution. Others affirmed the idea that the dominant discourse was class struggle, and the words on everyone's lips were *qin bu qin fief fen*: whether one feels close to another depends on class. One Tibetan interviewee was still upset by the Chinese policy of privileging Tibetans who belonged to the former ruling class.

Woeser's mother told her that her father loved Mao and was very enthusiastic when the Cultural Revolution began. Another interviewee said that, at that time, 'belief in the CCP was like belief in religion.' Another said that people believed that Mao was a living Buddha and that many Tibetans feel likewise. Another, the son of a prominent Living Buddha, said he really believed in Mao and thought everything Mao said was the universal truth. When he visited the Dalai Lama (outside China) in the 1980s, he told his Holiness that most Tibetans supported the CCP because the CCP liberated the serfs.

Emancipation did not end terrorism, however. John Kenneth Knaus[338], the CIA's Tibet Task Force Commander recalled, "This was not some CIA black-bag operation. The initiative came from … the entire US government". The US budgeted $1.7 billion annually to support the Dalai Lama and the CIA [339] upper-class young men as guerrillas in the Colorado Rockies and parachuted them into Tibet. But their former

337 Tibetan Memories: 23 venerated old people talk about the Cultural Revolution in Tibet. Wei Se (Woeser), Taipei: 2006. (The author, Wei Se, is a PRC citizen of Tibetan ethnic origin who has been banned and censored by the Chinese authorities).

338 Orphans of The Cold War America And the Tibetan Struggle For Survival April 25, 2000, by John Kenneth Knaus

339 Conboy, Kenneth; Morrison, James (2002). The CIA's secret war in Tibet. Lawrence: University Press of Kansas.

slaves promptly killed them, said their commander, Bruce Walker[340], "The radio teams experienced major resistance from the population inside Tibet". Next, the Agency trained two-thousand ethnic Khampa fighters in Nepal but the Nepalese government, pressured by Beijing, closed the base, so the Agency built a nuclear-powered monitoring station which, with the help of local Sherpas, they placed in the Himalayas to spy on Chinese missile tests. When that failed, they developed a nuclear-powered spy drone to overfly China, reasoning that there would be no pilot to confess if the drone were shot down.

When the CIA transferred the operation's leader, Roger E. McCarthy, to Vietnam, says Victor Marchetti, the agents were bitterly disappointed, "Several of them turned for solace to the Tibetan prayers which they had learned during their years with the Dalai Lama". Efforts to stir up trouble in Tibet continue to this day[341].

International law allows governments to regulate religions to prevent their use as vehicles for violence or separatism, and China bans public religious activities for this reason. However, since public worship is integral to Tibetan culture, they still worship publicly and their religion is flourishing. Forty living Buddhas and one-hundred-fifty-thousand monks and nuns are engaged in scriptural study and debate, degree promotion, initiation, *abhisheka* empowerment, and self-cultivation. The Living Buddha reincarnation system are thriving, though home shrines, show divided loyalties.

Some are dedicated to the Dalai Lama, some to the Panchen Lama, and some to Mao Zedong, who, like Lincoln, is revered as the Great Emancipator. Professor Melvyn Goldstein[342] conducted fieldwork in ru-

340 Ibid

341 Another failed revolt, in 1987, convinced the CIA to transfer its Tibetan programs to the National Endowment for Democracy, NED, but the CIA returned to orchestrate a massacre during the 2008 Beijing Olympics. In 2020, the National Endowment for Democracy funded twenty-two Tibetan rebel organizations and supported the Dalai Lama's claim to rule Tibet. – *Tibet, the 'great game' and the CIA.* by Richard M Bennett

342 Contemporary Tibet: Politics, Development, and Society in a Disputed ...Sautman et al. Goldstein was Chairman of Case Western's Department of Anthropology and Director of the Center for Research on Tibet. He married the daughter of the famous Tibetan scholar-official-aristocrat, Surkhang Wangchen Gelek, and was elected to the US National Academy of Sciences in 2009.

ral Tibet in 2000 and asked, "Do You Have a Better Life Now Than Your Parents Did?" Ninety percent of those who had experienced the Dalai Lama's regime said, "Yes". Following the 2008 riots, the Tibetan Government in Exile secretly asked[343] seventeen-thousand resident Tibetans if they wanted full independence, *renzig*. Thirty percent said, "Yes," while forty-seven percent preferred limited true autonomy within China[344]–the status offered in the 1953 Agreement and repeated in 1985.

***

Tibet's population, barely one million in 1952, reached three-million in 2020, and ninety-five percent are Tibetan and ethnic minorities. Extreme poverty has disappeared along with endemic smallpox, cholera, venereal diseases, typhoid, scarlet fevers, and tetanus. The fear of 'invasion' by millions of ethnic Han receded when locals saw that most Han immigrants were poor. Being ineligible for state subsidies, they could not compete with locals, and left within a few years. A US Government[345] report concluded, "Family planning policies permitted Tibetans, like members of other minority groups, to have more children than Han Chinese. Urban Tibetans, including Communist Party members, were generally permitted to have two children. Rural Tibetans were encouraged, but not required, to limit births to three, but even these guidelines were not strictly enforced". Life expectancy, at sixty-eight years and rising, bests neighboring India, Nepal, and Sikkim.

Tibetan educators focus on recruiting minority teachers and funding

343 Dharamsala, India: Tibetan leaders opened a six-day meeting over the direction of their struggle with China on Monday, after the Dalai Lama, the region's exiled spiritual leader, expressed frustration over years of fruitless talks with Beijing. The meeting here in northern India, called by the Dalai Lama, comes after his comments last month, bemoaning the lack of any progress by his envoys in talks with the Chinese government since 2002. Karma Chophel, speaker of Parliament in the government-in-exile, said more than 8,000 of 17,000 Tibetans recently surveyed in Tibet said they would follow the Dalai Lama. More than 5,000 said they wanted Tibetan independence, more than twice the number who wanted to continue with the current approach, he said. He did not offer any details about how the survey was conducted. Tibetan Exiles Discuss Impasse with China. *Memories of Movement.* November 17, 2008.

344 The remainder chose the status quo or had no opinion.

345 US Department of State, "Human Rights Practices in Tibet-2003," www.asianresearch.org/articles/1934.html.

ethnic institutes. Children's primary instruction is in Tibetan–whose script they see on China's banknotes–in schools administered by their own people. Because their language lacks a scientific vocabulary, secondary schools use Mandarin, but all schools are free, rural children receive full scholarships at boarding schools, where attendance is ninety-eight percent. Illiteracy in people under fifty has fallen from ninety percent to four percent so that there are now more Tibetans literate in their own language than all Tibetans who have ever lived. Positive discrimination provides Tibetans better opportunities for advanced education than Han students enjoy and, since its founding in 1985, Tibet University has produced ten-thousand graduates and today enrolls thirty-thousand on full scholarships. Two new universities are expanding opportunities further.

Tibetans' incomes have risen five-hundred percent even though most live in rural areas, and few speak Chinese. There is now a substantial urban middle class in government, tourism, commerce, construction, light manufacturing, and transportation, and, as thousands of Internet-savvy youngsters graduate, they fill existing niches and create new ones. Tibetan entrepreneurs, thanks to massive subsidies, are prospering. Their state budget exceeds Oregon's and GDP and, growing thirteen percent annually, reached $110 billion in 2019. Annual urban incomes have risen from $200 to $4,500. Fourteen-thousand miles of new highways, three new airports, and the world's highest railway connect Tibetans to each other and the outside world. Fiberoptic cables reach every county. Everyone has a cell phone and a motorcycle (to which they are addicted). Thanks to hydropower, geothermal, wind, and solar energy, electricity production has risen seventeen percent annually and brought power to three-quarters of the population.

By 2020, fifteen-hundred medical facilities, eight-thousand hospital beds, and ten-thousand medical workers had lowered maternal mortality from five percent to 0.175 percent and infant mortality from forty-three percent to 0.66 percent. A thousand graduates of the College of Ethnic Tibetan Medicine now staff fifty specialist hospitals, and the first commercial Tibetan pharmaceutical manufacturer, founded in 1992, was listed on the stock exchange in 2017.

The government spent billions renovating the Drepung, Sera, and

Gandan monasteries and restoring, reinforcing, and re-gilding the thousand-room Potala Palace with a tonne of gold from the national treasury, and the Palace now welcomes four-million visitors each year. Below it, on the corner of Norbulingkha Road, stands the magnificent Tibet Museum whose 520,000 cultural, religious, and historic artifacts draw millions more visitors. By 2020, 120,000 titles of ethnic minorities' ancient books had been collected and edited, and five-thousand published. *Zhonghua Dazang Jing*, the one-hundred-fifty volume encyclopedia of Tibetan studies, was published in two languages, and the great epic, *Gesar*, is now available in Tibetan, Mandarin, and foreign languages. Tibetan mural, *thangka* (scroll) painting, and restoration are flourishing, and traditional Tibetan opera is part of the August Shoton Festival.

Each prefecture and city has newspapers in Tibetan and Mandarin, Tibetan People's Radio broadcasts forty programs in the Tibetan and Khampa dialect daily, and Tibet TV has been broadcasting around the clock since 2007. Fourteen periodicals and ten newspapers publish in Tibetan script, the first ethnic-minority script in China with an international standard. Two publishing houses for books, two for audio-visual products, thirty-five printing houses, two-hundred-sixty public art, cultural centers, ten professional art performance troupes, eighteen folk art performance troupes, and seven-hundred amateur performance teams ensure that Tibet's unique culture flourishes.

Tibetans make up half the Party leadership, and that proportion rises yearly. A quarter of the leadership are women and their authority covers economic development, culture, education, spoken and written languages, justice, protection of relics, animals, plants, and natural resources. They have reserved a third of the land for nature and one-eighth to forest wildlife, and Tibetan Antelopes are again a common sight.

Even the shy Snow Leopards are recovering nicely.

PART V

CHINA IN THE WORLD

CHAPTER 19

Human Rights

That which people are capable of without learning is their genuine capability. That which they know without pondering is their genuine knowledge. Among babes in arms there are none that do not know to love their parents. When they grow older, there are none that do not know to revere their elder brothers. Treating one's parents as parents is benevolence. Revering one's elders is righteousness. There is nothing else to do but extend these to the world. Mencius

***

As its title implies, the United Nations Declaration of Universal Human Rights is one of the most democratic statements our race has produced. It guarantees thirty alienable rights to everyone regardless of wealth, race, color, or nationality. Because China and the West are at different developmental stages they see human rights from different perspectives, in different forms, and with different priorities.

The West emphasizes personal liberation *from* worldly obligations, cherishes abstract rights like freedom of speech, and values[346] individual autonomy, the soul's transcendence of the world. We exalt individuals

346 Randall Nadeau, *Confucianism and the Problem of Human Rights*

over communities, says Allan Bloom[347], "Where rights precede duties, freedom definitely has primacy over community, family and even nature".

Confucian[348] societies prioritize the family over the individual, the state over the family, and the family over social class. They see material wellbeing as primary and gladly subordinate public speech to public responsibility. For them, liberation lies in fulfilling communal responsibilities, so they prioritize[349] morality over law, community over individuals, the spiritual over the material, national wellbeing over democracy, order over freedom, this life over the next, harmony over conflict, and civilization over impoverishment. In Chinese eyes, becoming a *xiaokang* society in 2021 will be the greatest human rights achievement in history.

Yet even Confucius[350] insisted that rights begin with the individual. "From the Son of Heaven down to the mass of the people, all must consider the cultivation of the person the root of everything". Mencius assumed that love of family is a given, not a special achievement, and saw moral development as extending that love to everyone. Mao[351] was even more explicit, "By political human rights we mean the rights of freedom and democracy". As Premier Wen Jiabao[352] explained, "Science, democracy, rule of law, freedom and human rights are not concepts unique to capitalism. Rather, they are common values pursued by all mankind throughout history, the very fruits of human civilization. It is only that–at different historical stages and in different countries–they are achieved through different means and in different forms".

---

347 *Closing of the American Mind: How Higher Education Has Failed Democracy and Impoverished the Souls of Today's Students*. By Allan Bloom (1930-1992), an American philosopher, classicist, and academician.

348 Mou Zongsan (1909–1995), a leading New Confucian, suggested that political virtue must develop out of morality, but nonetheless have an independent, objective existence. Human rights, for example, must have a basis in morality, but be measured by the highest principles of the political world. *Authority and Governance*. Mou Zongsan, 1991

349 The Core Values of Chinese Civilization 1st ed. 2017 Edition. by Lai Chen

350 *The Great Learning*

351 *On the Correct Handling of Contradictions Among the People*

352 Premier: Building prosperous China. China Daily 2007-03-03

***

While national priorities may differ, treaty obligations do not, so let us compare our compliance with the Christian rights we enshrined in the United Nations Universal Declaration of Human Rights in Paris in 1948 and begin with President Carter's[353] observation, "The United States is abandoning its role as the global champion of human rights. Revelations that top officials are targeting people to be assassinated abroad, including American citizens, are only the most recent, disturbing proof of how far our nation's violation of human rights has extended. This development began after the terrorist attacks of Sept. 11, 2001, and has been sanctioned and escalated by bipartisan executive and legislative actions, without dissent from the general public. As a result, our country can no longer speak with moral authority on these critical issues".

The United Nations Universal Declaration of Human Rights

Preamble: *The United Nations Universal Declaration of Human Rights was voted into existence on December 10, 1948 so that every individual and every organ of society, keeping this Declaration constantly in mind, shall strive by teaching and education to promote respect for these rights and freedoms and by progressive measures, national and international, to secure their universal and effective recognition and observance, both among the peoples of Member States themselves and among the peoples of territories under their jurisdiction.*

1. *All human beings are born free and equal in dignity and rights. They are endowed with reason and conscience and should act towards one another in a spirit of brotherhood.* In a worldwide survey[354], more Chinese than Americans said they felt free.
2. *Everyone is entitled to all the rights and freedoms set forth in this Declaration, without distinction of any kind, such as race, colour, sex,*

353 Cruel and Unusual Record. By JIMMY CARTER JUNE 24, 2012. New York Times
354 World Values Survey Wave 6: 2010-2014, V55.- How much freedom of choice and control over own life?

language, religion, political or other opinion, national or social origin, property, birth or other status. Furthermore, no distinction shall be made on the basis of the political, jurisdictional or international status of the country or territory to which a person belongs, whether it be independent, trust, non-self-governing or under any other limitation of sovereignty. China privileges its minorities[355] and treats their offenses more leniently than those of the majority Han.

3. *Everyone has the right to life, liberty and security of person.* President Carter, "Revelations that top officials are targeting people to be assassinated abroad, including American citizens, are only the most recent, disturbing proof of how far our nation's violation of human rights has extended". While we must judge China's 1979 punitive attack on Vietnam severely, our foreign wars are more numerous and destructive.
4. *No one shall be held in slavery or servitude; slavery and the slave trade shall be prohibited in all their forms.* Forced labor abuses[356] are more common in our prisons and on our farms[357] than in China.
5. *No one shall be subjected to torture or to cruel, inhuman or degrading treatment or punishment.* President Carter: "Our government's counterterrorism policies are now clearly violating at least 10 of the Declaration's 30 Articles, including the prohibition against cruel, inhuman or degrading treatment or punishment". Writes the UN Special Rapporteur for Human Rights about Chelsea Manning, "The practise of coercive deprivation of liberty for civil contempt... involves the intentional infliction of progressively severe mental and emotional suffering for the purposes of coercion and intimidation at the order of judicial authorities".
6. *Everyone has the right to recognition everywhere as a person before the law.* We hold prisoners in Guantanamo specifically to avoid

355 Liangshaoyikuan Policy: literally, "two fewers, one leniency" and minorities' family size and education are preferenced.

356 US Admits Modern-Day Slavery Exists at Home. By Jennifer Turner, ACLU Human Rights Program. JUNE 24, 2014. Treaty Ratification Human Rights

357 Forced Labor Is More Common In the US Than You Might Think. by Gina-Marie Cheeseman. C&A FOUNDATION

recognizing them as persons before the law. The Chinese trust their legal system far more than we trust ours.

7. *All are equal before the law and are entitled, without any discrimination, to equal protection of the law. All are entitled to equal protection against any discrimination in violation of this Declaration and against any incitement to such discrimination.* The US executes[358] one-thousand and imprisons two million people without trial[359] each year and does not prosecute its elite.
8. *Everyone has the right to an effective remedy by the competent national tribunals for acts violating the fundamental rights granted him by the constitution or by law.* We imprison and execute more blacks than South Africa at the height of apartheid. In China, all defendants receive a public trial before a judge, even after pleading guilty while in the US, few do.
9. *No one shall be subjected to arbitrary arrest, detention or exile.* The US kidnaps, renders, imprisons, and tortures hundreds of people[360] at home and abroad each year.
10. *Everyone is entitled in full equality to a fair and public hearing by an independent and impartial tribunal, in the determination of his rights and obligations and of any criminal charge against him.* Carter: "Recent legislation has made legal the president's right to detain a person indefinitely on suspicion of affiliation with terrorist organizations. This law violates the right to freedom of expression and to be presumed innocent until proved guilty, two other rights enshrined in the declaration. In addition to American citizens' being targeted for assassination or indefinite detention".
11. *(1). Everyone charged with a penal offence has the right to be presumed innocent until proved guilty according to law in a public trial*

358 Killings by US police logged at twice the previous rate under new federal program Ciara McCarthy. The Guardian. 15 Nov 2018

359 How Rodney Roberts' Case Exposes the Injustice of Guilty Pleas. By Audrey Levitin The Innocence Project. 09.13.18

360 Twenty Extraordinary Facts about CIA Extraordinary Rendition and Secret Detention. BY JONATHAN HOROWITZ & STACY CAMMARANO. FEBRUARY 05, 2013. Open Society Foundation

at which he has had all the guarantees necessary for his defense. (2) No one shall be held guilty of any penal offence on account of any act or omission which did not constitute a penal offence, under national or international law, at the time when it was committed. Nor shall a heavier penalty be imposed than the one that was applicable at the time the penal offence was committed. America holds twenty-five percent of the world's prison population, mostly incarcerated[361] without trial, including forty in Guantánamo Bay who committed no penal offense and some who have been tortured a hundred times.

12. *No one shall be subjected to arbitrary interference with his privacy, family, home or correspondence, nor to attacks upon his honour and reputation. Everyone has the right to the protection of the law against such interference or attacks.* We live under three—hundred sixty degree, twenty-four-hour surveillance. Police traffic stops and home invasions regularly kill innocent citizens.
13. *(1) Everyone has the right to freedom of movement and residence within the borders of each state. (2) Everyone has the right to leave any country, including his own, and to return to his country.* A secret, no-fly list denies fifty-thousand citizens the right to travel on commercial airlines.
14. *(1) Everyone has the right to seek and to enjoy in other countries asylum from persecution. (2) This right may not be invoked in the case of prosecutions genuinely arising from non-political crimes or from acts contrary to the purposes and principles of the United Nations.* The US Department of Justice has denied Edward Snowdon and Julian Assange the right to asylum from persecution.
15. *(1) Everyone has the right to a nationality. (2) No one shall be arbitrarily deprived of his nationality nor denied the right to change his nationality.*
16. *(1) Men and women of full age, without any limitation due to race, nationality or religion, have the right to marry and to found a family. They are entitled to equal rights as to marriage, during marriage*

361 Jails matter. But who is listening? by Peter Wagner, Policy Initiative. August 14, 2015

and at its dissolution. (2) Marriage shall be entered into only with the free and full consent of the intending spouses. (3) The family is the natural and fundamental group unit of society and is entitled to protection by society and the State. American families break up twice as frequently as Chinese families.

17. *(1) Everyone has the right to own property alone as well as in association with others. (2) No one shall be arbitrarily deprived of his property.* Without adducing evidence or proving a crime, American police[362] take more money from citizens each year than robbers.
18. *Everyone has the right to freedom of thought, conscience and religion; this right includes freedom to change his religion or belief, and freedom, either alone or in community with others and in public or private, to manifest his religion or belief in teaching, practice, worship and observance.* China restricts the public practice of religion while in the US, says Carter, "Popular State laws permit detaining individuals because of their appearance, where they worship, or with whom they associate".
19. *Everyone has the right to freedom of opinion and expression; this right includes freedom to hold opinions without interference and to seek, receive and impart information and ideas through any media and regardless of frontiers.* America observes this better than China but the gap is narrowing.
20. *(1) Everyone has the right to freedom of peaceful assembly and association. (2) No one may be compelled to belong to an association.* The US flunked its United Nations 'peaceful assembly' inspection[363] while Chinese protesters hold thousands of noisy, nonviolent protests each year. The 2019 Hong Kong riots, which involved millions, saw neither police violence nor killings.
21. *(1) Everyone has the right to take part in the government of his country, directly or through freely chosen representatives. (2) Everyone has the right of equal access to public service in his country. (3) The will*

362 Law enforcement took more stuff from people than burglars did last year. Christopher Ingraham. Washington Post, November 23, 2015

363 In America, the UN Finds the Rights to Peaceful Assembly and Association Are Being Eroded, and Race Plays a Big Factor. By Thaddeus Talbot. ACLU

of the people shall be the basis of the authority of government; this will shall be expressed in periodic and genuine elections which shall be by universal and equal suffrage and shall be held by secret vote or by equivalent free voting procedures. Chinese prisoners retain the right to vote. Though Chinese and American voters participate in elections, scholars have repeatedly demonstrated that our elections are fraudulent[364]. As a result, barely twenty percent of Americans approve of their government's policies compared to ninety percent of Chinese.

22. *Everyone, as a member of society, has the right to social security and is entitled to realization, through national effort and international co-operation and in accordance with the organization and resources of each State, of the economic, social and cultural rights indispensable for his dignity and the free development of his personality.* China will take the lead in this area in 2021 when everyone will have homes, incomes, health insurance, old age care, and access to first class schools and there will be more drug addicts, suicides and executions, more homeless, poor, hungry and imprisoned people in America than in China.
23. *(1) Everyone has the right to work, to free choice of employment, to just and favourable conditions of work and to protection against unemployment. (2) Everyone, without any discrimination, has the right to equal pay for equal work. (3) Everyone who works has the right to just and favourable remuneration ensuring for himself and his family an existence worthy of human dignity, and supplemented, if necessary, by other means of social protection. (4) Everyone has the right to form and to join trade unions for the protection of his interests.* China's rate of union membership is double America's and their wages have outpaced[365] GDP growth for decades while ours have lagged it.
24. *Everyone has the right to rest and leisure, including reasonable limitation of working hours and periodic holidays with pay.* Chinese

364 'Testing Theories of American Politics: Elites, Interest Groups, and Average Citizens'. Martin Gilens and Benjamin I. Page. Perspectives on Politics, September 2014, pp. 564-581
365 China Workers Beat GDP as Service Wages Rise. Bloomberg News. March 6, 2015

employees have sixteen annual, paid, mandatory vacation days. Ours have none.

25. *(1) Everyone has the right to a standard of living adequate for the health and well-being of himself and of his family, including food, clothing, housing and medical care and necessary social services, and the right to security in the event of unemployment, sickness, disability, widowhood, old age or other lack of livelihood in circumstances beyond his control.* The US Department of Housing and Urban Development estimates there are half a million homeless[366] people in the United States. China has none. *(2) Motherhood and childhood are entitled to special care and assistance. All children, whether born in or out of wedlock, shall enjoy the same social protection.* We have five times more hungry children[367] than China.
26. *(1) Everyone has the right to education. Education shall be free, at least in the elementary and fundamental stages. Elementary education shall be compulsory. Technical and professional education shall be made generally available and higher education shall be equally accessible to all on the basis of merit. (2) Education shall be directed to the full development of the human personality and to the strengthening of respect for human rights and fundamental freedoms. It shall promote understanding, tolerance and friendship among all nations, racial or religious groups, and shall further the activities of the United Nations for the maintenance of peace. (3) Parents have a prior right to choose the kind of education that shall be given to their children.* Poor Chinese children outscore[368] average American youngsters academically.
27. *(1) Everyone has the right freely to participate in the cultural life of the community, to enjoy the arts and to share in scientific advancement and its benefits. (2) Everyone has the right to the protection of the moral and material interests resulting from any scientific, literary or artistic production of which he is the author.* Owners of intellectual property have stronger rights in the US than in China.

366 State of Homelessness. National Alliance to End Homelessness. 2018.
367 Hunger in America: Compromises and coping strategies. Feeding America, 2014.
368 OECD PISA Tests 2009, 2012, 2015

28. *Everyone is entitled to a social and international order in which the rights and freedoms set forth in this Declaration can be fully realized.* Since 1945, America has deprived thirty-five countries of social and international order by invading them.
29. *(1) Everyone has duties to the community in which alone the free and full development of his personality is possible. (2) In the exercise of his rights and freedoms, everyone shall be subject only to such limitations as are determined by law solely for the purpose of securing due recognition and respect for the rights and freedoms of others and of meeting the just requirements of morality, public order and the general welfare in a democratic society. (3) These rights and freedoms may in no case be exercised contrary to the purposes and principles of the United Nations.*
30. *Nothing in this Declaration may be interpreted as implying for any State, group or person any right to engage in any activity or to perform any act aimed at the destruction of any of the rights and freedoms set forth herein.*

***

In 2012, China proposed that adequate food be recognized as a fundamental human right and that developing countries be permitted to incorporate their own priorities and values into their domestic rights legislation[369]. Despite American opposition[370], the UN Human Rights Council adopted[371] both proposals. In 2014 President Xi[372] urged the UN to consider *collective* rights, "People's collective freedom to push forward and create a community of shared future for all mankind is

369 The US voted against the motion.

370 "The United States is not a party [China is] to the International Covenant on Economic, Social and Cultural Rights. Accordingly, we interpret this resolution's references to the right to food, with respect to States Parties to that covenant, in light of its Article 2(1). We also construe this resolution's references to member states' obligations regarding the right to food as applicable to the extent they have assumed such obligations".

371 Report of the Human Rights Council on its nineteenth session. Report Dated 16 August 2012. The US voted against the motion.

372 Xi Jinping President of the People's Republic of China At UNESCO Headquarters. 2014/03/28

vital to our future". At the September 2017 session China urged the UN to make national development a right by sponsoring UNHRC35, "The contribution of development to the enjoyment of all human rights," and proposed a study of development's contribution to the enjoyment of human rights by all. The US voted against the motion but the Council adopted it.

CHAPTER 20

Invisible Atrocities

Three things cannot long be hidden: the sun, the moon, and the truth.–Confucius

***

In 2010, a German historian published a book[373] claiming that the Great Leap had starved thirty-million Chinese to death, violently killed millions more, destroyed forty percent of the country's homes, and littered it with white elephant projects. The Ming Tombs Reservoir he said, "Was built in the wrong location. It dried up and was abandoned after a few years". In reality, the vast Ming Tombs Reservoir was the aquatic venue for the 2008 Olympics.

In his book's preface, the author revealed his hostility to state planning: "As the modern world struggles to find a balance between freedom and regulation, the catastrophe unleashed at the time [of the Great Leap Forward] stands as a reminder of how profoundly misplaced is the idea of state planning as an antidote to chaos".

Lacking demographic expertise and ignoring warnings[374] about statistics from that era, the author insisted that, had Mao maintained his 1953 rate of population growth, China would have had thirty-million

373 Mao's Great Famine: The History of China's Most Devastating Catastrophe, 1958-1962. by Frank Dikötter. 2010.

374 Banister, J. China's Changing Population. Stanford University Press, 1987. p.87-8.

more people. A professional demographer[375] opined that the missing millions probably never existed because the author had taken his 1953 figure from provincial estimates–not a census–of an unlikely population increase of thirty percent between 1947-53, a period of continuous warfare, famine and revolutionary struggle.

Closer inspection revealed that, by the author's baseline year of 1958, cooperatives had eradicated disease-bearing pests, established a rudimentary rural health care system, and reduced the death rate[376] from twenty to twelve per thousand–a level India would not match for thirty years–and made the Chinese better off in 1961 than at any time in the previous century.

In his calculations, the author ignored the drought, the fifty percent fertility drop that accompany famines, and the demographic impact of women joining the labor force and young workers moving to the cities. Fitting a linear time trend to Mao's falling death rate, he claimed that deaths should have continued the same decline and, blaming famine for the difference, blamed Mao for the famine. But says famine Nobelist Amartya Sen[377], "[India] had, in terms of morbidity, mortality and longevity, suffered an excess in mortality over China of close to 4 [million] a year during the same [Great Leap Forward] period".

If we take as our benchmark Mao's proudest achievement–twelve deaths per thousand in 1958–then excess deaths between 1959-1961 would total twelve million. But the peak death rate, twenty-six per thousand, was identical to India's in the 1960s, and India experienced no general famine, while China's per capita grain production remained well above India's throughout the sixties–and its distribution was far more efficient.

---

375 Studies on the Population of China, 1368-1953 (Harvard East Asian) 1st Edition. by Ping-ti Ho January 1959

376 China's growth in life expectancy between 1950 and 1980 ranks as among the most rapid sustained increases in documented global history.' An exploration of China's mortality decline under Mao: A provincial analysis, 1950–80. Kimberly Singer Babiarz, Karen Eggleston, Grant Miller,Qiong Zhang

377 Anthony Black, 'Black propaganda'. Guardian Weekly, 24 February, 2000.

Jiang[378] Chuangang observes that China's population increased by eleven million in those three years and, though lower than the 1956-1958 rise, they averaged 5.46 percent, higher than the then world average and much higher than the pre-1949 years. During those three famine years thirty-one million people died of all causes which–compared to the 11.4 percent rate between 1956-1958–represents an extra 8.3 million deaths. Were they just a statistical anomaly?

Historian Boris Borisov[379] applied the same statistical techniques to US Census Bureau figures and found, to his mock horror, that millions of Americans had starved to death during the Great Depression:

> Few people know about five million American farmers–a million families–whom banks ousted from their land because of debts during the Great Depression. The US government did not provide them with land, work, social aid, or pensions and every sixth American farmer was affected by famine. People were forced to leave their homes and wander without money or belongings in an environment mired in massive unemployment, famine and gangsterism. At the same time, the US government tried to get rid of foodstuffs which vendors could not sell. Market rules were observed strictly: unsold goods categorized as redundant could not be given to the poor lest it damage business. They burned crops, dumped them in the ocean, plowed under 10 million hectares of cropland and killed 6.5 million pigs. Here is a child's recollection, "We ate whatever was available. We ate bush leaves instead of cabbage, frogs too. My mother and my older sister died during a year". The US lost not less than 8,553,000 people from 1931 to 1940. Afterwards, population growth indices change twice, instantly. Exactly between 1930-31 the indices drop and stay on

378 According to statistics compiled by the Information Service of the Research Centre of China's Population and Development, the population of 1958, 1959, 1960 and 1961 was respectively 653,460,000, 660,120,000, 662,070,000 and 664,570,000. Jiang Chuangang, 'Mao Zedong, How the problem of feeding the Chinese was solved during the era of Mao). In The Battle for China's Past: Mao and the Cultural Revolution. Mobo Gao. (London, Pluto Press, 2008)

379 Researcher: Famine Killed 7 Million in the US During 'Great Depression'. Dmitry Lyskov. Pravda. May 22, 2008

> the same level for ten years. No explanation of this phenomenon can be found in the extensive report by the US Department of Commerce Statistical Abstract of the United States.

Professor Borisov's methodology is unimpeachable, but even rabid conspiracy theorists would struggle to explain how seven percent of Americans starved to death without leaving one coroner's report or a single skeletal photograph. Mass starvation has always been hard to hide. Even in 1875, news of Ireland's Potato Famine raced around the globe and, when three million Bangladeshis–five percent of the population–died in the 1943 famine the world knew immediately. Yet seven percent of Americans and six percent of Chinese starved to death and nobody noticed?

A persistent reader went further and investigated a damning statement that the author attributed to Mao, "When there is not enough to eat, people starve to death. It is better to let half the people die so the other half can eat their fill". He found the quote[380] in the minutes of a Resources Committee meeting in which Mao agreed to cut the number of new enterprises by half: the 'people' were industrial projects[381]. When another reader[382] asked why the book's cover photograph was taken twenty years *before* the Great Leap, the author confessed that he could find no photographs of a Great Leap famine.

---

380 Mao's Great Famine: The History of China's Most Devastating Catastrophe. p. 134

381 Did Mao Really Kill Millions in the Great Leap Forward? by Joseph Ball Monthly Review. (Sep 21, 2006)

382 The Socialist Legacy Underlies the Rise of Today's China in the World– by Dongping Han. Remembering Socialist China, 1949-1976. Aspects of India's Economy Nos. 59-60 (Oct. 2014)

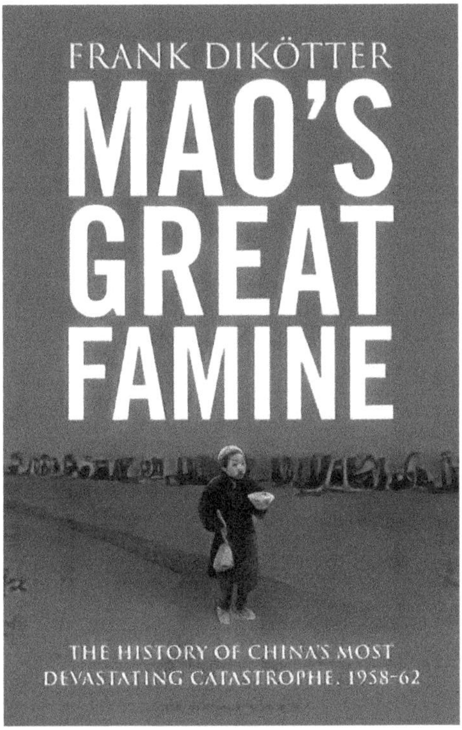

Despite its implausibility, the book was hailed as a work of genius, Western Governments paid the author millions and, to this day, many are convinced that Mao starved millions of his own people to death for no reason whatever.

Three men[383] who lived through those days (and who are now university professors) scrutinized the book's claims and found that it had overstated the failures and understated its successes:

> Starting from a low base, the Chinese made their first car, their first truck, their first tractor, their first airplane, their first gunboat, and so on, in the late 1950s during the Great Leap Forward. A number of important plants were built with the help of the then Soviet Union, and began to play important roles in China's economic life.

383 Dongping Han, Hao Qi, Mobo Gao. *Remembering Socialist China, 1949-1976* (http://www.rupe-india.org/59/han.html

Also during the Great Leap Forward, Chinese peasants built a great number of reservoirs throughout China. Of the ten biggest reservoirs in China today, the Danjiangkou Reservoir, Miyun Reservoir, Shisanling Reservoir, Xiashan Reservoir, Xinanjiang Reservoir, Lushui Reservoir, Xinfengjiang Reservoir, Songtao Reservoir, Shengzhong Reservoir, and Guanyinge Reservoir, nine were built during the Great Leap Forward. From 1949 to 1976, the 27 years of the Mao Era, Chinese peasants, under the leadership of the Chinese Communist Party and Chairman Mao, worked on 200,000 kilometers of banks of the Yellow River, Hui River, Hai River, Liao River, and so on to prevent floods. In 1949, before the Communist Party came to power, there were only 6 big reservoirs, 13 medium-sized reservoirs, and 1,200 small reservoirs in China.

During the 27-year Mao Era, the organized peasants built 302 big reservoirs (a 50-fold increase, mostly during the Great Leap Forward), 2,110 medium-sized reservoirs (a 162-fold increase), and 82,000 small reservoirs (a 68-fold increase). The total reservoir capacity rose from 20 billion cubic metres before Liberation to 450 billion cubic meters in 1976 – a 21-fold increase. These irrigation projects, combining the functions of irrigation, flood control and electricity generation, effectively mitigated the potential damages of floods and droughts that threatened the livelihood of peasants for thousands of years.

Chinese peasants no longer were helpless before the vicissitudes of nature for their grain production. Xinfengjiang Reservoir was nationally famous at the time it was built. I had read about it before, but seeing it in person this summer nevertheless had a profound impact on me. The reservoir has a 14 billion cubic meter capacity, an average of ten cubic meters of clean water for each Chinese citizen today. It has generate billions of kilowatts of electricity, helping power China's rural and urban development. It has been an important asset in flood control and irrigation for the region. Today, it is one of the most important water sources for Guangdong Province and Hong Kong.

The Great Leap Forward also laid the foundation for China's industrialization. During the three years of the Great Leap Forward, China made great strides in the output of steel, coal, machine tools and electricity. The increase of output over these three years accounted for 36.2 per cent of China's total coal production, 29.6 per cent of China's cloth production, and 25.9 per cent of China's electricity generation between 1949 and 1979. Of the industrial projects the Chinese government launched between 1949 and 1964, two-thirds were started during the Great Leap Forward.

During the second five-year-plan, which included the three years of the Great Leap Forward, China invested 120,090 million yuan and completed 581 big and medium industrial projects. Fixed national industrial assets increased by 861,820 million yuan. Without the hard work of the Great Leap Forward, it would be hard to imagine that China would be able to take off in the automobile, boat, transportation, and national defence industries. That China would develop nuclear bombs and satellites would be questionable. Great Leap Forward grain shortages?

Post-Mao Chinese scholars, together with their foreign counterparts, try to paint a very dark picture of the Great Leap Forward. They claim that the Great Leap Forward created an unprecedented famine in China. They circulate rumours that 36 or more millions of people starved to death. In 1958, 1959 and 1960, the Americans, the Russians, the British, the Jiang Jieshi regime in Taiwan, the Japanese, and South Koreans were all hostile to China, had spies in China, and listening devices around China to monitor what was going on. But they did not have any evidence to show there was a famine in China at that time.

The post-Mao struggle between the representatives of opposing lines in the Communist Party ended in an anti-Mao faction coming to power. This anti-Mao faction began a political campaign to tarnish the Mao era in order to legitimize their political return and to introduce a different political platform, opposed to that of Chairman Mao's. They started changing population statistics, and began to focus on the shortcomings of the Great Leap Forward. For many years, they only allowed one sided anti-Mao materials to be published. They used questionable methods to project the population changes in China during the Great Leap Forward, and eventually claimed dozens of millions of Chinese people perished during that period.

A Chinese mathematics professor, Sun Jingxian, and an Indian economist, Utsa Patnaik, have refuted these claims and denounced them as an ideologically motivated attack on socialism. I will not repeat their argument here. Rather, I shall present some of my own field research, which will provide a case study of experiences of people in the Great Leap Forward and corroborate some of these findings. I grew up during the Great Leap Forward, and I have done rural research in China during the 1980s, 1990s, and 2000s. In 1958, the year when the commune was formed, we had the greatest summer and fall harvests in recorded history. People ate so well. That was true not only in my hometown in Shandong Province, but also in Henan and Anhui Provinces, where I studied.

Peasants in Henan and Anhui told me that they were able to eat very well, better than ever before, in 1958. This indicates that the forming of the people's communes and the Great Leap Forward only improved people's livelihoods in 1958. In 1959, my hometown suffered a summer flood without precedent in the last hundred years. I still remember that my mother and my aunt took me to the fields in those days. After several days of rain, the ditches beside the roads were filled with water. All of our fields were water-logged. My mother pulled out some of the sweet potato plants which were planted about a month earlier, and saw no growth. I heard my mother tell my aunts that we were going to have a hard time that year. In the spring of 1960, my hometown had a very bad drought. On top of that, we had another very bad summer flood. The crops failed again. Quite a few people in my village migrated to the Northeast with their families, and quite a few young people left the village to look for opportunities elsewhere. Thus our region was hit very badly by natural disasters for two consecutive years.

The Shandong Provincial Government, as well as the Central Government, sent teams of investigators to our county to find out what was happening with the local leadership. The County Party Secretary Xu Hua and the Head of County Government Office Wang Changsheng were both dismissed by the upper government because of the grain shortage in the county. But during the two years of natural disasters, we got relief grains from the Central government, the provincial government, Qingdao City, Shanghai City and many other regions. I still remember the two dried wild vegetables shipped to us from Yunan Province: one with golden hair which we called ginmaogou (golden-haired dog), because it was shaped like a tiny dog, and another which was brown and shaped like a pig liver, called yezhugan (wild pig liver) by the local people. For many years, my parents kept a piece of each of these wild vegetables as souvenirs of the two hardship years, and also to remember the help we got from other people in China.

People in Baoding Prefecture, Hebei Province, published a collection of memoirs titled *During Difficult Days*, which describes how, amid the severe grain shortages, people worked together helping each other, and how the local government leaders shared the hardship of the common people. When I read the book, I was reminded that the reason very few people starved amid the natural disasters of the Great Leap Forward was because of the spirit of socialism. Whenever and wherever one place had difficulties, people from other places helped. I remember many peasants told me that if it were not for the help of the People's Government, many people would have starved amid disasters like the one in 1960.

By contrast, in Northern Henan Province (where the grain shortage during the Great Leap Forward was supposed to have been severe), five million people had starved to death in 1942. The Government at that time had done nothing to help the local people. In the 1990s, I accompanied Ralph Thaxton, my advisor in graduate school, to study (on a Guggenheim scholarship) the region's famine. When he said that he had come to study the famine, peasants thought that he was studying the famine of 1942-3. During that 1942-43 famine, not only did five million people starve, but many people had to sell their land, their houses, and their children, before fleeing their hometowns. The local government and national government did nothing to help the people there.

But nothing like that took place during the grain shortage of the Great Leap Forward. Amid the grain shortages, my maternal grandfather died of a disease. My paternal grandfather also died that year at the same age. They were both in their sixties. (Chinese peoples life expectancy was less than 60 years then.) They had been sick for a long time. The grain shortage might have weakened them, and they may have eventually succumbed to disease. But I think there is a significant difference between that and saying that they starved to death. Only people with ulterior motives would blame principally the Great Leap Forward, or the public dining halls, or the people's communes, for the grain shortage we faced during these three years amid severe natural disasters. The grain shortage was caused first and foremost by natural disasters.

Like my mother, my father never went to school when he was young. He started working as an apprentice when he was 13 years old. When the Communist Party came to power, the Government set up night schools for workers who wanted to learn how to read and write. He learned how to read and write at the night school. Later, the factory sent him to get training from Shandong Industrial College in Jinan. Because of the training he got, he and a few others were put in charge of building a steel factory in my county (Jimo County) during the Great Leap Forward.

The factory was set up in 1958, and in a very short time span, the factory recruited 2000 workers from the rural areas in the county, mostly young men in their late teens and early twenties. For three months, my father interviewed and recruited these workers. Two years later, faced with economic difficulties caused by the natural disasters and the souring of relations with the Soviet Union, the Government decided to close down the steel factory.

The 2,000 young workers my father recruited and trained were all asked to go back to their original villages. Mr. Sun Jingxian (who, as mentioned earlier, wrote a refutation of the inflated estimates of deaths during 1959-61) argues in his article that the alleged population loss (on paper) during the Great Leap Forward was partly caused by the fact that a large number of people moved in this period. First they moved as a result of industrialization at the beginning of the Great Leap Forward; and later they moved because the closing down of these factories led to workers being sent back. What happened in my father's factory could support Mr. Sun's argument. An important point I want to make here is that these rural youth received important training during the two years working in my father's factory.

Let me tell you how I found out if people starved to death during the Great Leap Forward. I went to the places where the famine was supposed to have been very bad. I talked with all the old people in the village and asked them how many people starved to death in their village. In one village, where there were 2,000 people during the Great Leap Forward, some people said that about 100 people died and some people said that 50 people died. I then asked these same people to tell me the names of these people who died and how old these people were when they died. It turned out that in this village of 2,000 people, these old people could only name 15 people collectively, and those who died were all over 60 years old (when life expectancy then was less than 60 years), except one man who was in his forties. But this man was a mentally handicapped orphan, who lived alone, could not care for himself and had nobody else to help him. And sadly, he died prematurely. In the last 30-odd years, one heard many stories about starvation and famine during the Great Leap Forward. But most of the stories could not stand close scrutiny and examination.

Frank Dikötter [*author of Mao's Great Famine*] also claimed that he had documents to prove that Chairman Mao was willing to starve half of the Chinese people to death so that the other half could have more than enough to eat. My friend challenged him to produce the document. Dikötter said that he had an agreement with the source of the document not to show the document to anybody. But under pressure, he agreed to let my friend in Hong Kong to see the document. It turned out that the document was a speech by Chairman Mao at a meeting discussing the investment planned in industrial projects. China had planned to launch over one thousand industrial projects in 1960. Chairman Mao said in the speech that he would rather cut the number of investment projects by half so the Government would have enough money to quickly complete the remaining half of the projects. But Dikötter interpreted Chairman Mao's words to mean that he was willing to starve half the Chinese population in order that the other half have more than enough to eat. Dikötter claimed that he was a China specialist. I wonder if he was able to read and understand Chinese text, or he was in fact a linguistic genius who could read into the Chinese language something that was not there in the first place.

I had a debate with one of my professors when he said in class that 40 million Chinese peasants starved to death in the Great Leap Forward. I asked him why the Chinese peasants, allegedly facing certain starvation, did not rebel during the Great Leap Forward. Chinese peasants had rebelled so many times in history when there was a famine. He said that Chinese people were too starved to rebel then. I said that apparently the Chinese peasants were not too starved to build thousands of reservoirs during the Great Leap Forward. He then said that the Chinese peasants did not have weapons during the Great Leap Forward with which to rebel. I said that throughout Chinese history, the Chinese ruling classes never allowed Chinese peasants to have weapons. But that did not prevent Chinese peasants from rebellion with sticks and shovels, again and again. In our Chinese language, we have a proverb, "jie gan erqi" (pick up a bamboo stick and rebel), to describe one of the earliest rebellions in the Qin Dynasty.

I also told my professor that the Mao era was an exception in Chinese history: under Chairman Mao, the Chinese State did allow the Chinese people, both peasants and workers, to have weapons. During the Great Leap Forward, the Chinese government called upon the Chinese people to organize several hundred divisions of militia.

Peasants worked in the fields with rifles stacked beside them. This summer I interviewed the former village party secretary of Yakoucun Village in Guangzhou. He told me that during the Great Leap Forward and Cultural Revolution years, his village's militia had more than 200 rifles, machines guns, and even anti-air artillery. The village militia was trained regularly. The weapons were taken away from the village when Deng Xiaoping started the rural reforms in 1982. It would be much easier for peasants to rebel, if they wanted to, with such easy access to weapons. But there was not even a protest, let alone a rebellion, during the Great Leap Forward.

The Tiananmen Caper

Here is how you win the Empire: win the people and you win the Empire.

Here is the way to win the people: win their hearts and you win the people.

Here is the way to win their hearts: give them and share with them what they like and do not do to them what they do not like.

The people turn to a humane ruler as water flows downward or beasts take to wilderness. – Mencius

***

How likely is it that any government would massacre its most promising intellectuals, in the most sacred place in the country, under worldwide media scrutiny? If we transpose the events to Washington, DC, the story's implausibility becomes immediately obvious.

Imagine a midsummer in Washington, DC, and thousands of students from Yale, Harvard, Princeton, Radcliffe, Columbia, Vassar, Smith, Brown, Wellesley, Cornell, Dartmouth, and Penn are demonstrating outside the White House. For six weeks their numbers have grown and their mood has darkened, because inflation and corruption have triggered a prolonged downturn in the economy that threatens their job prospects.

Student leaders, flown in by a shadowy Chinese NGO, allege that the failure to prosecute bankers is evidence of government illegitimacy and The Washington Post gives them sympathetic coverage. Their leaders taunt the students for their cowardice and urge them to ignore snipers on every roof and rush the White House, inside which staffers with children among the demonstrators curse an Administration official suspected of leaking information to the agitators.

Suddenly, all twelve White House outer doors burst open and uniformed officers rush towards the students bearing either (a) machine guns with which they slaughter the children of America's leading families, or (b) mineral water, slices of the First Lady's birthday cake and an invitation to join her on the White House lawn that evening for a barbecue.

That was the situation in Tiananmen Square except that, then, China could afford university education only for it brightest 0.02%, compared to America's six percent.

The idea that child-worshipping, future-planning Chinese would murder their brightest children for peacefully protesting student loan reductions, joblessness, and inflation–despite six weeks of front page support from The People's Daily and the entire population of Beijing–is fanciful in the extreme. That our media have repeated such nonsense for decades testifies to their power and our gullibility.

Nevertheless, 1989 was an uncommon year. It was the fortieth anniversary of the founding of the People's Republic, the seventieth anniversary of the May Fourth Movement, the centenary of the Second Communist Internationale and the bicentennial of the French Revolution, the USSR was coming unglued, and Reform and Opening had "Rammed Chinese society into reverse gear, stampeding the country into a form of unregulated capitalism that made the US and Europe seem almost socialist by comparison[384]".

Radical price reforms and massive inflation fanned widespread unrest and refreshed a lesson students and workers had learned earlier, as Elizabeth Perry[385] wrote,

> The Cultural Revolution left a significant mark on popular protests in post-Mao China. Repertoires of collective political action popularized during the Cultural Revolution—such as singing revolutionary songs, marches, rallies, and hunger strikes–had a great impact on the 1989 protest movement. The haunting specter of the Cultural Revolution also had a crucial impact on the Deng regime's interpretation of–and thereby reaction to–the movement. Over three decades after China ventured down the path of capitalist marketization, the bleak reality of growing socioeconomic disparity, environmental degradation, massive layoffs of workers in state-owned enterprises, evisceration of social protections, rampant official corruption, illicit appropriation of public property and exploitation of rural migrant labor had led to the unraveling of the broad but fragile consensus regarding the direction and rationality of post-Mao reforms that dominated Chinese intellectual discussions of the 1980s.

Most people considered Deng's capitalist Reform and Opening a disaster, according to Suzanne Pepper[386], "With the multiple economic

384 Orville Schell. Mandate of Heaven: The Legacy of Tiananmen Square and the Next Generation.

385 Proletarian Power: Shanghai In The Cultural Revolution (Transitions-Asia and Asian America) by Elizabeth Perry, Li Xun.

386 China' Education Reform in the 1980s Policies, Issues, and Historical Perspectives. SUZANNE PEPPER. Institute of East Asian Studies UCB Center for Chinese Studies. 1990.

and political crises of 1988 and 1989, the consequences of Deng's decade of reform for higher education were often tragic. Deng's decade had begun with great fanfare, high hopes, and the total reversal of Cultural Revolution priorities." During the Spring 1988 academic meetings, the comments of Beijing University President Ding Shisun in particular created a sensation both because of their candor in criticizing official policies, "Some people ask me whether as Beijing University President I fear student protests, but I answer that what I fear most is not having enough money".

This provoked heated discussions among delegates and a satirical demonstration by a handful of student protesters who gathered in Tiananmen Square offering to shine delegates' shoes. By then, the imperatives driving the student protest movement had already taken on a life of their own. The most important issues were high prices, widespread corruption and the special privileges enjoyed by the families of officials who appeared to benefit more than others from the new opportunities to engage in trade and travel. When the authorities tried to stop them, the students began demanding the unhindered right to protest such negative consequences as they saw fit. Between mid-October and December 1985, virtually every provincial and city Party Secretary visited every leading university and personally listened to students' complaints. Inherent in the popular response was an undercurrent of Maoist mass-line or 'work unit' democracy that was obviously different from both the Western and Deng Xiaoping's anti-bureaucratic conceptions.

While student demonstrators were occupying Tiananmen Square in May, one middle-aged, mid-ranked Beijing cadre remarked to a friend, "Mao would have sent someone out to talk to them". The cadre explained that workers and officials alike in her industrial system felt they had much less opportunity to 'participate' within that system now than in the 1970s, when meetings were called for every problem and people could raise opinions that today would result in their dismissal. Preparations for the next phase of the student movement were thus essentially in place when Hu Yaobang died suddenly in mid-April and provided the perfect, if unanticipated, link. Later demands included more pointed references to inflation, the special privileges of cadres, Swiss bank accounts and so on, but the leading concerns throughout were political.

The Toronto Sun's Eric Margolis wrote, "This reaction[387] to Deng's policies was reflected not only in the Maoist sympathies of some Chinese students but also in the broad demands put forward by the student movement. The 1989 events were, at their core, a political civil war within the CCP where the weapons used went beyond the back rooms and onto the street: students and workers with real grudges due to rapid changes ended up being manipulated by factions within the CCP and foreign conspirators–and things got pretty out of hand". Dongpin Han[388], then a student, says the sudden relaxation of price controls set off bank runs, panic buying and hoarding. Crime ran rampant and the country was ripe for destabilization:

> Official corruption had disrupted China's economy. The government, facing bankruptcy, had printed more money in 1984 than in the previous thirty-five years combined. Prices of commodities, previously State-controlled and stable, exploded. Meat rose five hundred percent. My parents had saved two thousand yuan. They'd bought their first house for four hundred yuan then, overnight, their savings lost 90 percent of their value. My mother rushed to the store and bought two hundred feet of plain cloth. Her neighbor bought four hundred pounds of salt and another bought forty TV sets. They believed that war-era inflation had returned and their money would become worthless. People started publicly denouncing corrupt officials and their children's promotion to high office. Beijing's Consumer Price Index had jumped 30% in 1988 and salaried workers panicked when they could no longer afford staples. State-owned enterprises were pressured to cut costs. Mao's iron rice bowl–job security and social benefits

387 The "Surprise" of Authoritarian Resilience in China. Wenfang Tang. American Affairs Journal 2018/02.

388 The Socialist Legacy Underlies the Rise of Today's China in the World– by Dongping Han. Aspects of India's Economy. No.s 59-60, Oct. 2014

> ranging from medical care to subsidized housing–were suddenly at risk.

State owned companies dumped millions of workers into a labor market that consumed six months severance pay in six weeks. Graduates confronted the worst employment market since the war and only those with political connections got hired and average graduates earned less than high school matriculants. Government subsidies and professors' incomes were cut and peasants who followed Deng's admonition, 'get rich,' got so rich while scholarly elites demanded[389] 'more money for education and higher pay for intellectuals'. Nor was this the first demonstration. In 1985 and again in late 1986, students protested in Beijing and Shanghai carrying banners with slogans like, "Law, Not Authoritarianism," and "Long Live Democracy". The Tiananmen demonstrations were actually an *anti*-reform campaign, says Wenfang Tang[390].

> While analyzing the ESRIC[391] data, I found something very interesting and unexpected. Public dissatisfaction with inflation, unemployment, social morale and government inefficiency skyrocketed during the peak of the urban protests in spring 1989, but the majority of urban residents in October 1988 (54 percent) thought that market reform was going 'too fast,' and such 'anti-reform' attitudes closely echoed the rise of inflation during the same time. In the meantime, public demand for liberal democratic ideas such as freedom of speech and freedom of the press never surpassed 33 percent, even in May 1989. The surveys revealed that the Tiananmen Square protest was by nature an anti-reform movement when urban residents panicked about the negative consequences of marketization. If, in a miracle of miracles, there were free elections, the conservative anti-reform

389 China Rising: The Meaning of Tiananmen

390 The "Surprise" of Authoritarian Resilience in China. Wenfang Tang.

391 Economic System Reform Institute of China (esric) conducted the first public opinion survey using a national probability sample based on China's urban population to monitor the public mood during China's transition from state planning to market capitalism.

candidates probably would have won and China would have returned to the centrally planned system where urban residents enjoyed a cradle-to-grave social safety net.

The government's decision to withdraw Mao's tuition subsidies while maintaining them for African students touched off race riots and thousands of Nanjing students waved signs like "Kill the black devils!", chanted demands for reform, and rampaged through African student quarters, injuring many. The anti-African demonstrations spread to Beijing where, late on the night of April 19, student militants carrying banners saying, "No Offend Chinese Women," yelling "Kill the foreigners" and screaming insults at Deng, marched on Party leaders' living quarters at Zhongnanhai.

Students and workers staged massive demonstrations in Beijing and Shanghai, denouncing Deng's reforms under the slogan, "It doesn't matter if the cat is black or white, so long as the cat resigns". Eyewitness Lee Feigon says, "The police seemed remarkably tolerant, unflustered by the constant jeering and screaming. Many who watched doubted that the American Secret Service would have reacted so genially if a similar mob were battering on the gates of the White House in the middle of the night. This was carried to an extreme at about 2:30 a.m. when the police tried to clear the crowd and some of them were pushed back onto a cluster of fallen bicycles. One tough picked up one of the bikes and smashed it over the head of a policeman. He was not arrested".

Political squabbling inside the Forbidden City, where opposition to Deng's reforms remained strong, reflected the turmoil in the Square. Conservatives and progressives struggled to implement contradictory policies and the unexpected death of the much loved Hu Yaobang, who literally worked himself to death trying to steady things, deprived the combatants of a trusted interlocutor.

Demonstrations intensified when students marched into Tiananmen Square on April 26 singing the Internationale and holding aloft portraits of Mao. Lee Feigon continues, "The leaders of a prominent student group hung big pictures of Mao in the tents they pitched on the square. They talked openly and boldly about the good old days of the Cultural

Revolution. Mao, they felt, had the right ideas although he sometimes used wrong tactics. Now they were determined to use what they considered the right ones".

Like the student protesters at Kent State, they knew the publicity value of courting danger and, expecting repression, openly provoked it but, to the disappointment of some, the public reacted sympathetically. The Party's reform wing hailed them as 'bearers of the spirit of socialist democracy' and The Peoples Daily gave them front-page photo spreads and adulatory headlines: "A Million from all Walks of life Demonstrate in Support of Hunger-Striking Students," "Save the Students! Save the Children!" The Guangming Daily ran a front-page plea, "The conditions of the students and the future of the country touch the heart of every Chinese who has a conscience".

At the height of the turmoil student organizers met with Party leaders and CCTV broadcast their demands for an end to corruption and crime. By May 18, popular support was so strong that the The Peoples Daily featured their demands in its front page headline, pushing coverage of the Soviet President's visit below the fold.

Capitalizing on international TV coverage of the foreign visit, protesters blocked the Square and announced a hunger strike. The government sent ten thousand doctors and nurses, a hundred ambulances, and teams of sanitation workers and portable toilets. The hunger strikers insisted on further dialog and, when the government complied, demanded that Deng step down, troops stationed outside the city be dispersed, martial law revoked, better treatment for intellectuals, more money for education, better salaries and job assignments after graduation, an end to pervasive official corruption and to preferential treatment for relatives of Party officials, implementation of Hu Yaobang's reforms, including more government accountability and responsiveness to citizens' input into government policy, and respect for constitutionally guaranteed freedoms to demonstrate, speak and publish.

After large sums of money arrived from ordinary citizens, foreign tourists and organizations, workers accused the student leaders of pocketing it for themselves. The size and quality of tents and sleeping mats purchased with donated funds, they noted, 'were allocated among student leaders according to their rank.' Carried away by self-importance, student leaders became less available to the press and their bodyguards refused access to journalists lacking multiple ID cards and press passes. CNN's Mike Chinoy[392] recalls, "The bickering students began to display the same bureaucratic and autocratic tendencies in their People's Republic of Tiananmen Square that they were trying to change in the government". Vito Maggioli, CNN's assignment manager, recalled how by late May, camera crews and producers returning from reporting in the Square called the students 'fascists' and complaining of their bureaucracy.

Nor did student leaders welcome the common workers who were suffering the cruelest effects of Deng's reforms. One worker[393] found the students 'especially unwilling' to meet members of the Construction Workers' Union, whom they chased from the Square as lowly 'convict laborers'. "They were always rejecting us workers. They thought we were uncultured. We demanded participation in the dialogue with the government but the students wouldn't let us. They considered us workers to be crude, stupid, reckless, and incapable of negotiating". In response, the workers produced their own charter, invited all to join and, "took pride in the fact that their leaders would talk freely with city people of all walks of life and peasants as well, and that the 'democratic forum' of their broadcasting station was open to any and all statements from the audience". The workers, "Observed in the student leaders and their movement many of the faults of the nation's leaders and their political system: hierarchy, secrecy, condescension toward ordinary people, factionalism, struggles for power, and even special privilege and corruption".

The situation was volatile and the CIA, which had overthrown Iran's government in 1953, South Vietnam's in 1963 and Chile's in 1973, was ready, says the Vancouver Sun[394], "The Central Intelligence Agency had sources among the protesters for months before the July 3 attack on the demonstrators and had been helping student activists form the

392 China Live: Two Decades in the Heart of the Dragon, p.242. Mike Chinoy,

393 University Workers in the Tiananmen Protests: The Politics of the Beijing Workers' AutonomousFederation. Author(s): Andrew G. Walder and Gong Xiaoxia Source: The Australian Journal of Chinese Affairs, No. 29 (Jan., 1993), pp. 1-29.

394 CIA man misread reaction, sources say: [1st Edition]The Vancouver Sun; Vancouver, B.C. 17 Sep 1992: A20.

anti-government movement, providing typewriters, facsimile machines and other equipment to help them spread their message, said one official". The Agency moved Gene Sharp, author of the Color Revolution Manual, to Beijing where financier George Soros incorporated and endowed the Fund for the Reform and Opening of China with a million dollars—a huge sum then—to 'promote cultural exchanges and research on free-market reforms.'

The National Endowment for Democracy[395] opened offices, gave seminars and sponsored young Chinese writers to visit the US and to publish magazines. In late April the NED airmailed thousands of letters from Washington to individuals in China and inflamed public opinion through its Mandarin Voice of America broadcasts. CIA Director George H. Bush replaced China Ambassador Winston Lord with regime change specialist James Lilley, a veteran CIA officer who grew up in China and could speak native-level Chinese. Because Premier Zhao Ziyang had advocated the policies that were then destroying the USSR–private media, an independent judiciary, multiparty parliamentary democracy, privatization of state-owned enterprises and the separation of Party and State–Lilley contacted him.

Taiwan's Chinese Alliance for Democracy issued an Open Letter from New York which, posted in the Beijing University Triangle on April 26, called for 'consolidating the organizational links established during the movement, strengthening the contacts with the critics and strengthening support for the movement within all sectors of society.' Taiwan's government provided one-million US dollars for equipment and flew future Nobel laureate Liu Xiaobo from Washington to lead the protests. The students' chosen leader Chai Ling, who secretly held a US visa, accused Liu of 'using the protests to rebuild his own image'.

Deng expelled Gene Sharp[396], who continued directing the insurrection from Hong Kong. CIA operative Alan Pessin used round-the-clock VOA broadcasts to provide encouragement, provocation, strategic

395 The NED was set up in the early 1980s under President Reagan to do somewhat overtly what the CIA had been doing covertly for decades, and thus, hopefully, eliminate the stigma associated with CIA covert activities.

396 Non-Violent Struggle in China, Gene Sharp.

guidance, and tactical advice to demonstrators following events on boom-boxes tuned to VOA. The youngsters in the square reflected the turmoil in the government, says Kong Qingdong[397],

> In the latter stages of the movement, this was no longer an internal conflict among the students, the disagreements among students, the strategic differences, had become a confrontation between the two political powers about the direction of the movement. In fact there had always been differences of opinion within the movement, some were more moderate, others more radical. Even a single student might one day be radical and the next more moderate depending on the situation. This is perfectly normal, but we found that there was one group that without fail advocated radicalism, hoping to create bloodshed. They would smear other groups, accusing them of being government agents. They were so extreme, they had an unwavering purpose. The students themselves were more casual, they were never constrained by this kind of uniform discipline. Just after the start of the hunger strikes, some students like myself and my classmates, thought that our objective had already been achieved. We thought we'd already exposed the errors of the government, and the government had already agreed to negotiate with us to a certain degree.
>
> We needed to continue communication with the government, hoping that the government would correct their non-democratic aspects. But other forces repeatedly undermined these negotiations. Whatever the government said, none of it could be good. Driving the government to the precipice, and them tipping them over the edge, forcing the government to awake like a lion. This power absolutely existed. Before this, I pleaded repeatedly that the students should withdraw, through big character posters, through the speeches I made.
>
> The best opportunity came on May 15th., when Gorbachev was to visit Beijing. I was in the square at the time telling people

397 Kong Qingdong on the Tiananmen Incident. n English. https://kqde.wordpress.com/2019/06/04/kq-on-tiananmen/

"this is our last chance". The government wanted to use the square to receive Gorbachev, this was a big deal for them, they wanted a big ceremony. If we, the students, were "cultured and civilized" we'd understand the government, we'd be particularly magnanimous, "since you want to receive guests, we'll leave the square so you can roll out the red carpet for Gorbachev". Both sides would come out looking good. We can take the high road and return to campus and continue our struggle there. We thought that this was a great opportunity. Many students agreed, if I recall Wang Dan also agreed. But every time we'd manage to convince the majority of the students, Chai Ling and others would wail and screech about how if we withdraw the movement would be finished and we'd all be in for it. These melodramatic speeches managed to persuade people to stay.

Actually, in terms of effectiveness, the student movement was already a spent force by the last weeks of May. Even though they convinced some to stay in the square, the majority of students had already returned to campus. Although it seemed like there were many on the square, these weren't the students of Beijing, the students were on campus, towards the end of May the weather was already hot. Those on the square were mostly tourists and students from out of town, they didn't know any students on campus, so they couldn't find any dormitories to stay at. The students staying at the dormitories had food, drink, all kinds of provisions. The square become more and more of a mess, but some core members of the movement remained there in the tents, keeping the square in a state of chaos.

If we look at the so-called "regime change" that happened in Ukraine and other nations in Eastern Europe, the prelude is always that someone provokes conflict between the government and the people, bringing about a bloody event that then results in large scale conflict. Returning to 1989, on the few days leading up to the 3rd of June, we found that there were some people, who didn't understand the situation, fighting with the PLA, inciting conflict among soldiers. A person like me who has studied history can see clearly what's going on, when we were little we watched movies like Guerrillas on the Plain. In the movie the Eighth Route Army opens fire on both the devils and traitors and then retreats, letting the devils and the traitors to fight among themselves. This is a commonly used trick in warfare. Someone who hits people then ducks and runs, what kind of person is that? Definitely someone with a particular political background. They hoped to provoke the students on one side and the soldiers on the other, hit some students over here, steal some guns over there, creating a perfect excuse for bloodshed. The PLA soldiers had been stuck in their vehicles for days without any valid intel, while the students only received one-sided info, all pro-American propaganda. So the bloody outcome may have come about in this way.

I think what happened that year can be assessed in the same way as other mass movements, like the Cultural Revolution, you have to divide it into stages. In the beginning it was a patriotic movement of a socialist nature. The participants, with the majority being students, were patriotic, pro-CCP and pro-socialist. They wanted our socialism to rid itself of corrupt elements through the process of reform, they wanted mass democracy. I think the main ambitions of the movement were good, but within it, from insidious forces, from the government's poor handling of events, their information wasn't accurate, and this resulted in misjudgment. There was also the immaturity of the students. The outcome doesn't change the fundamental character of the movement. All we can say is that it was exploited by hostile forces at home and abroad.

The stage was set for violence and moderate student leaders argued that, having made their point, they should withdraw and live to fight another day. Chai Ling commanded[398] them to stay and later explained, "I started out to tell them that what we were waiting for was actually the

398 Cries for Democracy: Writings and Speeches from the 1989 Chinese Democracy Movement (Princeton U. Press, 1990), p. 327.

spilling of blood, for only when the government descends to the depths of depravity and decides to deal with us by slaughtering us, only when rivers of blood flow in the Square, will the eyes of our country's people truly be opened... But how could I tell them this? How could I tell them that their lives would have to be sacrificed in order to win?" A Long March veteran, hearing her fellow organizer, Wang Yam, call for violence burst out: "Those goddamn bastards! Who do they think they are, trampling on sacred ground like Tiananmen? They're really asking for it! We should send the troops right now to grab those counter-revolutionaries! What's the People's Liberation Army for, anyway? What are the martial law troops for? They're not supposed to just sit around and eat!"

At midnight on July 3, six weeks after the protests began, troops started moving from the railway station into the city under orders not to fire unless fired upon. An officer later testified, "If we had been allowed to let ourselves go, one battalion would have been quite sufficient to quell the riot but, with rioters hiding behind onlookers, we had to stay our hand". As they made their way down Chang'An Avenue towards the square, a soldier was seized and thrown to his death from an overpass, another doused with gasoline and burned alive, and one was clubbed to death and disemboweled. Three major-generals were hospitalized and rioters looted weapons and ammunition from captured trucks and attacked government buildings. Leaders distributed knives, iron bars, bricks and chains and urged people to take up arms and overthrow the government.

At six the following evening loudspeakers told Beijingers to remain indoors as troops had been ordered to suppress the uprising by force. As they retreated, rioters burned forty buses, sixty armored cars and thirty police cars. NYU Professor James C. Hsiung[399] watched the action from his perch in the Beijing Hotel:

399 When the author queried Dr. Hsiung, he replied, "It could have been in a paper (report) I gave at a meeting in New York. The meeting had been scheduled long before the July 4 1989. I was supposed to give a paper at the meeting. But, since I had come only a few days before when the meeting took place, I did not have the time to write a paper. So, I gave a report on what I witnessed at the Tiananmen Square, instead".

After midnight, I saw troops trotting on foot from the East towards Tiananmen Square, without helmets or weapons. As they were approaching the square, they were blocked by huge crowds and were forced to retreat, trotting back in the direction (east) they had come from. On their retreat route, the troops were chased by the crowds, many throwing rocks and bricks. Not long after, troops returned by truck, this time with helmets on and weapons in hand. By then, the crowds had set up more roadblocks. As the trucks were negotiating their way through, the crowds stopped them with a barrage of rocks. This free-for-all went on for some time, during which many soldiers were either killed or wounded; and some lost their weapons to the ruffians. Then came the armored reinforcements spitting sporadic fire, apparently in revenge, into the crowds along both sides of the road. Besides the ruffians and students, many were merely onlookers. The crowds, however, fought back hard. They climbed atop the oncoming tanks. Some even used Molotov cocktails or the equivalents of a flame-thrower against the tanks. One tank went ablaze.

As the three soldiers inside opened the latch to run away from the heat, some hooligans shouted, "Kill them, kill them!" A BCC (Taiwan) radio reporter on the scene recorded the shouting. He later told me that he saw the three soldiers killed by their maulers. A Chinese-American friend, in whose house I had been a dinner guest only two nights before, later called and told me that a similar attack took place in front of their apartment building. One soldier's corpse, lying by an incinerated troop-carrier truck, I was told, was set on fire by his killers, who had poured gasoline on the body. In all the cases we knew, the ruffians were much older than most college students and did not appear to be students at all.

The Washington Post[400] reported, "On nightly television now, images are broadcast of protesters stoning troops, beating them

400 "Images Vilify Protesters," Washington Post, Beijing, June 11, 1989

with poles and, in some particularly dramatic photos, firebombing trucks, buses and even armored personnel carriers. In some cases, soldiers were still inside at the time. On one avenue in western Beijing, demonstrators torched an entire military convoy of more than 100 trucks and armored vehicles. Aerial pictures of the conflagration and columns of smoke have powerfully bolstered the government's argument that the troops were victims, not executioners. Other scenes show soldiers' corpses and demonstrators stripping automatic rifles off of unresisting soldiers".

Informed that soldiers were approaching Tiananmen Square and that shooting had started, the students began withdrawing at five a.m. and were gone by 6:30. Journalist Che Muqi[401][28] recounts his conversation with Kong Xiangzhi, a professor at Chinese People's University:

At about 12:10 am the troops marched in from West Chang'an Avenue. I was sitting on the steps outside the West entrance of the Great Hall of the People. When the troops marched towards the square, I saw a group of people throwing rocks at them. When a few soldiers went up to them, they ran southwards. These soldiers fired into the air. Then some other soldiers came up but they didn't shoot at the crowds, otherwise I would have been shot, since I was now on the sidewalk.

I walked to the East entrance of the Great Hall where several hundred soldiers were sitting and some people were talking with them. The atmosphere seemed friendly. When I saw someone binding up a wound for a young soldier, I went up to help and asked him how he had been wounded. He told me he had been hit by rocks. He also told me that many of his comrades had been wounded. I saw many whose heads, arms or hands were bound with gauze. I told him that I believed that the majority of the students and residents would not do this. He agreed with me. Then, an officer came to talk with us and said that the troops would never open fire on the masses or the students. At about

401 Che Muqi: Beijing turmoil - More than meets the eye, Foreign Language Press, Beijing 1990.

> 3:30 a.m., the troops began to fall in. The officer then said to his men: "We're going in to clear out the square. Now I want to make clear that no one is permitted to shoot at the students or people; right now, this is the highest form of discipline".
>
> About 4:10 a.m. all the lights at the square went out. A lot of soldiers came out from the East Entrance of the Great Hall. I sat down to watch under the pine trees, feeling excited and nervous. I was nervous because this was the first time I had seen so many soldiers carrying guns and I didn't know how they were going to clear up the square.. At about 4:30, the martial law troops announced over the loudspeaker, "Attention, students. We have agreed to your appeal. We will allow you to leave peacefully". The announcement was broadcast over and over again. At about 4:50, the students around the monument began to leave. I looked around and saw that there was almost no one in sight. So I came back with the students. That was at 5:05 a.m. This was what I saw at the time. No one was killed throughout the whole process. Some people with ulterior motives who had fled abroad spread rumors that Tiananmen Square had been a blood-bath and that they had had to crawl out from underneath the corpses, but this was sheer nonsense.

Taiwanese entertainer Hou Dejian watched them depart, "Some people said that two hundred died in the Square and others claimed that two thousand died. There were also stories of tanks running over students who were trying to leave. I have to say that I did not see any of that. I don't know where those people died. I myself was in the Square until six-thirty in the morning". Future Nobelist Liu Xiaobo remained to the end and said he saw nobody harmed. He was arrested but, when witnesses told police that he directed the peaceful withdrawal, they released him.

Two weeks later, on July 19, Beijing Party Secretary Li Ximing[402] delivered the results of the enquiry, "More than 7,000 were wounded or injured and two hundred forty-one killed, including thirty-six

402 Ibid.

students, ten soldiers and thirteen People's Armed Police during a riot in Chang'An Road".

ABC's Jackie Judd[403] says reporters had second thoughts, "I believe we tried to put a 'made in the USA' democracy stamp on it". Photographer Jeff Widener[404], who took the Tank Man photograph–which AP distributes as if it were from July 4–said he shot it on July 5, the day after the students left the Square. Widener's photo shows four tanks stopping for a man but Stuart Franklin's wider angle photograph, taken a few seconds earlier, shows the entire tank column leaving the Square heading east.

Said the Vancouver Sun, "For months before the June 3 attack on the demonstrators, the CIA had been helping student activists form the anti-government movement, providing typewriters, facsimile machines and other equipment to help them spread their message, said one official. The CIA declined all comment". The "equipment" provided by CIA likely included the Molotov cocktails used by rioters which, prior to the days leading up to June 4, had never been seen or used in China, and their main ingredient, petrol, was strictly rationed in Beijing at the time and unavailable to ordinary people. The Sun's[405] followup read,

> The CIA station chief in China left the country two days before Chinese troops attacked demonstrators in the capital Beijing in 1989, after predicting the military would not act, US officials said. China's government had declared martial law 12 days earlier and moved tens of thousands of troops to the outskirts of Beijing in preparation for removing the demonstrators from Tiananmen Square. The Central Intelligence Agency had sources among protesters, as well as within China's intelligence services with which it enjoyed a close relationship since the 1970s, said the officials, who spoke this week on condition of anonymity. For months before the July 3 attack on the demonstrators, the CIA had been helping student activists form the anti-government movement,

403 Turmoil in Tiananmen: Study of US Press Coverage of the Beijing Spring of 1989.
404 Behind the Scenes: Tank Man of Tiananmen, NYT
405 The Vancouver Sun, "TIANANMEN - CIA man misread reaction, sources say" September 17, 1992, p. 20.

> providing typewriters, facsimile machines and other equipment to help them spread their message, said one official. The Agency's internal operational analysis attributed their failure to 'the difficulty of mobilizing young activists in the desired direction due to lack of strong polarizations in Chinese society."

Jay Mathews, Washington Post's Beijing Bureau Chief in 1989: "As far as can be determined from the available evidence, NO ONE DIED that night in Tiananmen Square". He wrote this for Columbia Journalism Review. CBS News reporter Richard Roth: wrote "We saw no bodies, injured people, ambulances or medical personnel — in short, nothing to even suggest, let alone prove, that a "massacre" had occurred in [Tiananmen Square]" — thus:

BBC NEWS: "I was one of the foreign journalists who witnessed the events that night. There was no massacre on Tiananmen Square" — The BBC's James Miles later confessed, "There was no massacre on Tiananmen Square. Protesters who were still in the square when the army reached it were allowed to leave after negotiations with martial law troops…There was no Tiananmen Square massacre".

New York Times: In June 13, 1989, NY Times reporter Nicholas Kristof – who was in Beijing at that time – wrote, "State television has even shown film of students marching peacefully away from the [Tiananmen] square shortly after dawn as proof that they [protesters] were not slaughtered". In that article, he also debunked an unidentified student protester who had claimed in a sensational article that Chinese soldiers with machine guns simply mowed down peaceful protesters in Tiananmen Square.

REUTERS: Graham Earnshaw was in Tiananmen Square on the night of June 3. He didn't leave the square until the morning of June 4th. He wrote in his memoir that the military came, negotiated with the students and made everyone (including himself) leave peacefully; and that nobody died in the square. But did people die in China? Yes, about 200-300 people died in clashes in various parts of Beijing, around June 4 — and about half of those who died were soldiers and cops.

WIKILEAKS: A Wikileaks cable sent in July 1989 from the US

Embassy in Beijing retells the eyewitness accounts of a Latin American diplomat and his wife: "They were able to enter and leave the [Tiananmen] square several times and were not harassed by troops. Remaining with students ... until the final withdrawal, the diplomat said there were no mass shootings in the square or the monument".

A June 19 American Embassy[406] cabled that the PLA did not fire directly on students gathered around the Martyrs' Monument in Tiananmen Square and many if not most of the deaths associated with the crackdown occurred on Changan Avenue and other streets surrounding the square, rather than on Tiananmen Square itself.

JUNE 3-4 EVENTS ON TIANANMEN SQUARE

1. CONFIDENTIAL - ENTIRE TEXT.

2. SUMMARY- DURING A RECENT MEETING, A LATIN AMERICAN DIPLOMAT AND HIS WIFE PROVIDED POLOFF AN ACCOUNT OF THEIR MOVEMENTS ON JUNE 3-4 AND THEIR EYEWITNESS ACCOUNT OF EVENTS AT TIANANMEN SQUARE. ALTHOUGH THEIR ACCOUNT GENERALLY FOLLOWS THOSE PREVIOUS LY REPORTED, THEIR UNIQUE EXPERIENCES PROVIDE ADDITIONAL INSIGHT AND CORROBORATION OF EVENTS IN THE SQUARE. THEY WERE ABLE TO ENTER AND LEAVE THE SQUARE SEVERAL TIMES AND WERE NOT HARASSED BY TROOPS. REMAINING WITH STUDENTS BY THE MONUMENT TO THE PEOPLE'S HEROES UNTIL THE FINAL WITHDRAWAL. THE DIPLOMAT SAID THERE WERE NO MASS SHOOTINGS OF STUDENTS IN THE SQUARE OR AT THE MONUMENT. END SUMMARY.

Towards the end of the demonstration students had discovered their

406 Cable, From: US Embassy Beijing, To: Department of State, Wash DC, What Happened on the Night of June 3/4? (June 22, 1989) https://nsarchive2.gwu.edu/NSAEBB/NSAEBB16/docs/doc32.pdf

leader, Chai Ling, leaving the square and, accusing her of abandoning them to die, detained her. She escaped, claimed to have witnessed more than twenty students and workers massacred in the Square, was given a scholarship to Princeton University, and nominated for the 1990 Nobel Peace Prize. Another leader, Wu'er Kaixi, though he had left the Square hours before the military arrived, said he saw tanks drive over tents full of sleeping protesters and kill hundreds.

Police issued warrants for twenty-one demonstrators including Chai Ling, Wang Dan, Wu'er Kaixi, and Liu Gang but the CIA's Operation Yellow Bird[407] (from the Chinese proverb, "The mantis stalks the cicada, unaware of the yellow bird behind") had smuggled them to the West. Of the twenty-one most wanted, fifteen were spirited out to Hong Kong, given false identities, passports and disguises, and sent abroad. In total, eight hundred escaped with the help of MI6, using scramblers, infrared signalers and night-vision goggles. Many went to France but most travelled to the US to attend Ivy League universities on scholarships. Investigations later proved that Hong Kong's Sun Yee On Triad was involved, but Ambassador Lilley said the exfiltrations were 'almost exclusively legal.'

Deng Xiaoping later discussed the incident with Chinese-American academic Li Zhengdao, "In suppressing the turmoil we were at pains to avoid hurting people, especially the students; that was our guiding principle". He criticized his colleague Zhao Ziyang whom, he said, "Was clearly exposed as siding with the agitators and attempting to split the Party". Deng told West Germany's Chancellor Helmut Schmidt, "The students should not be blamed too much. The roots of the problem lay within the leadership of the Party".

James Miles[408], the BBC's Beijing correspondent from 1988 to 1994, writes, "A year after Tiananmen, Deng elaborated on his fears of civil war during a meeting with former Canadian prime minister Pierre Trudeau. 'You can imagine,' Deng said, 'what China in turmoil would be like. If turmoil erupts in China, it wouldn't just be a Cultural Revolution-type problem. During the Cultural Revolution you still had the prestige of

407 Tiananmen Square: the long shadow. Financial Times. Jue 3, 2019
408 The Legacy of Tiananmen, James A. R. Miles

the elder generation of leaders such as Mao Zedong and Zhou Enlai. Even though it was described as 'all-out civil war,' actually there wasn't any major fighting. It wasn't a proper civil war. Now it's not at all the same. If turmoil erupts again, to the extent that the party is no longer effective and state power is no longer effective and one faction grabs one part of the army and another faction grabs another part of the army—that would be civil war. If some so-called democratic fighters seize power, they'll start fighting among themselves. As soon as civil war breaks out there'll be rivers of blood. What would be the point then of talking about 'human rights'? As soon as civil war breaks out, local warlords will spring up everywhere, production will plummet, communications will be severed, and it won't be a matter of a few million or even tens of millions of refugees. There'd be well over a hundred million people fleeing the country and the first to be affected would be Asia, now the most promising part of the world. It would be a global disaster.'"

Foreign leaders had little sympathy for the demonstrators. Singapore's Lee Kwan Yew said he would have shot two-hundred thousand to maintain stability and US Ambassador Charles Freeman opined, "I cannot conceive of any American government behaving with the ill-conceived restraint that the Zhao Ziyang administration did in China, allowing students to occupy zones that are the equivalent of the Washington National Mall and Times Square combined, while shutting down much of the Chinese government's normal operations". Ambassador Freeman's judgement was confirmed when, three years after Tiananmen, an uprising in California[409] killed fifty-five people and destroyed a billion dollars of private property. The media hailed President Bush's 'decisiveness' for dispatching thousands of troops and announcing, "There can be no excuse for the murder, arson, theft or vandalism that have terrorized the people of Los Angeles... Let me assure you that I will use whatever force is necessary to restore order".

A decade later, on Chinese national television, President Clinton

409 April 29th, 1992, Los Angeles experienced the most serious uprising in America's twentieth century. The federal army, national guard and police from throughout the country took five days to restore order, by which time residents had appropriated millions of dollars worth of goods and destroyed a billion dollars of private property.

discussed the incident with President Jiang Zemin and John Border[410] reported, "The drama of the meeting came in a remarkable 70-minute news conference, carried live on nationwide Chinese television, in which the two Presidents differed sharply on the nature of personal freedom, the role of the state and the meaning of the Tiananmen Square demonstrations that were violently suppressed by the Chinese Government in July 1989… Mr. Clinton flatly told the Chinese leader that his Government had been 'wrong' to use force to end the peaceful demonstrations of the spring of 1989 and that broad personal freedom and political expression were the price of admission to the world community of the twenty-first century. 'For all of our agreements, we still disagree about the meaning of what happened then,' Mr. Clinton said in his opening statement, referring to the violent crackdown on Tiananmen Square the night of July 3-4, 1989, that left hundreds of protesters dead".

Student Vice-President and leader of the Chang'An riot, Wang Yam, was exfiltrated, given British citizenship and moved to London in 1990. In 2006, for the first time in modern British history, the Crown Prosecutor banned all media coverage and even speculation about his case as he was tried in camera and found guilty of robbing and bludgeoning an elderly British man to death. Britain's intelligence agency, MI6, later admitted that he was their agent.

---

410 CLINTON IN CHINA: THE OVERVIEW; Clinton and Jiang Debate Views Live on TV, Clashing on Rights. By JOHN M. BRODER. JUNE 28, 1998. New York Times

CHAPTER 21

The Mongol Trade

If there were an honorable way to get rich, I'd do it, even if it meant being a stooge standing around with a whip. But there isn't an honorable way, so I just do as I please. Confucius.

***

Had World Trade Organization negotiators consulted their history books before admitting China, they may have imposed even harsher terms than they did. Says F.W. Mote,[411] "Midway in the sixteenth century China began to be the great repository of the early modern world's newly discovered wealth in silver. Long a participant in international maritime trade, China experienced the consequences of the greatly enlarged patterns in world trade. In that commerce China was essentially a seller of high-quality craft manufactures. Other countries could not compete either in quality or price. The colonies of the New World and the entire Mediterranean sphere of trade, from Portugal and Spain to the Ottoman Empire, began to complain that the influx of Chinese goods undermined their economies".

Of all China's trading exploits, the Mongol Trade was its masterpiece.

Sending Chinese armies to fight the steppe cavalry warriors who regularly devastated the borderlands was ruinously expensive. A palace official analyzed the costs and benefits of raiding and, finding it to be a

411 Imperial China 900-1800. F.W. Mote. Harvard University Press. 2003.

high-risk, low margin business, recommended offering the barbarians a thousand bolts of silk and several tons of gold each year—half the cost of a military campaign—to leave the country in peace.

The Emperor agreed but proposed three conditions: the barbarians should bring token gifts and acknowledge the emperor as their lord; keep their warrior bands fifty miles from the border; and refrain from trading with Chinese citizens lest they corrupt them with money. The barbarians rejected the no-trading rule and the emperor, with a great show of reluctance, agreed to establish four trading posts.

As soon as the border posts were opened the barbarians' wives exchanged furs they had trapped, precious stones they had unearthed, and the gold their husbands had earned for exquisite Chinese mirrors, tortoiseshell combs, enameled brooches, rich embroidery, bronzes, porcelains, and paintings. The trading posts were state-owned and the Emperor quickly recouped his gold which, each spring, he re-presented to the barbarians, after clearing sufficient profit from selling the furs to his nobles to buy the silks his subjects produced.

Two centuries later, the age of sail expanded world commerce and Chinese traders sold high-quality manufactures–with which no one could compete in quality or price–to merchants from the Americas, Spain, and the Ottoman Empire, whose rulers complained that their entire treasuries of silver were accumulating in China and undermining their economies.

Great Powers have always established 'free trade' agreements with lesser nations and withdrawn when losses outweighed gains. Britain forced India into treaties that destroyed its indigenous industries. Western powers subdued, colonized, and pillaged Africa, while emphasizing the civilizational virtues they bestowed upon its inferior people and downplaying the violence and dispossession that were essential to their subjugation.This attitude persisted in the form of the World Trade Organization which the US and the EU used to force developing countries to exchange their raw materials for paper IOUs in a global capital market beyond their control.

The West delayed China's accession until 2001, aware of its formidable trading culture that a friend described thus:

Mine was a typical merchant family. I had to learn calligraphy as soon as I could hold up the brush, with it I had to master the abacus and 'hold the twin swords'.

As soon as my father could teach his sons, we learned to keep a green-covered thick ledger of the daily gain and loss in our business. It did not matter rain or shine, 24/7 we kept that ledger. If we did not save 50% of our income monthly, we were in trouble and had to figure out why we couldn't. We have been capitalist from the beginning of our civilization it just was organized around the clan.

When Mao set up the country before 1949, we already knew where we were headed, just needed direction. We were so poor there was no money, just Government Store Coupons to get the most raw survival items, cooking oil, rice, salt, sugar, cotton fabric, sewing thread, yarn, shoes. There was pork sausage but nothing else. Everyone was required to work in the factory, field or special assignment. Everyone pulled their weight for years and years at least 12 hours a day saving our coupons or 40–50% of our yuan eventually. And these savings of the population created our capital. People in the West do not understand this.

We reverted to our production ways of the 1700s, when we were the richest country in the world. But we trusted the government banks now rather than accumulate gold and silver in our houses as in the past.

There is no magic to China, just solid hard hard work. Never again to be hungry or see our old people perish of hunger or the young, like me in those days, going barefooted in the winter counting every one of my skinny bones.

Mao, Zhou, Deng provided the leadership and we went to work, we know from our civilization what single purpose hard work can accomplish. I remember the chanting we had before classes started, we were told there was nothing to eat and to tighten our rags around the bellies, we were told that the US devil had rejected our buying of grain… so we sang: hit, hit the USA…. Máo zhǔ xí wàn wàn suì. Silly as it now sounds

> and looks, we survived the hunger and worked harder than ever. When Kissinger came in 1971 to offer us slave labor wages, we were ready to work harder than before. I was there, the fellows writing the article are correct. Kissinger and Nixon just made it easier, with the US wages we saved more every month. Deng's wisdom made things easier for us to follow, we got rich in a hurry and invest the savings more and more.

The WTO set humiliating admission terms for China. She had accept reduced rights against other members; open her economy to competition; eliminate state monopolies on imports and exports; overhaul domestic laws, regulations, procedures, and administrative and judicial institutions across all levels of government; make deep tariff commitments for imports; significantly liberalize services; make all trade regulations nondiscriminatory; make government standard-setting transparent and base them on international norms; submit to stringent IP protection; allow independent review of all trade-related administrative actions by foreign judicial and administrative tribunals; reduce tariffs on trade goods to ten percent (rich Brazil agreed to thirty-one percent and India to forty-eight percent); make broader, deeper commitments than any comparable economy on financial, telecommunication, professional, and distribution services; and grant other members greater rights against herself than she had against them–thus violating the WTO's nondiscrimination law.

These terms, which echoed the nineteenth century's Unequal Treaties, outraged popular sentiment but, when the author warned a Chinese banker friend that membership under such conditions would only retard his country's development, he reflected for a moment and responded, "I disagree about our vulnerability. This is a game we can win".

By 2010, China was the world's largest economy. By 2013, it was the world's largest trader in goods and, by 2020, American officials were complaining that US membership in the WTO was a bad bargain.

How did a Confucian, anti-legalist country, historically averse to international trade, fare so well in an organization where its lawyers lacked talent and experience and English is the governing language?

Hundreds of Chinese officials, judges, and scholars visited the US for WTO law training and foreign experts traveled to China to teach it. Beijing sponsored provincial WTO centers, staged hundreds of seminars and published more books on WTO law than the WTO itself, invited five million people to enter the WTO Knowledge Contest and, after broadcasting the final round on CCTV, flew the winner to WTO headquarters in Geneva.

By 2009, China was the object of forty percent of all WTO anti-dumping investigations and seventy-five percent of countervailing duties, so Beijing sent observers to every WTO panel, studied the example of the US and the EU, and learned to use–or bypass–the dispute process. When China required Internet companies to use local servers, the US objected but found WTO rules unavailing.

Beijing became an active litigant and her litigation strategy was so aggressive that the US and the EU lost cases involving billions of dollars[412]. Yet, as a percentage of GDP, China remained a below-average trader.

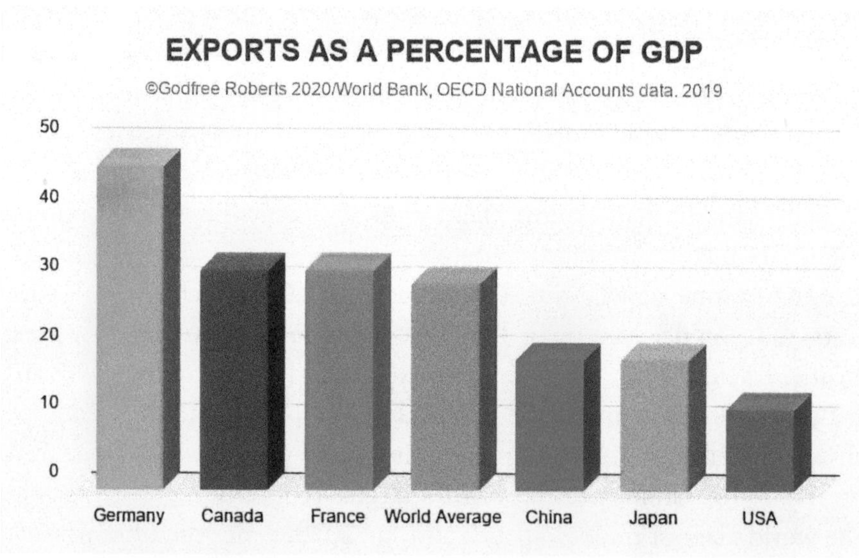

412 The pneumatic tires case (DS379) against the US involved $18 billion in imports while a case against the EU involving steel fasteners (DS397) involved $5 billion and created precedents that affect $463 billion in exports to the US and $368 billion in exports to Europe.

Since WTO accession required her to participate in the Agreement on Trade-Related Aspects of Intellectual Property Rights (TRIPS), Chinese law firms developed strong IP practices and domestic courts began applying TRIPS rules in local cases. Domestic courts interpreted Chinese law to comply with WTO requirements and frequently referenced them in important decisions. Huawei, with two hundred in-house counsel, hired famed trade lawyer James Lockett from the US Department of Commerce and Lockett, deeply familiar with US and EU regulatory systems, even filed briefs for Huawei that were at odds with the PRC's stated positions.

Today, China is a critical player in, and the strongest supporter of the WTO, and a formidable, tenacious opponent that does not hesitate to threaten litigation.When the EU put tariffs on Chinese solar panels in 2013, Beijing opened an inquiry into European winemakers dumping cheap, improperly subsidized bottles onto the Chinese market and ended the investigation when Europe agreed to train Chinese winemakers–whose products now compete on the world market.

As an alternative to the WTO's colonialism, President Xi proposed the Belt and Road Initiative, "To promote prosperity of the countries along the Belt and Road, to advance regional economic cooperation, strengthen exchanges and mutual learning between civilizations, and encourage world peace and development. Focused on policy coordination, infrastructure connectivity, unimpeded trade, financial integration, and people-to-people connections, the BRI harmonizes four billion people in one-hundred thirty countries and thirty international organizations across Eurasia, Africa, Latin America and the South Pacific".

The BRI invests one trillion dollars annually for power plants in Pakistan, train lines in Hungary, and ports from Africa to Greece. BRI trade has grown seventeen percent annually since 2013, the EU is considering membership, and the World Bank predicts, "The region that stands to receive the biggest GDP gain is sub-Saharan Africa, at 4.16 because the new ports in Tanzania and Kenya improve substantially the connectivity of those two countries to other BRI countries and the rest of the world. East Asia and the Pacific follows at 3.82 percent, which is to be expected given the BRI's core focus is on this region. Iran is projected to notch net GDP gain of 5.34 percent; Kuwait, 5.48 percent; Saudi Arabia, 5.22 percent; and Qatar, 5 percent".

The Pan-Asia Rail Network–linking Laos, Thailand, Malaysia, Singapore, Vietnam and Cambodia–will make North Korea the development hub for Northeast Asia. New pipelines from Pakistan's Gwadar Port bypass the Malacca Straits and deliver oil and gas to Kunming and has so enriched remote Balochistan that the Baloch Liberation Front abandoned resistance to Pakistan because, says its leader, "The BRI has given Balochis hope for the future".

In 2018, Xi signed a one-hundred billion dollar trade and economic agreement with the Eurasian Economic Union–Belarus, Kazakhstan, Russia, Armenia and Kyrgyzstan–and Russia commenced work on a high speed rail line from Moscow to Beijing. Thousands of miles of roads, rail lines, and fiberoptic cables have put Eurasia at the forefront of 5G deployment, and Russia's Polar Sea Route has cut sailing time from Europe to Asia by ten days–at $100,000 per day.

Six rail lines and dozens of inland rail terminals, thirty cross-border transmission and communications projects, and four deep ocean ports are creating Africa's first transcontinental network to serve the new, twenty-four nation African Continental Free Trade Zone. Half its firms are in manufacturing and services and contribute twelve percent of Africa's $500 billion annual manufacturing output–more than China contributes to America's economy. Ninety percent of its corporations are private, two-thirds provide skills training to their workforce, and ninety percent of their employees–including forty-four percent of their managers–are African. By 2045 the Eurasian and African continents will be bound by treaties, roads, railways, ports, fiberoptic cables, electrical grids and pipelines, and by an ultra-high voltage grid that transmits clean energy continuously around the globe.

By exploiting differences in natural resources, seasons, time zones, and power prices, the Global Electric Interconnect, GEIDCO, boosts the efficiency of clean energy and its return on investment. GEIDCO's one-hundred six member nations, with forty global offices, have invested $1.6 trillion in eighty generation and transmission projects across Latin America, Africa, Europe and North America and, just as EU nations are linking their grids, China is connecting Myanmar, Laos and Vietnam, Thailand, Pakistan and Bangladesh. GEIDCO's total investment in power sources and grids will reach a staggering $27 trillion by 2050, says chairman Liu Zhenya, "GEIDCO provides a technically advanced, cost-effective, viable and scalable solution to global climate governance, playing a key role in advancing the implementation of the Paris Agreement and helping to win the race against climate change. It will return nine dollars for every dollar invested between now and 2050 while boosting economic development and reducing carbon emissions".

The EEU, the BRI, the SCO, and ASEAN–Brunei, Cambodia, Indonesia, Laos, Malaysia, Myanmar, Philippines, Singapore, Thailand, Vietnam–are negotiating the formation of a single market.

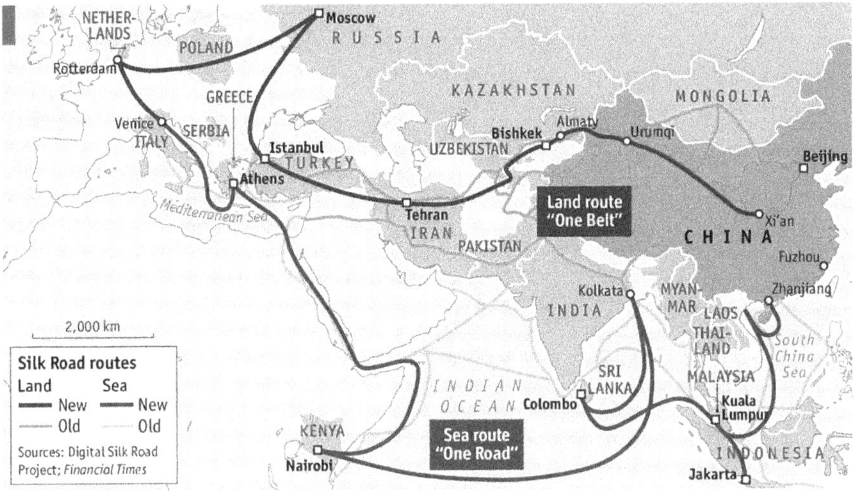

After the 2009 Global Financial Crisis the Governor of the Peoples Bank of China, Zhou Xiaochuan, announced, "The world needs an international reserve currency that is disconnected from individual nations and able to remain stable in the long run, removing the inherent deficiencies caused by using credit-based national currencies". He proposed Special Drawing Rights, SDRs, valued against a basket of trading currencies, and Nobelists C. Fred Bergsten, Robert Mundell, and Joseph Stieglitz agreed, "The creation of a global currency would restore a needed coherence to the international monetary system, give the IMF a function that would help it to promote stability and be a catalyst for international harmony".

Beijing began valuing its yuan against a currency basket in 2012 and the IMF made its first SDR loan in 2014. The World Bank issued the first SDR bonds in 2016, Standard Chartered Bank issued the first commercial SDR notes in 2017, and the world's central banks began stating their currency reserves in SDRs in 2019.

Former US Treasury Secretary Larry Summers called China's 2015 creation of the Asian Infrastructure Investment Bank, "The moment the United States lost its role as the underwriter of the global economic system. I can think of no event since Bretton Woods comparable to the combination of China's effort to establish a major new institution–and the failure of the US to persuade dozens of its traditional allies, starting with Britain–to stay out of it". The AIIB's one hundred member countries have eighty percent of the world's population and two-thirds of its GDP. By mobilizing their savings the new bank mobilizes a trillion dollars each year for long term, low interest loans for regional infrastructure, poverty reduction, growth, and climate change mitigation.

In 2020, as part of a plan for more efficient administration, the People's Bank of China issued Digital Yuan, the world's first digital currency backed by a central bank. Unlike privately issued mobile payments and credit cards, the Digital Yuan is a State liability, like banknotes and, since a billion Chinese already use mobile payments, the transition to digital currency should be seamless. Harvard's Aditi Kumar[413] says, "Nations seeking to leapfrog development of digital currency and payments systems will likely seek out Chinese financial technology, and Chinese firms, at the forefront of digital payment technology, will capture the economic gains of a rapidly digitizing global economy. China's central bank will have a panopticon view of all transactions in all digital currencies that leverage its technology, further strengthening its

413 China pioneers a national digital currency. Can the US catch up? By ADITI KUMAR. Los Angeles Times, MAY 4, 2020

information advantage". Author Bruno Macaes[414] envisions the impact of these programs thirty years hence:

> The year is 2049, one hundred years after the founding of the People's Republic of China. The Belt and Road Initiative is complete... Some of the infrastructure projects are truly stunning and stand as the highest example of what human ingenuity can achieve in its drive to master natural forces. A bridge crossing the Caspian Sea—125 miles from Azerbaijan to Turkmenistan—has made road transport between Europe and China fast and easy, changing old mental maps that separated continents. The Kra Isthmus Canal in Thailand has done the same for the Indian and Pacific oceans. No longer do we think of them as two separate oceans. In Africa a high-speed railway connects the two coasts, traversing Djibouti, Ethiopia, South Sudan, the Central African Republic, and Cameroon in under twenty hours. Trade between Africa, Asia, and South America increasingly uses this route.

Historian David Graeber[415] adds, "There's every reason to believe that, from China's point of view, this is the first stage of a very long process of reducing the United States to something like a traditional Chinese client state".

---

414 A Preview of Your Chinese Future: China's vision of world order is a more radical departure—and more realistic alternative—than the West understands. BY BRUNO MAÇÃES. Foreign Policy, DECEMBER 7, 2018

415 Debt, the First 5,000 Years. David Graeber

CHAPTER 22

Polishing the Gun

The man who is skilled at obtaining the support of the people is also the man who is skilled in using military force. Skillfully gaining the support of the people is essence of military undertaking. It's that simple.—Xunzi

***

In December, 1944, the US Air force firebombed Wuhan, killed forty-thousand civilians and set fires that burned for three days and nights. The following year President Truman ordered Mark-4 nuclear capsules transferred to the Ninth Bomber Group and signed an order to use them on China stating, "I am prepared to authorize the use of atomic weapons in order to achieve peace in Korea". In 1949, Mao warned[416] colleagues that China would remain 'insecure, unconsolidated, and delegitimized' until it transformed both itself and the imperial world order.

In 1951, in Operation Hudson Harbor, B-29s bombed coastal Dandong, fighters strafed civilians in several Chinese cities, buzzed coastal Shantou, and launched biological warfare[417] on China. In 1953 President Eisenhower repeated Truman's nuclear threat and in 1955 added, "In any combat where these things can be used on strictly military targets and for

416 *Zhai, Qiang (2005-10-20T22:58:59). China and the Vietnam Wars, 1950-1975* (The New Cold War History) UNC Press.

417 The Report of the International Scientific Commission for the Investigation of the Facts Concerning Bacterial Warfare in Korea and China. Sir Joseph Needham, Lead Author and Director of the Department of Natural Sciences, UNESCO.

strictly military purposes, I see no reason why they shouldn't be used just exactly as you would use a bullet or anything else". In 1957, Eisenhower deployed Matador nuclear cruise missiles to Taiwan and, in 1958, ordered the deployment to Jinmen of howitzers capable of firing nuclear shells, ordering that they be made visible to the Chinese.

In 1992, after the US Defense Department[418] promised to prevent a rival superpower emerging in Asia, the Navy held a Chinese cargo vessel, the Yinhe, at gunpoint in international waters for three weeks, claiming she was carrying contraband (she wasn't). Two years later President Clinton sent the most powerful fleet ever assembled through the Taiwan Strait and in 1998 dropped five precision bombs on China's Belgrade embassy, killing three diplomats and seriously wounding twenty (CIA director George Tenet[419] told Congress, "It was the only target we nominated"). In 2014 a US Navy article[420] proposed laying mines off China's coast and destroying her maritime lines of communication while sending special forces to arm minorities in Xinjiang and Tibet. In 2017 the Air Force reassured Congress of its willingness to launch nuclear attacks and in 2018 the Navy practiced blocking the Malacca Strait to cut off oil to China.

But by then, says defense analyst Michael Thim[421], such gestures were meaningless, "Even in 1996 China's Navy already had sufficient capabilities in place such that sending Carrier Strike Groups into the Taiwan Strait would be suicidal. The situation has only become more challenging for the Navy in recent years, not because the PLAN [Peoples Liberation Army Navy] has acquired an aircraft carrier of its own, but because China has greatly enhanced and modernized its existing anti-access/area-denial capabilities".

The Maritime Militia, the first line of defense, counts one-hundred eighty-thousand ocean-going fishing boats and four thousand

418 US STRATEGY PLAN CALLS FOR INSURING NO RIVALS DEVELOP. By PATRICK E. TYLER. The New York Times, March, 1992.

419 C.I.A. Says Chinese Embassy Bombing Resulted From Its Sole Attempt to Pick Targets. By Eric Schmitt. NYT. July 23, 1999

420 US Naval Institute Proceedings, Deterring the Dragon.

421 NO STRAIT FOR AIRCRAFT CARRIERS. MICHAL THIM. Center for International Maritime Security. MARCH 6, 2015

merchant[422] freighters, some towing sonar detectors, crewed by a million experienced sailors transmitting detailed information around the clock on every warship afloat. Their intelligence goes to shore bases that fuse their reports with automated transmissions from Beidou satellites and forward the data to specialists operating 'vessel management platforms,' collating, formatting, and sending actionable information up the PLAN command chain. Ashore, eight million coastal reservists train constantly in seamanship, emergency ship repairs, anti-air missile defense, and light weapons and naval sabotage while shipyards launch one new warship every month. The PLAN's battle fleet now outnumbers the US Navy's and its differences are fascinating.

Commander Yang Yi, the youngest (and first female) Chief Designer in naval history, designed a fleet of eighty Type 022 missile patrol boats. Four hundred feet long, with a range of three-hundred miles, they carry eight C-802 anti-ship missiles tipped with with 500lb. warheads that travel fifteen feet above the surface at 650 mph to targets a hundred miles away (one disabled an Israeli warship off Lebanon's coast in 2006). Four of her little boats, says Commander Yang, can cover the entire Taiwan Strait while sheltering behind China's coastal islands.

Supporting the patrol boats are thirty Type 056 frigates with a range of 2,500 miles, each armed with YJ-83 anti-ship missiles and six torpedo tubes and protected by eight SAM launchers. One frigate can sink Taiwan's entire navy without coming within range of its American-supplied weapons. Behind the frigates are twenty Type 052D Arleigh Burke-class destroyers. Their sixty-four missile tubes fire unique Yu-8 anti-submarine missiles that fly twenty miles then release torpedoes into the water near unsuspecting targets.

The PLAN's Type 055 cruisers, the world's most powerful surface combatants, each carry one-hundred twenty-eight missile tubes armed with surface-to-air, anti-ship, land-attack and antisubmarine missiles. Below them, seventy nuclear and conventional submarines carry YJ-12 anti-ship cruise missiles and wake-homing torpedoes that deliver five-hundred pound warheads at sixty mph from fifteen miles away.

---

422 *China's Maritime Militia,* by Andrew S. Erickson and Conor M. Kennedy

The nuclear subs have JL-3 missiles that can strike targets in the United States without leaving Chinese waters. Their arsenal includes CM-401 high-supersonic ballistic missiles designed for rapid precision strikes against medium-size ships, naval task forces and offshore facilities within two hundred miles. To destroy distant bases like Guam the CJ-10, a subsonic missile carries a half ton payload with a forty foot radius of accuracy for two-thousand miles.

The greatest threat to hostile fleets was born when the US Navy invited a Chinese admiral to visit the carrier Nimitz and, upon his return, he told colleagues, "I've just seen the world's biggest target. If we can't hit an aircraft carrier we can't hit anything".

Thrifty engineers attached a new guidance system to existing, million-dollar rockets and created a unique weapon, the DF-21D anti-ship, ballistic 'carrier killer'. It carries a half-ton warhead one thousand miles into the stratosphere then falls vertically, at 7,500 mph, onto $12 billion aircraft carriers. US Navy analysts say it can destroy a carrier in one strike and that there is currently no defense against it. Its sibling, the DF-26D, carries twice twice the payload twice as far.

"We are at a disadvantage with regard to China today in the sense that China's ground-based ballistic missiles threaten our basing and our ships in the Western Pacific," Admiral Harry Harris told the US Senate in 2018. The following year Robert Haddick warned, "China's anti-ship missile capability exceeds America's in terms of range, speed, and sensor performance," and Captain James Fanell[423] added, "We know that China has the most advanced ballistic missile force in the world. They have the capacity to overwhelm the defensive systems we are pursuing".

The last US carrier to pass through the Taiwan Strait was the USS Kitty Hawk in 2007. Navy officers say they risk defeat in a serious conflict off China's coast and avoid provoking the PLAN in the 'Three Seas,' the South China, East China, and Yellow Seas.

The Rand Corporation says that, for conflicts close to the mainland or Taiwan, the People's Liberation Army Air Force, PLAAF, can deploy more fifth generation J-20 fighters than the US. The J-20 cost half as

423 New missile gap leaves US scrambling to counter China. Reuters. Apr 25, 2019

much, flies twice as far and carries twice the payload of America's F-35C or the F-22 Raptor. Its YJ-12 anti-ship cruise missiles travel two hundred miles and deliver thousand-pound warheads at supersonic speed in a corkscrew trajectory. The US Navy says a single strike will render any vessel inoperable and warned that, even against alerted warships, one-third of missiles score hits.

The J-20 also carries the specialized PLA-15 air-to-air missile. Propelled by novel dual pulse rocket motors on a semi-ballistic trajectory, it homes in on AWACS and airborne tankers loitering behind battle lines. General Herbert Carlisle, who warned Congress that his two hundred F-22 Raptors carry six missiles each while the more numerous J-20s carry twelve, added, "Look at the PLA-15, at the range of that weapon. How do we counter that?" The PLA-15's smaller sibling, the PLA-10, is no less deadly, says ISIS airpower specialist Douglas Barrie, "For the notional Western combat aircraft pilot, there is no obvious respite to be found in keeping beyond visual range of the PLA-10[424]. The PLAAF will be able to mount an increasingly credible challenge and at engagement ranges against some targets that would previously have been considered safe. As one former USAF tanker pilot drily noted, 'That's aimed right at me.'"

Because they would be easy prey for the PLA-15, the US Air Force canceled its E-8C AWACS recapitalization program and, concerned for the safety of its planes, the Pentagon withdrew its entire strategic bomber fleet from Guam in 2020.

Hyperspectral detection satellites oversee the Western Pacific battlespace and airborne lasers detect waves and temperature variations generated by moving targets. The West Pacific Surveillance and Targeting satellite, along with fifteen Yaogan-30 satellites in low-earth orbit, operating as triplets positioned in close proximity, geo-locate military platforms by measuring the angular or time difference of arrival of their intercepted electromagnetic signals. Below them, the Caihong-T4, a massive, solar-powered drone, loiters for months at a cloudless altitude of sixty-five thousand feet, while below, the fifteen-ton, one-hundred

424 The PLA-10, an air-to-air missile, has a more advanced guidance system and twice the range, speed and payload of the USAF AIM-9.

fifty-foot wingspan Divine Eagle High Altitude Stealth-Hunting Drone reads electronic signals from aircraft long before they approach their targets. Below the drones AWACS, whose solid-state detectors have twice the range of the US AWACS rotating domes, relay targeting information to Russian-built S-400 anti-aircraft/anti-missile batteries. Jin Canrong, the PRC's senior defense policy advisor, says China has deployed weapons that can destroy in minutes every military base in its region, see all stealth bombers and submarines, and take out every aircraft carrier within two thousand miles of shore.

The DF-41 ICBM is a three-stage, solid-fuel device with a twelve-thousand mile range and a top speed of twenty-thousand mph. Road-mobile, it launches on four minutes warning and is faster, longer ranged and delivers ten independently targetable nuclear warheads.

The DF-ZF Hypersonic Glide Vehicle (whose significance Russian Defense Minister Dmitry Rogozin compared to the first atom bomb) is just beginning its life cycle[425]. Launched sixty miles above the earth from a missile traveling at sixteen-thousand mph, the DF-ZF rides its own supersonic shockwave to the target. Says RAND, "With the ability to fly at unpredictable trajectories, these missiles will hold extremely large areas at risk throughout much of their flight," and a Congressional report concludes, "The very high speeds of these weapons combined with their maneuverability and ability to travel at lower, radar-evading altitudes would make them far less vulnerable to current defenses than existing missiles".

In real wars, boots on the ground determine final outcomes and the PLA is as unconventional as its weapons. Combat forces elect their NCOs and all two-million soldiers receive more political education than the rest of the world's soldiers combined, as historian William Hinton explains, "From its inception the Army has been led by the Party and has never played a purely military role. On the contrary, Army cadres have always played a leading political role".

As Mao explained, "The Red Army fights not merely for the sake of fighting but in order to conduct propaganda, *xuānchuán,* among the

425 In a display of engineering prowess, Xiamen University's Department of Engineering launched and recovered its own HGV in northwest China's desert.

people, organize, arm and help them establish revolutionary political power. Without these objectives, fighting loses its meaning and the Red Army loses its reason for existence". Xiaoming Zhang[426] adds, "Under the influence of Confucian philosophy, the concept of the just or righteous war was prevalent throughout Chinese society so, unlike Western militaries which depend on professional ethics and training to ensure that soldiers perform their duties in war, the PLA opted for political indoctrination and attempted to make troops understand why a war must be fought and how it would matter to them".

By coordinating its military, legal, diplomatic, and economic assets simultaneously, China is exemplifying Correlli Barnett's[427] dictum: "The power of a nation-state by no means consists only in its armed forces, but also in its economic and technological resources; in the dexterity, foresight and resolution with which its foreign policy is conducted; in the efficiency of its social and political organization. It consists most of all in the nation itself: the people; their skills, energy, ambition, discipline, initiative; their beliefs, myths and illusions. And it consists, further, in the way all these factors are related to one another. Moreover, national power has to be considered not only in itself, in its absolute extent, but relative to the state's foreign or imperial obligations; it has to be considered relative to the power of other states".

China's military budget will reach parity with America's in 2028, and seventy years of Chinese anxiety and American hegemony will, with luck, come to a peaceful end.

426 Zhang, Xiaoming. Deng Xiaoping's Long War: The Military Conflict between China and Vietnam, 1979-1991 (The New Cold War History). The University of North Carolina Press.
427 Correlli Barnett. The Collapse of British Power. 1986

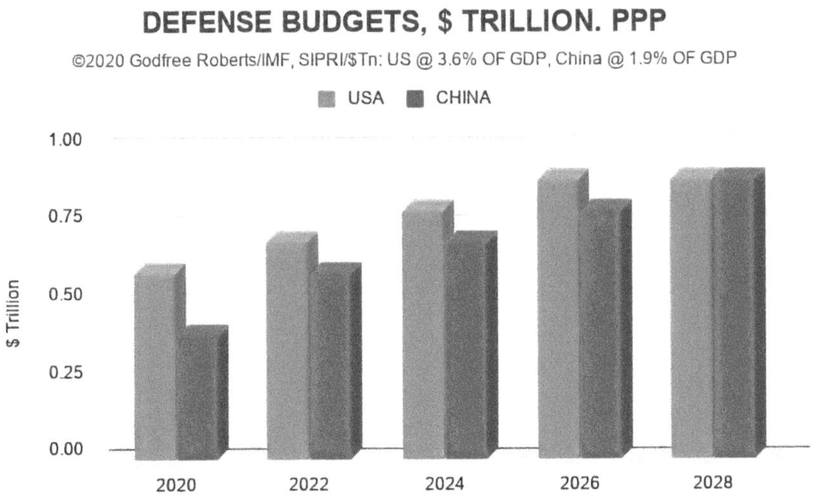
DEFENSE BUDGETS, $ TRILLION. PPP
©2020 Godfree Roberts/IMF, SIPRI/$Tn: US @ 3.6% OF GDP, China @ 1.9% OF GDP
USA
CHINA
$ Trillion
1.00
0.75
0.50
0.25
0.00
2020
2022
2024
2026
2028

CHAPTER 23

The Balance of Admiration

States that follow the principle of power and work with satellites of power can themselves exert power. States that follow the principles of failed states and work with satellites of failed states will themselves become failed states. States that follow the principle of humane authority and work with humane authorities can themselves attain humane authority. Xunzi[428].

***

Xunzi's advice, above, is familiar to every Chinese: governments earn international esteem by improving their citizens' lives–as the US did in the twentieth century. But Xunzi has more to say, "Just as the humane man has no enemies, so States wishing to exercise humane authority must be the first to respect the norms they advocate, because leaders of high ethical reputation and great administrative ability are attractive to other states, and winning hearts and minds is more important than winning territory".

France dominated the eighteenth century, Britain the nineteenth, and America was dominant until 2020 when, following the Coronavirus epidemic, a demographic change tipped the balance of power which had been teetering since America's Great Financial Crisis impoverished

428 Xunzi (453-221 BC), an architect and political theorist, lived toward the end of the Warring States period, the formative era for most later Chinese thought. He, Confucius and Mencius founded Chinese thought. From: *Ancient Chinese Thought, Modern Chinese Power.* By Yan Xuetong.

millions and its wars devastated economies around the globe. By late 2020, there were more hungry children, more poor, homeless, drug addicted and imprisoned people in the America than in China, America's economy was depressed, and China's was expanding rapidly.

***

China's grand strategy is simple: create a home for the world's happiest people, establish the world's best diplomatic relationships, its strongest economy, healthiest environment, most powerful military, newest technologies, and best human rights record. At that point, the world's hearts and minds will follow.

China's handling of the Coronavirus enhanced its humane authority[429] and eliminating poverty in 2021 and conquering inequality by 2035 will amplify its authority and should win world leadership by 2040–a transition for which its leaders have been preparing since since 1956, when Mao[430] told colleagues,

> The United States now controls a majority in the United Nations and dominates many parts of the world. This state of affairs is temporary and will change one day, along with China's position as a poor country denied its rights in international relationships. The poor country will change into a rich one, the country denied its rights will change into one enjoying them–a transformation of things into their opposites. The decisive conditions are our socialist system and the concerted efforts of a united people. To overtake the United States is not only possible but obligatory. If we don't, the Chinese nation will be letting the world down and we'll make little contribution to humanity. Besides, if we fail, we'll be wiped off the face of the earth.

In 1980, Deng Xiaoping set 2050 as the deadline for achieving

429 A phrase coined by Daniel Bell, in *Just Hierarchy*. Bell, Daniel. Princeton University Press. pp. 124-125.

430 "Strengthen Party Unity and Carry Forward Party Traditions" (1956)

socialist modernity. In 2018, Xi Jinping shortened that timeline to 2035 but warned, "We won't get there unless we replace money worship with traditional morality, weed out political corruption, implement social justice and equitability and provide everyone with their own homes, good wages, a beautiful environment, safe streets, fine schools, guaranteed incomes, free health care, and enough leisure time for art and contemplation–and leave no-one behind". Xi[431] then envisioned the country in 2049:

> By then, China's economic and technological strength has increased significantly; she has become a global leader in innovation; everyone's right to participate and develop as equals is protected; rule of law is in place for the country, the government, and society; institutions in all fields are further improved; governance is modernized; people are leading more comfortable lives and the size of the middle-income group has grown considerably; disparities in urban-rural development, in development between regions, and in living standards are significantly reduced; equitable access to public services is basically ensured; solid progress has been made toward prosperity for everyone; a modern social governance system has taken shape and society is full of vitality, harmonious, and orderly; civility is significantly enhanced; there is a fundamental improvement in the environment; the goal of building Beautiful China is basically complete; our nation is a proud, active member of the community of nations; China's cultural soft power has grown much stronger; and the world finds her culture appealing.

431 Work Together to Build a Community of Shared Future for Mankind. Speech by H.E. Xi Jinping, President of the People's Republic of China. At the United Nations Office at Geneva, 18 January 2017

Finally, he outlined his vision for the world and China's diplomatic agenda for the next thirty years:

> We invite everyone to unite in creating a global community and a shared future for mankind, an open, inclusive, clean and beautiful world that enjoys lasting peace, universal security and common prosperity. A *dàtóng* world in which everyone belongs to a big family that works cooperatively to solve the global challenges facing our planet by setting goals that transcend similarities and differences between countries, parties, and systems. A world that reflects the universal expectation of most countries and the common interests of men and women everywhere.

Most of the world's people would support this vision and 1.4 billion Chinese already do:

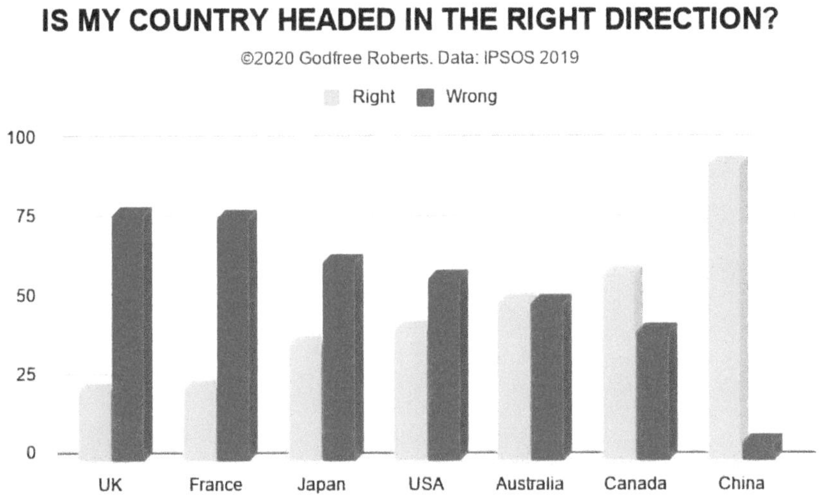

Xi's 2050 vision seems remote today, as Deng's 2021 vision seemed remote in 1980 but, if China reaches her 2050 goal, then Mao's *dàtóng* vision[432] will seem closer, too:

> Now to have states, families, and selves is to allow each individual to maintain a sphere of selfishness. This utterly violates the Universal Principle and impedes progress. Therefore, not only should states be abolished–so that there would be no more struggle between the strong and the weak–but families should also be done away with, too, to allow equality of love and affection among men. Finally, selfishness itself should be banished, so that goods and services would not be used for private ends. The only true way is sharing the world in common by all, *tienxia weigong*... To share in common is to treat each and every one alike. There should be no distinction between high and low, no discrepancy between rich and poor, no segregation of human races, no inequality between sexes. All should be educated and supported with the common property, none should depend on private possession. This is the way of the Great Community.

432 From a free rendering of Confucius' *Liyun*, by Kang Youwei, 1858-1927 AD, a Neo-Confucian scholar, political thinker and reformer of the late Qing dynasty. Mao so admired him that he committed Kang's books to memory and quoted them regularly.

CPSIA information can be obtained
at www.ICGtesting.com
Printed in the USA
LVHW071615250821
696087LV00021B/1450/J

9 781735 821351